DEVELOPMENT OF ACCOUNTING AND AUDITING SYSTEMS IN CHINA

Development of Accounting and Auditing Systems in China

XU-DONG JI
La Trobe University, Australia

Ashgate

Aldershot • Burlington USA • Singapore • Sydney

Published by
Ashgate Publishing Limited
Gower House
Croft Road
Aldershot
Hampshire GU11 3HR
England

Ashgate Publishing Company
131 Main Street
Burlington, VT 05401-5600 USA

Ashgate website: http://www.ashgate.com

British Library Cataloguing in Publication Data
Ji, Xu-Dong
    Development of accounting and auditing systems in China. -
    (The Chinese economy series)
    1.Accounting - China - History
    I.Title
    657'.0951

Library of Congress Control Number: 2001093266

ISBN 0 7546 1684 3

Printed and bound in Great Britain by Antony Rowe Ltd.,
Chippenham, Wiltshire.

Contents

List of Figures

List of Tables

Preface

One question which has been asked by many accounting scholars concerns the value of doing Chinese accounting research. Is it worthwhile to conduct research into Chinese accounting? The majority of accounting research has focused on accounting theory, especially normative and positive accounting theory. Even in international accounting research, the emphasis has been on developed countries, such as the United States, the United Kingdom, Germany, Japan, Netherlands, France and Australia. Less attention has been paid to developing countries. With the progress of international accounting harmonisation, the need for research on developing countries should be recognised. In the case of China, there are several reasons for doing accounting research.

Firstly, there is an historical value in conducting research into Chinese accounting. Research into Chinese accounting history will make a great contribution to world accounting history. Accounting in China has a long history and its systems are quite different from those of the western world. Chinese accounting reached a peak of sophistication in the Western Zhou Dynasty (1100-771 B.C.), at which time it was more advanced than elsewhere in the world. After that, during the long centuries of feudal society, accounting in China developed slowly. However, there were some advances: for example, the Bi-Bu auditing system developed in the Tang Dynasty (618-907 A.D.), and the invention of the elaborate government accounting system in the Song Dynasty (960-1279 A.D.), both of which can be regarded as significant achievements in Chinese accounting.

Research into Chinese accounting history also gives us a better understanding of world accounting history. For example, it shows that early double-entry bookkeeping is not the sole province of the Italians and there is strong historical evidence that other double-entry systems were devised in both China and India. A comparative study of different double-entry systems invented by the Italians, the Chinese and the Indians could possibly throw some light on the social, political and economic environments from which they emerged.

Secondly, there is an academic value in conducting research into Chinese accounting. A number of international organisations are involved in efforts to harmonise accounting and financial reporting across the world, including the European Community (EC) and at professional level, the International

Accounting Standards Committee (IASC). Questions arise about the extent to which such efforts have had an impact on practice. What are the political and organisational processes involved? Do the benefits of harmonisation outweigh the costs? Are comparative international investment pressures more effective than harmonisation by regulation? How can international pressures and local accounting and cultural values be coordinated? Accounting development and reform in China has had and will continue to offer some answers to these questions. China has had a centrally planned economy and a strong eastern cultural background. The internationally oriented accounting reform that has been carried out by the Chinese constitutes a good experiment in the harmonisation of accounting practice and theory. Constant monitoring and observation of this harmonisation progress will benefit accounting research, especially in the international accounting research area.

Finally, there is a practical value in conducting research into Chinese accounting. China has over one billion people and is one of the biggest markets in the world. Since China re-opened the door to other countries, particularly Western nations, foreign investment has increased greatly. Many joint ventures and foreign companies have been set up in China and large international accounting firms are now operating in the Chinese market. The Western business community has urgently needed to gain an understanding of different accounting and legal systems in China. Accounting research in this area will offer guidelines for doing business between China and Western countries.

I would like to take this opportunity to thank all the people who encouraged and helped me to write this book. Firstly, I would like to thank Professor Max Aiken for his support throughout the research and writing of this book. I am grateful for his constant encouragement and invaluable suggestions during my research. Secondly, I would like to thank my family members, my father and mother, my father-in law and mother-in-law for supporting me to write this book. Finally, I would like to thank my wife, Wei Lu, for her endless encouragement and support. Without her, this work would never been completed.

I would like to thank Australian Accounting Review and International Thomson Publishing Company for the permission to include my two previous papers published in their journal and book.

I would like to dedicate this book to my lovely son and daughter, Andrew Moning Ji and Katharine Morong Ji.

Introduction

With the increasing importance of the role of China in the international, political and economic arena, Chinese accounting has attracted more foreign attention. Since economic reforms were carried out in the late 1970s, the Chinese economy has grown rapidly. It may become the largest market in the world in the next century (World Bank, 1996). Foreign investment has increased greatly. Many joint ventures and foreign companies have been set up in China and the six largest international accounting firms are operating in the Chinese market. With the growth of the economy and the opening-up of the Chinese market, accounting systems in China have been changing. The purpose of this book is to examine major events and reforms which occurred in Chinese accounting within this transformation period and then to assess critically the impact of politics, the economy and culture on the development of Chinese accounting. Four tasks have been carried out in order to achieve this purpose.

Firstly, a survey of the application of western management accounting in China was conducted by the author in 1995/96 to examine how the Chinese adopted to western accounting techniques, and whether there is also a gap between management accounting and practice in China. According to the survey, traditional Chinese cost methods have been predominant in practice. The adoption of western management accounting techniques is slow, except for short-term decision methods. Also, the Chinese accountants' attitude towards western management accounting is positive and they are willing to accept many techniques. The major obstacles in absorbing western ideas are now technical factors rather than political factors.

Secondly, an empirical model was established to examine the impact of politics, economy and culture on the development of Chinese accounting in the transformation period. It was found that there is a significant correlation between the development of recent accounting and changes of the political, economic and cultural environments.

Thirdly, major accounting reforms in China have been examined comprehensively and critically. These reforms include promulgation of the Chinese accounting standards, promulgation of the Chinese auditing standards, the developments of the accounting profession, and the establishment of auditing systems. Also, accounting education and research in China have been reviewed.

3

Fourthly, some weak areas in Chinese accounting research have been explored by the author. These include cost accounting systems and the development of management accounting in China. The aims of cost and management accounting in China are different to these in western countries and several case studies have been constructed to help understand these systems.

The book contains ten chapters. Chapter 1 is a literature review which examines research on Chinese accounting and indicates that management accounting and cost accounting systems are weak areas of research. Chapter 2 gives a brief review of developments of the Chinese economy and of accounting since the revolution in 1949. This chapter emphasises the economic reforms, which have had a direct influence on accounting and also accounting reforms carried out by the Chinese since 1979. Chapter 3 examines in more detail the first accounting standard issued by the Ministry of Finance (MOF) in 1992 and its impact on the future development of Chinese accounting. It also discusses the relationship between accounting standards and the uniform accounting system, showing the recent development of accounting standards. Chapter 4 reviews the development of the accounting profession in China, the contents of *The Certified Public Accountants Act 1993*, and the issuing of auditing standards. Chapter 5 evaluates the accounting education system and the feasibility of future accounting education reforms. Chapter 6 examines the costing system used in China and its similarities and differences with that of western countries. Chapter 7 briefly reviews western management accounting developments in the modern era and critically examines management accounting techniques, especially the responsibility accounting systems, used in China from 1949 to the present. Chapter 8 evaluates the western influence and Chinese reactions to adopting western management accounting methods. Chapter 9 studies the empirical environmental factors which include political, economic, cultural, technical and outside factors, on the development of Chinese accounting. A multivariate model is used to examines these impacts.

Chapter 10 is the Conclusion. After evaluation of the main accounting reforms, such as the promulgation of Chinese accounting and auditing standards, reorganisation of the Chinese accounting profession, and the development of cost and management accounting, the thesis concludes that, firstly, Chinese accounting development is becoming more internationalised. Secondly, accounting developments in China are influenced strongly by the nation's political structure, economic system and culture and the development of technology. Outside influences, especially from the Soviet Union, Japan and the United States, have also impacted on this development. Finally, Chinese accounting has and will continue to maintain its own characteristics with internationalism and nationalism being entwined in the future developments. Some Chinese characteristics shown in the development of accounting are the government domination in accounting affairs, the concurrence of uniform accounting systems and accounting standards, diversity in bookkeeping methods, and predominance of accounting in public sectors and state-owned enterprises over the private sectors. With the future development of Chinese accounting, some of these characteristics will disappear due to the harmonisation of accounting practices around the world, the entrance of China to the World Trade Organisation (WTO) and changes of ownership structures in enterprises. However, some characteristics will remain even though substantial changes will occur in economy.

1   Literature Review

Accounting Research and Chinese Accounting

Accounting in China has had a long history that can be traced back 6,000 years (Aiken and Lu, 1993). However, because post-revolution China implemented a closed-door policy until 1979, little was known by Western accounting scholars about Chinese accounting. There were few publications on the subject in English. One contribution of note was Philip Fu's PhD dissertation, *A Study of Governmental Accounting in China: with Special Reference to the Sung Dynasty (960-1279)*, at the University of Illinois (1968). Fu later published a paper, "Government Accounting in China During the Chou Dynasty" in the *Journal of Accounting Research* in 1971. An earlier paper by Ching-Wen Kwang, entitled "The Economic Accounting System of State Enterprises in Mainland China", was published in the *International Journal of Accounting Education and Research* in 1966.

In 1979, China re-opened its door to the outside world and implemented a series of economic reforms. Since then, economic growth and China's proportion of total world trade have increased significantly. The accounting system has also been changed in order to meet the needs of economic reform and international trade. Western accounting scholars have shown increasing interest in Chinese accounting, and China has sent a number of accounting scholars and students to industrial countries to learn advanced accounting techniques and theory. These scholars have undertaken many joint research projects with foreign scholars on Chinese accounting issues, and the number of articles on Chinese accounting published in English has increased steadily. This paper reviews published research in English from 1966 to 1998. The scope of this study includes articles from referred journals and edited books. Details of these are as shown in Table 1-1.

Table 1-1 The Books and Articles on Chinese Accounting Issues

Titles of the Books and Articles	Authors or Editors	No. of Article
Edited Books:		
1. Accounting and Auditing in the People's Republic of China: A Review of Its Practices, Systems, Education and Developments	Shanghai University of Finance and Economics and The University of Texas at Dallas (1987, 1989 an supplementary)	13
2. Perspectives on Accounting and Finance in China	Blake and Gao (1995)	19
3. Recent Accounting and Economic Developments in the Far East	Centre for International Education and Research in Accounting, University of Illinois (1988)	5
4. The Academy of Accounting Historians Working Paper Series	Jong (1979)	1
5. Advances in International Accounting	Lin (1989), Hy and Marts (1991), Taussig et al (1994), Xiao et al (1995), Roberts et al (1995), Fuglister (1997), Chan and Lee 91997), Epps and Chen (1998)	8
6. Research in Accounting in Emerging Economies (3 Vols) Vol.1-2 published as Research in Third World Accounting	Maschmeyer and Yang (1990), Skousen et al (1990) Skousen et al (1993) and Scapens and Hou (1995)	4
7. Studies in Accounting History	Xu (1995)	1
Referred Accounting journals:		
1. Abacus	Aiken and Lu (1998)	1
2. Accounting and Business Research	Chow et al (1995)	1
3. Accounting History	Aiken and Lu (1993), Scorgie and Ji (1996)	2
4. Accounting Horizons	Winkle et al (1994), Davidson et al (1996)	2
5. Accounting, Organisations and Society	Skousen and Yang (1988), Zhou (1988), Firth (1996)	3
6. Asian Review of Accounting	Taylor and Liu (1992), Chen and Tran (1995), Chow et al (1997)	3
7. Australian Accounting Review	Aiken et al (1997)	1
8. British Accounting Review	Aiken and Lu (1993)	1
9. Issues in Accounting Education	Watne and Baldwin (1988), Winkle et al (1992)	2
10. Journal of Accounting and Economics	Chan and Chow (1997)	1
11. Journal of Accounting Research	Fu (1971)	1
12. Journal of International Accounting, Auditing and Taxation	Yang and Kao (1995)	1
13. Management Accounting Research	Scapens and Meng (1993)	1
14. The Accounting Historians Journal	Lin (1992), Aiken and Lu (1993), Chen (1998)	3
15. The Accounting Historians Notebook	Guo (1988)	1
16. The International Journal of Accounting	Kwang (1966), Hoyt and Maples (1980), Tsun (1981), Farag (1988), Lefebvre and Lin (1990), Lau and Yang (1990), Briomwhich and Wang (1991), Fang and Tang (1991), Lin and Deng (1992), Tang (1993), Macve and Liu (1995), Graham (1996), Chen et al (1997), Graham and Li (1997), Xiao and Pan (1997)	15
17. The Journal of Financial Research	Chui and Kwok (1998)	1
Total		91

The total sample of this study is 91 articles, which can be broken into three periods: (1) 1966-1977, Pre-reform period; (2) 1978-1992, Pre-internationalisation period; and (3) 1992-1998, current period. During the second period in 1992, China promulgated the first accounting standard, which indicated that accounting reform entered into a new era and showed the willingness of the Chinese government to harmonise its accounting regulations with those implemented internationally.

Table 1-2 Periods of Articles on Chinese Accounting Issues

	1966-1977	1978-1992	1992-1998
Articles in edited books		23	28
Articles in referred journals	2	15	23

Three Books about Chinese Accounting

There are three books specifically devoted to Chinese accounting issues. The first is *Accounting and Auditing in the People's Republic of China: A review of Its Practices, Systems, Education and Developments*, which was published in 1987 as the result of a joint research project carried out by Shanghai University of Finance and Economics and the Center for International Accounting Development of the University of Texas, in Dallas. Professor Lou Er-Ying, who is well-known in China, and Professor Adolf J.H. Enthoven, an expert in international accounting from the USA, participated in the project. Their work covers every aspect of accounting: financial accounting and reporting (chapter 2); cost and management accounting (chapter 3); auditing (chapter 4); taxation (chapter 5); foreign investment (chapter 6); governmental accounting (chapter 7); accounting education (chapter 8); accounting research (chapter 9); Chinese political and economic systems (chapter 10) and Chinese accounting history (chapter 11), while the final chapter contains Professor Adolf J.H. Enthoven's evaluation of the development of Chinese accounting. Because this book focuses mainly on the accounting systems of the centrally planned economy, most of it is now out of date. However, it does give us some valuable information about the Chinese accounting systems of that period. From a historical point of view, this book deserves to be studied by academics and researchers who are interested in Chinese accounting.

Another joint project was undertaken in 1984 by Shanghai University of Finance and Economics and the University of California. Its results were published under two titles: *Comparative Research on Accounting in China and The United States*, and *Accounting Terminologies in Use in the People's Republic of China and in The United States*. Unfortunately, the former is not available in English while the latter is only a Chinese-English dictionary of accounting.

The second major work on the subject is *Accounting and Finance in China: A Review of Current Practice* by Tang Yun Wei, Lynne Chow and Barry J. Cooper, three accounting scholars from China, Hong Kong and Australia. This book attempts to keep pace with the recent reform and development of Chinese accounting, and provides up-to-date information. Its twelve chapters are concerned with: the traditional accounting system; accounting standards; enterprises with foreign investment; the share capital system; contemporary accounting issues; management accounting; government accounting; taxation; auditing; the accounting profession and education. This book covers a wider range of Chinese accounting topics, although its analysis and evaluation of the development of the Chinese accounting system is unfortunately brief.

The third book is *Perspectives on Accounting and Finance in China*, which is based on the proceedings of the International Symposium on Chinese Accounting and Financial Management held at the University of Central Lancashire in United Kingdom. Many scholars from China and overseas made great contributions to this work. Most of the articles in the collection not only describe Chinese accounting issues but also provide the reasons for the transformation and development of Chinese accounting. Many of the scholars involved critically evaluated that landmark of accounting reform, the promulgation of the first Chinese accounting standard, and the future direction of Chinese accounting.

In addition to these three major works, there are also several edited books which contain useful references to Chinese accounting.

International accounting has become a popular research topic among accounting academics and practitioners worldwide. It is the main course taught at both undergraduate and postgraduate levels in most universities in the United States. Some Australian universities have started to integrate international accounting into undergraduate and postgraduate courses. There are three leading international accounting textbooks. The authors of one, Frederick D.S. Choi and Gerhard G. Mueller (1992), observed the impossible mission of simplifying of accounting systems in Mao era and concerned the future directions of accounting reforms in China. They comment:

> What will emerge from this is still unclear. While it is likely to be a system whose procedures and outputs are understandable and useable in world commerce and international financial markets, chances are that it will be a system unique to its native country (p.56).

In *International Accounting and Multinational Enterprises*, Radebaugh and Gray (1993) do not comment directly on Chinese accounting, but mention the issue indirectly. They highlight the differences between Chinese accounting systems and the Western accounting systems:

> Accounting in a centrally-planned context is perceived as having primarily a record-keeping function and is not decision-oriented or concerned with efficiency at the enterprise level. Rather it is used as a means of centralised control. At the same time, there is a tendency to emphasise the receipts and payments approach rather than the accruals approach used in western accounting systems with resulting differences in measures of profit (p.227).

Comparative International Accounting, edited by Nobles, C. and Parker, R. (1998) devotes more attention to Chinese accounting. They discussed accounting reforms carried out in China and raised an issue that Chinese culture may constrain China to adopt the Western accounting systems:

> It is important to note that the regulatory framework (in China) also remains quite unlike that of Anglo-American countries. The 'standards' come from a government ministry, and the Chinese Institute of Certified Public Accountants (CICPA) is also controlled by the ministry. ... It is argued that cultural constraints will slow China down in its move towards Anglo-American accounting (p.301).

Besides two main editorial books, *Accounting and Auditing in the People's Republic of China* and *Perspectives on Accounting and Finance in China*, there are also several editorial books which include a large amount of information about Chinese accounting issues. One example is the paper by Jong, H.H. (1979) entitled "The Traditional Accounting Systems in the Oriental Countries - Korea, China, Japan" which appeared in The Academy of Accounting Historians: Working Paper Series edited by Edward N. Coffman (1979).

Another example is *Recent Accounting and Economic Development in the Far East* (1988) which presents the proceedings of a conference held at the University of Illinois in 1988. Presenters at the conference included academics and practitioners from North America and the Orient. Each of the 12 papers published provides an historical perspective of accounting and/or auditing practices in the country as a whole or in a specific geographical region. Authors then utilised this background to compare and contrast practices in various countries with related accounting practices in the West. Four papers, the largest number in the book, comment upon China's practices. Two of the papers were written by Chinese scholars and two by western scholars and both western and eastern academics have interpreted Chinese issues from different points of view. Simyar (1988) comments:

> It will become essential for Western managers to understand the underlying cultural and environmental aspects of the Chinese business climate (p.196).

Berry (1988) emphasises that "cultural reasoning" has directed accounting developments in China and then concludes:

> The synergistic effect of pluralism in the PRC's marketplace today could lead to more experimentation to develop the accounting function. However, the PRC will also be searching for ideological explanations for the changes now being introduced so that its view of scientific management will exist in its appropriate cultural framework (p.25).

Yu (1988), on the other hand, states:

> The intrinsic difference between socialist and capitalist accounting existed only in the sense of the difference between the socialist system and the capitalist system. That is, all socioeconomic phenomena differ intrinsically under these systems;

11

naturally, accounting is no exception. However, some concrete things (events) that exist in a different social system may have certain general characteristics and some common objective laws embodied in them.

Other edited books which include many articles on Chinese accounting are: *Research in Accounting in Emerging Economies* edited by Wallace, R. S.O. et al (1990, 1993, 1995); *Advances in International Accounting* edited by Timothy, S.J.; Salter, S.B. and Sharp, D. J. (1987-1998) and *Studies in Accounting History* edited by Tsujui, A. and Garner, P. (1995).

Accounting Journals on Chinese Accounting

Most leading accounting journals have published papers on Chinese accounting issues. One that has been particularly active is *The International Journal of Accounting,* in which fifteen papers on Chinese accounting have appeared so far. Some of these are: "Auditing in China: Historical Perspective and Current Developments", by Lau, A.H.L. and Yang, J.L. (1990); "Management Accounting in China: A Current Evaluation", by Bromwich, M. and Wang, G.Q. (1991); "Internationalisation of Financial Accounting Standards in the Peoples' Republic of China", by Lefebvre, C. and Lin, L. Q. (1990); and "Problems of Accounting Reform in the People's Republic of China", by Chen, Y., Jubb, P. and Tran, A. (1997). Each of these papers was written jointly by Western and Chinese accounting academics working in collaboration while the latter were either studying or undertaking research in Western countries. These articles provide up-to-date information about Chinese accounting developments.

Other journals that are active in publishing Chinese accounting issues are: *Accounting, Organisations and Society; Accounting Horizons; The Accounting Historians Journal; Asian Review of Accounting; Issues in Accounting Education; and Accounting History.* Each of these journals has published more than two papers relating to Chinese accounting issues. For example, two papers relating to Chinese accounting appeared in the *Accounting, Organisations and Society* in 1988 (Skousen and Yang, 1988; Zhou, 1988). These papers provided an introduction to the role of accounting in China, the Chinese regulatory environment and accounting methods. These two papers have been cited frequently by academics.

Subjects of Research on Chinese Accounting

Needles (1995, 1997) classified the subjects of international accounting research into Accounting Education, Accounting History, Accounting Theory, Auditing, Economic & Development, Financial Accounting & Reporting, Governmental, Information Systems, Managerial Accounting, Miscellaneous, Professional Development, Public Accounting, Social Effects of Accounting, and Taxation. This classification has been adopted with some changes in current study of research on Chinese accounting: Financial Accounting & Reporting have been subdivided into Accounting Standards and Financial Accounting; Public Accounting and Governmental have been merged into Governmental and Public Accounting. Table 1-3 shows the subjects of the articles on Chinese accounting research.

Table 1-3 Subjects of Research on Chinese Accounting

Subjects	1966-77	1978-92	1993-98
1. Accounting Education and Research		5	3
2. Accounting History	1	4	6
3. Accounting Theory			
4. Auditing		4	3
5. Economics and Development		3	5
6. Accounting Standards		1	13
7. Financial Accounting and Reporting		8	7
8. Governmental and Public Accounting		1	1
9. Information Systems and Computers			1
10. Managerial Accounting	1	6	4
11. Professional Development			4
12. Social Effects of Accounting		2	4
13. Taxation		1	
14. Miscellaneous		3	
Total	2	38	51

Financial Accounting and Reporting

There are fifteen papers in relation to financial accounting and reporting. Traditional financial accounting and reporting in the centrally planned economy is reviewed in "Financial Accounting and Reporting" by Wang and Qiang in *Accounting and Auditing in the People's Republic of China: A Review of Its Practices, Systems, Education and Developments* and "An Overview of Traditional Accounting Systems and Practices" by Tang, Chow and Cooper (1994). A paper by Lefebvre and Lin (1990) "Internationalisation of Financial Accounting standards in the People's Republic of China", and another by Fang and Tang (1991) "Recent Accounting Development in China: An Increasing Internationalisation" give up-to-date information about reforms carried out in financial accounting and reporting up to 1991. More recent information on this topic has appeared in Roberts et al. (1995) "Chinese Accounting Reform: The Internationalization of Financial Reporting". The formats and contents of current financial accounting and reporting have changed significantly, e.g. the categories in the current balance sheet consist of assets, liabilities and owners' equity rather than total fund application and total fund sources, which were the categories in the balance sheet for planned economy. However, the users of financial reports have not yet changed substantially. The main users of financial reports are governmental authorities, managers of enterprises and creditors from banks. The purposes of financial reporting are not clarified even in the new accounting standards.

Managerial Accounting

A paper, entitled "Management Accounting in China: A Current Evaluation", by Michael Bromwich and Guo-Qi Wang (1991) makes a significant contribution in this area. Bromwich and Wang review the evolution of management accounting in China and assess the Western influences on its development. They conclude that the future development of Chinese management accounting will depend largely upon the direction and pace of economic reforms. Particularly, it will depend on future changes in the pattern of enterprise operations and management perceptions and skills. This may cause a cultural cleavage.

Traditional management accounting methods used in China attracted westerners' attention very early. Kwang's article (1966) "The Economic Accounting System of State Enterprises in Mainland China" explained the Economic Accounting System (EAS). This system was the forerunner of Responsibility Accounting Systems used in China from the middle of 1980s. The evolution of responsibility accounting in China has been documented by Mascmeye and Yang (1990) and Scapens and Hou (1994). However, the internal operating mechanism of a responsibility accounting system is not fully understood by western academics. The relationship between financial accounting systems and responsibility accounting systems has not been described clearly. The study by Scapans and Meng (1993) outlines the economic reforms and describes current management accounting systems in China, especially systems of responsibility accounting. It also examines the differences between the Chinese and Western socio-economic systems, and the implications for management accounting research in China. Scapans and Meng conclude that there is not an entirely satisfactory western management accounting framework for the needs of China. Nevertheless, agency theory and behavioural science may help to give direction to Chinese management accounting research in the future.

There is also some empirical research on Chinese managerial accounting. The most recent by Firth (1996) hypothesizes that the accounting systems employed by joint venture operations, which are invariably designed by foreign partners, will have a significant influence on the development of, and content of, management accounting in the Chinese partner. The research approach involved the design of a questionnaire which elicited information on the management accounting techniques used by other parties to a joint venture, the joint venture itself, and a control group consisting of state-owned manufacturing organisations which were not involved in a foreign joint venture relationships. Survey results show those Chinese enterprises which participated in foreign partnered joint ventures made more changes to their management accounting system compared to similar Chinese companies who had no collaborative venture operations with foreign firms.

Auditing

Not until 1982 did China establish an auditing system for the whole country. The introduction of an auditing system has caused much controversy in China, especially over the role of governmental auditing, public auditing and internal auditing. There are seven articles relating to this topic, for example, Lau and Yang (1990)'s "Auditing in China: Historical Perspective and Current Developments"; Skousen, Yang and Dai's (1991) "Auditing in China: Recent Developments and Current Problems" and Graham's (1996) "Setting a Research Agenda for Auditing Issues in the People's Republic of China". These articles discuss the history of auditing in China, the current functions of the State Audit Department and auditing regulations. The functions of State Audit Department overlap with the functions of other governmental agencies, especially with the Ministry of Finance. This overlap has caused many problems in the development of governmental auditing as well as in the development of the public accounting profession.

Accounting History

Accounting in China has a long history which has caught the attention of many scholars in China, as well as overseas. Two recognised experts on accounting history in China are Daoyang Guo and Youliang Zhao. Guo's (1988) books, *Chinese Accounting History* (Volume 1 and 2) and *The History of Accounting Development*, and Zhao's (1992), *The Accounting and Auditing History in Ancient China* are regarded as classics of accounting historical research. However, none of these are available in English. Fortunately, the authors have published some papers in English: for example, Guo's "The Historical Contributions of Chinese Accounting" (1984) and "Confucius and Accounting" (1992); and Zhao's "A Brief History of Accounting and Auditing in China". The research styles of these two scholars differ; Guo's approach being more constructive while Zhao's is more conservative, emphasising the historical evidence.

There are many overseas historians studying Chinese accounting history. Philip Fu started his research on Chinese accounting history in the 1960s and his PhD dissertation, *A Study of Governmental Accounting in China: with Special Reference to the Sung Dynasty (960-1279)*, was completed in the University of Illinois in 1968, under the supervision of Professor V.K. Zimmeon. In 1971, Fu published a paper, "Government Accounting in China During the Chou Dynasty", in the *Journal of Accounting Research*.

More recent research on Chinese accounting history has been carried out by Max Aiken, Wei Lu, Lin Zejun, and Chen Siming. They include Aiken and Lu's (1993a, 1993b) "Perception, Culture and Research Method in Accounting History: Its Evolution in Modern China" and "Historical Instances of Innovative Accounting Practices in the Chinese Dynasties and Beyond", and Chen's (1998) "The Rise and Fall of Debit-Credit Bookkeeping in China, History and Analysis".

The innovation and evolution of Chinese double-entry bookkeeping is the significant contribution of Chinese accounting towards the development of accounting in the world. Three papers have discussed this issue. They are Jong's (1979) "The Traditional Accounting System in the Oriental countries – Korea, China and Japan", Lin's (1992) "Chinese Double-entry Bookkeeping Before the Nineteenth Century", and Aiken and Lu's (1998) "The Evolution of Bookkeeping in China: Historical Trends Shaping Western Influences of the Modern Era". They review the emergence of Chinese double-entry bookkeeping and evolutionary trends from single-entry to double-entry. The argument focuses on whether the principles of Chinese double-entry bookkeeping are similar to those of western double-entry bookkeeping. Lin believes that the principles between two methods are basically the same. Aiken and Lu contest that the underpinning of western bookkeeping method is the property right and the fundamental basis of the Chinese bookkeeping method is the cash movement.

Governmental Accounting

China has been a centrally controlled country for more than 2,000 years. The government has dominated society and had a strong influence on accounting developments. The development of governmental accounting was much faster than that of non-government accounting. The history of the development of Chinese government accounting systems has been documented by Aiken and Lu (1993). The current government accounting systems are discussed in Tang, Chow and Cooper's (1994) "Government Accounting" and Chen's (1987) "Budgetary Unit Accounting". The current development of accounting for government and not-for-profit organisations can be found in Epps and Chen's (1998) paper "A Comparison of the Development of Financial Reporting Standards for Not-for-profit Organisations in China and the United States". There is a set of separate accounting regulations for governments on different levels and not-for-profit organisations in China. These regulations adopted the cash-based rather than accrual-based recognition criteria.

Accounting Education

Accounting education has a long history in China. It is said that Confucius was an accountant nearly 2000 years ago. This great philosopher and educator taught accounting as a main subject in his classes. Some of his students found accounting positions in various self-independent governments and in rich family businesses after they graduated from his school. However, accounting was not a subject in education until early last century. It was regarded as a handcraft skill, which needed to be learned using the master-apprentice method. The modern accounting education system has also been interrupted and has suffered much criticism. Descriptions of present day accounting education systems can be found in Wang and Qian's (1987) paper

"Education and training of accounting and auditing personnel", Watne and Baldwin's (1988) "University-Level Education of Accountants in the People's Republic of China", and Lin and Deng's (1992) "Educating Accounting in China: Current Experiences and Future Prospects". They all pointed out there was a wide gap between Chinese and Western accounting education systems. Accounting research is a most disadvantaged area in education in China. They suggested there is a need to import some new ideas and methods to modify the current model, which is still based on the Soviet Union's accounting education system.

Accounting Profession

Compared with its counterparts in the Western countries, Public Accountants are quite young and vulnerable in China. They were separated into two campuses: the Chinese Institution of Certified Public Accountants (CICPA) and Chinese Association of Certified Public Auditors (CACPA) for more than a decade. Two papers, entitled "Auditing in China: Historical Perspective and Current Developments" by Lau and Yang (1990) and "Auditing in China: Recent Developments and Current Problems" by Skousen et al (1990) present a one-sided story, the development of social auditors in the ASCPA campus. Another paper, entitled "The Development of the Certified Public Accountant System in the People's Republic of China" by Xu (1995) describes the CPA's system in CICPA campus. The struggles and even vicious attacks upon each other have been well documented by Macve and Liu (1995) in the paper "A Proposal to Form a Unified Chinese Public Accountancy Profession: An Academic Perspective". They suggested that bureaucrats in the public finance and state audit sectors generally ignore firms headed by each other in their publications and official addresses although they have been marketing their own regulated firms. However, the existence of both accounting and auditing firms has led to many problems in the public accountancy/audit market (e.g. abnormal competition and duplicate audits), which have been widely acknowledged.

The CICPA and CACPA have been merged into new CICPA since June 1995. However, the battle between financial and auditing department has not yet finished.

China's first accounting standard was formally promulgated in 1992 by the Ministry of Finance. It indicated a willingness by the Chinese government to adopt the American-British model of accounting regulations. Since the promulgation of the first Chinese accounting standard in 1992, the Ministry of Finance has endeavoured to set up a new accounting regulation system by issuing the specific accounting standards. However, this procedure is more complicated because of the coexistence of the unified accounting systems and accounting standards (Chen et al, 1997). So far about thirty specific accounting standards have been drafted and circulated for public comment. The major criticism of those drafts of accounting standards is that they are not suitable for Chinese situations because they are mainly copied from the International Accounting Standards and GAAP from the United States. In 1993 the Ministry of Finance in 1993 planned to establish an accounting standards system with 32 specific standards in three years (Aiken et al, 1995). However, so far only 9 specific standards have been formally promulgated. These are:

- Changes of Accounting Policies; Estimations and Mistakes;
- Accounting for Revenues;
- Accounting for Investments;
- Accounting for Construction Contracts;
- Accounting for Re-organisation of Debt;
- After-Balance Date Events;
- Cash Flow Statement;
- Disclosure of Related-party Transactions and Accounting for Non-cash Transactions.

The promulgation of accounting standards has attracted international attention. Fourteen papers have been published on this issue. Most of them discuss the changes brought by the new accounting standards and difficulties found with implementation of the new system. Some scholars (Davidson et al, 1996, Liu and Eddie, 1995, Taussig et al, 1994, Xiao and Pan, 1997) have compared the first Chinese accounting standard with conceptual frameworks in the Western countries. They found that the Chinese accounting framework is similar to that in the West and the two sets of frameworks do not have significant differences. However, the implementation of new accounting standards has caused many problems. Chen et al (1997) observed the state of accounting reform in China since the promulgation of *Chinese Accounting Standard for Enterprise* and concluded that "Anglo-American accounting principles and standards … cannot be successfully transplanted overnight to the PRC" (p.150). There are three reasons for this: (1) a large part of commercial activity is conducted through state-owned enterprises and collectively owned enterprises, both having pubic ownership; (2) China's socialist market economy is still in its pre-mature stage and the legal system needs to be refined; and (3) the government has set up rigid accounting systems for different types of enterprises as well as accounting standards. In Western countries, accounting standards are established by professional accounting bodies.

Although many scholars have provided insights into determining the problems facing accounting reforms in China, they usually fail to analyse those problems under a historical and cultural framework. The main features of the historical and cultural framework in China are as follows:

- domination of governments in all aspects in the society;
- a relatively weak private sector in the economy;
- distinguishing Eastern culture resisting external influences.

In the near future, China will complete its proposed accounting standards. However, this is not to suggest that the Chinese accounting system will be fully comparable with the systems in western countries. If we view that the accounting standard is just another set of governmental regulations, and the environment in which the accounting standards are implemented is not substantially changed, the hope that promulgation of new accounting standards will improve the quality of accounting information may be diminished.

Other Subjects

Taxation is a legal issue rather than an accounting issue in China. Therefore the materials on taxation in accounting texts is weaker than in taxation texts. Two of the Chinese accounting books mentioned before both contain a chapter on the taxation issue, however these are very brief. For taxation issues, one should refer to legal texts such as *Taxation in the People's Republic of China* and *Taxation of Foreign Investment in the People's Republic of China*.

China officially opened two stock exchange markets in Shanghai in 1990 and in Shenzhen in 1991. By the end of 1998, 438 and 413 companies were listed on the Shanghai Exchange and Shenzhen Exchange, respectively. There are three papers on the subject of Chinese stock markets. Two of them, Ayling and Jiang's (1995) "Chinese and Western Stock Market: international Influences and Development" and Brayshaw and Zeng's (1995) "Re-emergence of Chinese Stock Market", describe the development of the Chinese stock market. Chui and Kwok (1998) studied the correlation of share prices between A shares and B shares. So far the research on Chinese stock markets is relatively weak. There have not been any articles on the impact of accounting information on share prices.

Research Methods Used in Chinese Accounting Research

Needles (1995, 1997) suggested that the types of research methodology used in international accounting research could be classified as follows: Capital Market, Deductive Descriptive, Empirical Descriptive, Empirical Statistical, Historical, Modeling and Theoretical.   According to the classification provided by Needles, the methodology used in Chinese accounting research is shown in Table 1-4. From 1966-1977 there were two papers published. One used the deductive descriptive method and the other used the historical method. From 1978 to 1992, there were 37 papers published, all of them were either descriptive or historical. The range of methodologies applied increased after 1992. Of 52 papers published after 1992, the majority of papers applied descriptive or historical methodology. However, some of the papers have adopted empirical methodology. As shown in Table 1-4, the most popular method applied in Chinese accounting research is the descriptive method. There are several reasons for the use of this method. Firstly, research into Chinese accounting is still at an early stage, and Chinese accounting is not yet fully understood by Western scholars, particularly in the areas of management accounting and accounting administration. There is a lot of work to be done to explain and describe Chinese accounting systems to the world. Secondly, most data concerning accounting information is confidential in China and it is difficult to obtain relevant data for research purposes. This situation is gradually changing with the introduction of the shareholder system, which requires enterprises to disclose certain accounting information to the public. Thirdly, most accounting researchers in China are under the influence of Marxist theory and prefer ideological debate. Scientific research methods are quite new for most accounting researchers and it will take time for them to become familiar with western research methods and styles. Their papers, even when co-authored by western scholars, are still restricted by their research methods.

Table 1-4 Research Methods Used in Chinese Accounting Research

Research Methods	1966-1977	1978-1992	1993-1998
1. Capital Market			1
2. Deductive Descriptive	1	33	40
3. Empirical Descriptive			3
4. Empirical Statistics			1
5. Historical	1	4	6
6. Modelling			
7. Theoretical			1
Total	2	37	52

Some empirical papers have appeared in the English literature. For example, Firth's (1996) "The Diffusion of Managerial Accounting Procedures in The People's Republic of China and The Influence of Foreign Partnered Joint Ventures", published in *Accounting, Organisations and Society*. Firth used survey and multi-regression methods and found that Chinese enterprises which participated in foreign partnered joint ventures made more changes to their management accounting system when compared to similar P.R.C. companies that had no collaborative venture operations with foreign firms. Chui and Kwok (1998) in their paper, "Cross-Autocorrelation Between A Shares and B Shares in the Chinese Stock Market", use multi-regression modelling to demonstrate that returns of B shares are correlated with those of A Shares and that this correlation depends upon the information transmission mechanism at work. Chan and Chow's (1997) "An Empirical Study of Tax Audit in China on International Transfer Pricing" shows that Chinese tax audits on transfer pricing are confined mainly to medium and small sized foreign investments, lower technology companies and transfer of tangible goods, and tend to focus on certain nationalities and forms of foreign investment.

Research Methodology

The narrative analytical approach is the major approach used in this book. This approach can be either deductive or inductive. Deductive reasoning begins with basic propositions and proceeds to derive logical conclusions about the subject under consideration. Inductive reasoning begins with observations and measurements and moves towards generalised conclusions. In inductive reasoning, the observation does not necessarily result in statistical data; it can comprise descriptions of the subject observed. In the case of this study on Chinese accounting, the subject of Chinese accounting has been observed from different points of view. Its accounting systems include financial, cost and management accounting. Its institutional arrangements are set up to promote accounting standards and the status of accountants, and its statutory requirements provide for professional organisations to be formally recognised. These observations have been conducted over time from the past to the present and on some occasions, future developments are also predicted. Attention has been given particularly to the changes occurring over time. These changes then have been analysed under a broad social framework and the impacts of political economic and cultural factors on accounting have been highlighted. The development of Chinese accounting has also been contrasted with the accounting system in western countries. Simple observations, however, cannot be regarded as research. Where these observations have been analysed critically and then generalised into conclusions, it becomes research by narrative language. The narrative analytical approach can be useful in exploratory research. Much of the subject being studied has not been fully understood and knowledge is needed to put more effort into the explanation of the nature and characteristics of the subject. The research about Chinese accounting is in its early stage. Often, the mechanism and the features of the Chinese accounting systems remain mysterious to westerners. Therefore, Chinese accounting should be explained in detail and then contrasted with western models.

The historical approach has been used in Chapter 7 of this book. In Chapter 7, the development of Chinese management accounting is examined, especially for historical aspects. It reveals that the present management accounting system in China is a product of a centrally planned economic system adopted by the Chinese from the early 1950s to late 1970s. The Chinese economic systems have been changed dramatically by the economic reforms carried out since 1978 and western management accounting theories and practices have been introduced into China for more than two decades.

However, in the present, Chinese management and cost accounting systems remain stable and only a few changes have been made. Compared with the financial accounting systems in China, which are closer to the western model, management accounting systems may need to be improved substantially.

The case study approach adopted in Chapter 5, is mainly descriptive and exploratory. In chapter 5, two cases are chosen in the comparison between research of accounting education systems in Australia and China. One university in China, Shanghai University of Finance and Economics, and one university in Australia, La Trobe University have been chosen as representatives of respective accounting education systems. The reason why only one university is selected from each country is there is a similarity of education systems and patterns among the universities in each country as well as unifying requirements of professional bodies. Therefore, the results of this case study will have significant scientific generalisation.

The survey approach has been used in this book. A survey of the application of western management accounting in China was carried out. There are 22 questions in the questionnaire that covered all aspects of management accounting methods, from short term to long term decision models and from budgeting methods to responsibility accounting. The questionnaire was translated into Chinese and sent to 150 financial managers, financial controllers and chief accountants and a total of 52 responses was received. Besides mailing the questionnaire directly to Chinese enterprises, 21 interviews were conducted in three different cities in China.

The multiple regression technique is used in Chapter 9 to identify the influences of political, economic and cultural factors on the development of accounting in China. The percentage of CPA in the total population of China is selected as the dependent variable for the development of accounting. Rates of real gross domestic production per person are chosen as the independent variable for economic influence; the percentage of trade value between the United States and China in the total Chinese trade value is used as a surrogate of the political influence; and the percentage of the employment of non-state sectors in total employment is selected as the independent variable for cultural influence.

Conclusion

In this chapter, the studies on Chinese accounting issues have been examined. Most accounting textbooks and journals which include Chinese accounting issues are reviewed from two aspects: the research contents and the methodologies applied. Secondly, the historical, academic and practical values of doing research into Chinese accounting are evaluated. It has been argued that studies on Chinese accounting topics will bring significant contributions to the development of accounting in the world. Finally, the methodologies to be used in this book are examined in detail. They include the narrative analytical approach, the historical approach, the case study approach, the survey approach and the regression analysis approach. Thus the thesis is a multi-dimensional and multi-technical study on Chinese accounting. It will attempt to provide a comprehensive analysis of all the key dimensions of accounting development in China.

2 Development of the Chinese Economy and Accounting after the 1949 Revolution

The Development of the Chinese Economy from 1949 to 1979

The People's Republic of China was established in 1949. From 1949-1952, the Chinese Communists rehabilitated the war-torn economy. They brought inflation under control, nationalised the industries, established a new monetary system and carried out land reforms in the countryside. During the rehabilitation period, outputs in both industry and agriculture rose quite rapidly and were restored to the past levels (Lippit, 1987).

The First Five-Year Plan was carried out by the Chinese with great help from the Soviet Union during 1952-1957. Industry output continued to rise strongly and gross industry output value was 2.3 times the 1952 level (Xue, 1982). However, this achievement was based on the extraction of surplus production from the countryside and could not be sustained in a long run because the surplus from agriculture was limited.

From 1958 to 1960, China attempted to bring about a "Great Leap Forward" (GLF) in economy. The Five-Year Plan (1953-1957) had been successful and had created an atmosphere of great optimism, which led the leaders to make wild plans for the future. The famous campaign of the Great Leap Forward, launched by Mao Zedong in February 1958, called for a doubling of output within one year. The Great Leap Forward led to serious imbalances in the economy, and the natural catastrophe which later hit agriculture further hampered development. During the second Five-Year-Plan (1958-1962) the average growth rate of the economy was 3.8 per cent, compared with 18 per cent during the First Five-Year Plan (Lippit, 1987). Another setback hit the Chinese economy in 1960, when Soviet aid ended suddenly. The Russian technicians and experts, including accounting experts, were withdrawn from China. As there had been between 10,000 and 20,000 Soviet experts and advisers in all economic areas in China during the 1950s, the withdrawal with their detailed plans was deeply felt in Chinese economy for some years afterwards.

26

China started its recovery plan in 1962 under the leadership of Liu Shao-Chi and his supporters, including Zhou En-Lai, Deng Xiao-Ping and Chen Yun. Moderate economic policies were introduced by them, such as reducing the accumulation rate, emphasising material incentives and increasing living standards. Mao, however, had lost his dominant position in the party with the collapse of the GLF. He tried to regain power again and found his support from youth activities, the red guards. With help from his wife, Jiang Qing and the Gang of Four, he launched the Great Proletarian Cultural Revolution in 1966.

The Great Proletarian Cultural Revolution had lasted for ten years by 1976 when Mao Zedong died and the Gang of Four was arrested. In this ten year period, governmental organisations were destroyed, the economy was broken down and the Chinese culture was seriously damaged.

Accounting Development from 1949 to 1979

Introduction of the Soviet Union Accounting System (1949-1957)

After the foundation of the PRC the economic structure began to follow the Soviet Union with the introduction of central planning. The capitalist enterprises of the economy were gradually replaced by state-owned and collective enterprises. State-owned enterprises were considered a leading force in a socialist economy and therefore all private enterprises were transferred to public ownership. The Ministry of Finance was established as the department in charge of accounting affairs and commenced to unify, based on the Soviet model, the variety of accounting systems inherited from the old society. The Ministry of Finance issued thousands of regulations to ensure the implementation of uniform accounting systems. The complexity and the inflexibility of the Soviet style uniform accounting system were discovered at this stage, and some simplifying suggestions were proposed by accounting academics and practitioners. Accounting research was focused on translation of Soviet Union accounting theories and an attempt was made to distinguish the different natures of capitalist accounting and socialist accounting.

Simplification and First Collapse of Accounting Systems (1957-1961)

The "Great Leap Forward" was a catharsis for accounting and led to the virtual collapse of the infant accounting systems established in enterprises. In

Mao's philosophy, the creative talents of the masses were unlimited, and if the abilities of the masses could be liberated and encouraged, they could create a miracle. Therefore all regulations were to be abolished, to let the masses do as their will directed and create a new China. This irrational thinking resulted in a severe contraction of the economy and caused a catastrophe. Accounting suffered under this deregulation movement. Lack of accounting during this period is illustrated in the following two statements:

1. Not only were the functions of accounting neglected as a result of the deviation from the principles of scientific management, but many absurd accounting concepts and practices were also encouraged and applied. A notable example was the practice of "accounting without books", a reference not to the use of a computer but to the elimination of accounting journals and ledgers. Such a system might work briefly, over time, however, original documents such as invoices, receipts, and other documents accumulated, resulting in great confusion and disarray in accounting departments (Zhao, 1988, p.28).
2. Drastic simplifications of accounting systems and procedures were made in order to make it possible for workers in the factories and peasants in the People's communes to participate in such work (Kwang, 1966, p.65).

Reshaping and Nationalising Accounting Systems (1961-1965)

Because of the confrontation with the Soviet Union and the still cooling relationship with the United States, China adopted a policy of self-reliance in the recovery period from 1961-1965. It was not surprising that a nationalising movement occurred in accounting and other disciplines. Chinese-authored accounting textbooks and curricula were proposed and published in order to establish a new accounting system with Chinese characteristics. New accounting regulations and disciplines were gradually installed in the country and the practice of accounting without books was criticised and abandoned. Accounting academics and practitioners tried to create for China its own accounting system, and several bookkeeping methods were proposed. These replaced the debit/credit double entry bookkeeping method. The ideological reason for this movement was that the debit/credit method was practised by the United States and other western countries and therefore was a capitalist method. It had also been adopted by the Soviet Union and therefore was a revisionist method. China was to use its own socialist bookkeeping method. The only direction the accounting academics and practitioners could go was to look back to traditional bookkeeping methods. Several new bookkeeping methods were created as a result. The increase/decrease method and receipt/disbursement method were the most popular and practicable methods among the proposed methods.

The increase/decrease method was implemented first in state owned commercial enterprises and then was adopted by many industrial as well as commercial enterprises. It was considered easy to learn and master. Also, it overcame much of the confusion associated with the debit/credit method. Several receipt/disbursement methods were innovated and used. The cash receipt/disbursement method was used for banking industries, the property receipt/disbursement method was used in people's communes and the fund receipt/disbursement method was used by government units and social organisations. The fund receipt/disbursement method is still used in government organisations.

Accounting in the Great Proletarian Cultural Revolution Period (1966-1976)

The Great Proletarian Cultural Revolution began in 1966 and introduced a ten-year period of chaos. The Cultural Revolution shook all of Chinese society profoundly, and was often very painful. Accounting practice was terminated because the masses and the Red Guards thought it represented the vestiges of capitalism and federalism. Accounting education and training were dropped totally from the education system. Some Chinese and overseas scholars have made the following comments:

> By the time of the great proletarian Cultural Revolution (1966-1976), intellectuals had become one of the primary targets for revolutionary charges of elitism. Most academicians were humiliated and branded as reactionary academic authorities because of their "inappropriate thinking" and "bourgeois attitudes". Intellectuals came to be known as the "stinking ninth category" of class enemies (Watne and Baldwin, 1988, p.141).

> Many accountants later complained that during this period they could not do their routine bookkeeping during office hours because that time was supposed for the "unprecedented revolution". Many accounting teachers were forced to perform manual labor in the countryside, and record-keeping and statistical services which were vital for central planning were virtually abandoned. Any accounting measures designed to aid management, such as the regular comparison of major ratios among enterprises of the same industry and of similar size, were denounced as running counter to the revolutionary line and were dropped (Zhao, 1988, p.29).

Mao died in September 1976, and his powerful widow Jiang Qing and the other three radicals in the so-called "Gang of Four" were arrested quite soon after Mao's death. This signalled the end of the ten-year trauma of the Great Proletarian Cultural Revolution. Deng Xiao-Ping took power at the Third Plenum of the Eleventh Central Committee of the CPC in December 1978, and a new era began.

Economic Reforms since 1979

It now has been 22 years since China first carried out reform of its economic structure. Reforms conducted can be divided into the following four phases.

The first phase covers roughly the period from the Third Plenary Session of the 11th CPC Central Committee in December 1978 to the Third Plenary Session of the 12th CPC Central Committee in October 1984. Reform in this phase was focused on rural areas. During this period, a contract responsibility system on a household basis with remuneration linked to output was introduced. Vast numbers of peasants were granted adequate operational autonomy so as to arouse their enthusiasm in production. The rural economy was rejuvenated with rapid development of town and township enterprises. Meanwhile, preliminary reforms also were conducted in urban areas, aimed at (1) developing diversified economic elements, (2) granting greater decision-making power to enterprises, and (3) improving the financial structure.

The second phase covers roughly the period from the Third Plenary Session of the 12th CPC Central Committee to October 1992, that is, before the convocation of the 14th party congress. The CPC Central Committee's "Decision on Economic Structure Reform", which was adopted by the Third Plenary Session of the 12th CPC Central Committee, marked the beginning of a shift in the focus of reform from rural areas to cities. During this phase, efforts were centred on injecting greater vitality into enterprises, and especially on enlivening state-owned large and medium-sized enterprises. Coordinated reforms were instigated for management systems, including prices, planning, investment, material supplies, finance and taxation, the monetary system, and foreign trade. Political and social reforms were also initiated in many fields including science and technology, education, culture, and legal systems. However, these attempts slowed down after the Tian An Men Square event in 1989.

The third phase begins with the convocation of 14th Chinese Communist Party Congress. According to the famous speech of Deng Xiao-Ping on his southern tour, CPC adopted a new party line to develop the socialist market economy. Under this concept, a socialist economy can also be a market economy. The successful experience of managing a market economy in capitalist countries can be adopted and used in the Chinese environment. But the Chinese still put a "socialist" condition on the market economy. This is because China as claimed by its leaders has different cultural and political systems. With the deepening of reform and the widening of the open door, the Chinese economy will be capitalist in appearance but with market differences.

The fourth phrase is also called the post-Deng era or Jiang's era. After the death of paramount leader of Deng Xiao-Ping in 1997, the chosen successor, the President Jiang Zie-Ming controlled powers. The legacy of Deng's reforms and open-ups was inherited and carried out forwards. Although China experienced many difficulties in this phrase, such as the financial crises in the southeastern Asia, the economic policies were maintained consistently according to the principles set up by Deng.

Over 20 years since 1978, reform made tremendous progress. This has been attracting worldwide attention, although China still suffers criticism from the West, such as for human rights abuse. Gao (1996) summarised the major changes in Chinese economic structure as follows:

1. Popularly owned enterprises have begun to transform themselves into independent commodity producers; and managers with the power of decision making in the original organisations are taking up positions within administrative organisations.
2. Fully nationalised ownership has given way to various forms of shared interest with a majority public component.
3. The mechanism of economic operation has begun to be transformed from that of mandatory allocation and distribution to a combination of planned economy and market regulation.
4. The form of economic policy making has been changed from the former centralised strategic command system, with its lack of distinction between the responsibilities of state and the enterprises, to one involving a redefinition of governmental functions and the introduction of multi-level responsibility.
5. The principle of social provision has begun to shift from the former egalitarian system - everyone "eating from a big common pot" to a variety of forms that operate on the basis of distribution according to contribution.
6. The former principle of economic association based on a vertical division among government agencies has given way to a series of lateral relations.
7. The style of economic management has been gradually transformed from a direct to an indirect practice.

8. Employment policy and personnel management in the enterprises, based on the maintenance of a permanent work force, and a system of commissioned cadres, has given way to the introduction of a competitive element, to the practice of open recruitment and to the optimum organisation of labour.

9. China's economic relations with other countries are no longer determined by the long-standing closed-door policy, but follow an open style of economic activity that allows full participation in the system of international trade and cooperation (p.11-12).

Comparing 1998 with 1978 from a macroscopic view, China's achievements can be found as follows according to *China Statistical Yearbook* (1999):

1. The Chinese national economy had been tremendously strengthened. The gross national product (GNP) had been increased from 362.4 billion yuan to 7,801.8 billion yuan, with an average annual growth of 16.6 per cent. After deducting the inflation rate, the real average annual growth is 9.8 per cent. The gross domestic product (GDP) had increased from 362 billion yuan to 7,939.6 billion yuan, with a real average annual growth rate of 9.9 per cent. GDP per Capita rose from 379 yuan to 2,451.7 yuan.

2. Industrial production had been accelerated. Over 20 years, the gross output value of industry rose from 423.7 billion to 11,904.8 billion yuan, with an average annual growth rate of 18.1 per cent. Major industrial products have increased rapidly. The output of coal doubled; Steel increased from 31.8 million tons to 115.6 million tons; the annual growth rate of the output of electricity is 7.9%.

3. Agriculture has made significant progress. The output of agriculture rose from 139.7 billion to 2,451.7 billion yuan, with an average annual growth rate of 15.4 per cent. The output of major farm crops all increased substantially. The Chinese have got rid of the biggest problem of how to feed 1 billion people. China now can produce more than sufficient foods to sustain the growth of its population. The noteworthy development in the agriculture sector is the emergence of village and township enterprises (VTE). Currently, the output from VTE have over-weighted the output for agriculture in the total rural gross output value. The value-added output from village and township enterprises is 2,218.7 billion yuan in 1998 and its proportion in the total gross value of value of agriculture is more than 90 per cent.

4. The socialist market economic framework was established successfully in China. Domestic and foreign trade increased vigorously. The total value of retail sales of consumer goods increased from 155.9 to 2,915 billion yuan, with the annual growth rate of 15.8 per cent. The annual inflation rate for the general retail price is 6.8 per cent. After allowing for inflation, the real growth rate for retail sales is 9 per cent per annum over 20 years. Foreign trade has continuously expanded. The total value of import-export was 2,685.4 billion yuan (323.9 billion US dollars) in 1998, which was 75.6 times of that in 1978. The average annual growth rate of foreign trade was 24.1 per cent. Foreign direct investment (FDI) surged from 4.6 billion US dollars in 1985 to 58.6 billion US dollars in 1998. The average annual growth rate was 16.2 per cent. In 1990 and 1991, China established the stock exchange markets in Shanghai and Shenzhen. By 1998, there were 851 listed companies and listed stocks totalled 931. The negotiable market value of stocks is 574.6 billion yuan.

5. The living standards have been improved substantially. Ordinary people in China enjoyed benefits brought by the economic reforms and open-ups over the last 20 years. Per capital annual income of rural householders increased from 133.6 yuan to 2,028.4 yuan. The annual growth is 8.1 per cent after considering the effect of inflation. Per capital annual disposable income of urban householders increased from 343.4 yuan to 5,081.7 yuan with a real annual growth of 8 per cent. The consumption power in 1998 increased by 15 times of that in 1978. In 1978, the savings deposit was 21.1 billion yuan. However, this figure increased to 5,319.6 billion yuan in 1998, 252 times of that in 1978. The developments in other areas, such as culture, public health, sports and leisure, tourism and sciences all make significant progress. The Comprehensive Indexes of Chinese National Economy from 1978 to 1994 are shown in Table 2-1.

The accomplishments scored in the 20-year reform are significant. However, some problems have emerged in the course of development. The economic reform has not been carried out in a comprehensive way, but in one step after another, as in Deng's maxim: "feeling the stones in order to wade across the river". Therefore reform has inevitably been restricted in breadth, as well as depth. The state's ability in macro economic regulation and control

Table 2-1 Comprehensive Indexes of the Chinese National Economy from 1978 to 1998

	1978	1980	1985	1990	1995	1998	Increase/decrease	Annual growth
1. Gross National Product (GNP) *	362.4	451.8	898.9	1,859.8	5,749.5	7,801.8	7,439.4	16.6%
2. Gross Domestic Product GDP)*	362.4	451.8	896.4	1,854.8	5,847.8	7,939.6	7,577.2	16.7%
3. Per Capita GDP (yuan)	379.0	460.0	853.0	1,634.0	4,854.0	6,392.0	6,013.0	15.2%
4. Gross Output Value of Agriculture *	139.7	192.3	362.0	766.2	2,034.1	2,451.7	2,312.0	15.4%
5. Yield of Major Farm Crops								
Grain (million tons)	304.8	320.6	379.1	446.2	466.6	512.3	207.5	2.6%
Oil-bearing Crops (million tons)	5.2	7.7	15.8	16.1	22.5	23.1	17.9	7.7%
Cotton (million tons)	2.2	2.7	4.1	4.5	4.7	4.9	2.7	4.1%
6. Gross Output Value of Industry *	423.7	515.4	971.6	2,392.4	9,189.4	11,904.8	11,481.1	18.1%
7. Output of Major Industrial Products								
Coal (billion tons)	0.6	0.6	0.9	1.1	1.4	1.3	0.7	3.9%
Grude Oil (million tons)	104.1	106.0	124.9	138.3	150.0	161.0	56.9	2.2%
Steel (million tons)	31.8	37.1	46.8	66.4	95.4	115.6	83.8	6.7%
Cement (million tons)	65.2	79.9	146.0	210.0	475.6	536.0	470.8	11.1%
Electricity (billion kwh)	256.6	300.6	410.7	621.2	1,007.0	1,167.0	910.4	7.9%
Cloth (billion m)	11.0	13.4	14.7	18.9	26.0	24.1	13.1	4.0%
8. Total Retail Sales of Consumer Goods *	155.9	214.0	430.5	830.0	2,062.0	2,915.0	2,759.1	15.8%
9. Per Capital Annual Income of Rural	133.6	191.3	397.6	686.3	1,577.7	2,162.0	2,028.4	14.9%

Households (yuan)								
10. Per Capital Annual Disposable Income of Urban households (yuan)	343.4	477.6	739.1	1,510.2	4,283.0	5,425.1	5,081.7	14.8%
11. Household Consumption (yuan)	184.0	236.0	437.0	803.0	2,236.0	2,972.0	2,788.0	14.9%
Rural Householders	138.0	178.0	347.0	571.0	1,434.0	1,895.0	1,757.0	14.0%
Urban Householders	405.0	496.0	802.0	1,686.0	4,874.0	6,182.0	5,777.0	14.6%
12. Savings Deposit in Urban and Rural Areas *	21.1	40.0	162.3	703.4	2,966.2	5,340.7	5,319.6	31.9%
13. General Retail Price Index	100.0	108.1	128.1	207.7	356.1	370.9	270.9	6.8%
14. Total Investment in Fixed Assets	n	91.1	254.3	451.7	2,001.9	2,840.6	2,749.5	25.8%
15. Total Value of Imports and Exports	35.5	57.0	206.7	556.0	2,350.0	2,685.4	2,649.9	24.1%
16. Total Amount of Foreign Capital Used	2.9	2.9	4.6	10.3	48.1	58.6	55.7	16.2%
17. Stock Market								
Number of Listed Companies	n	n	n	10	323.0	851.0		
Number of Listed Stocks	n	n	n	10	381.0	931.0		
Total Negotiable Market Capitalisation*	n	n	n	n	93.8	574.6		
Total Trading Volume (billion shares)	n	n	n	n	40.4	215.4		

* Amounts in Billion Yuan

Source: *China Statistical Yearbook*, 1999, State Statistical Bureau, The People's Republic of China

is weak; energy resources, transportation, and important raw materials have always been "bottlenecks" that restrict the development of the national economy; agriculture has lacked sufficient staying power, and the peasants' burden is too heavy in many aspects; the uniform free market has not formed and the dual price system still exists, especially in raw materials, such as steel, grain and cotton; inflation has been a serious problem and in some stages prices have risen over 20 per cent. A more serious problem is the reform goal, to enliven state-owned enterprises, has not been reached. The situation of state-owned enterprises has got worse and worse. According to a report by Hong Kong journalist, Shao Ling (1994):

> At present, however, some 40 percent of the large and medium state-owned enterprises on the Chinese mainland are running in the red, and the situation is rather serious. In Liaoning Province, the country's major heavy industrial base with a large number of state-owned enterprises, in recent years, nearly half (46.2 percent) of the state-owned enterprises have been running in the red, and nearly 700,000 workers could not receive their wages on time. The situation of Heilongjiang Province, another major heavy industrial base, was even worse. The large and medium enterprises in Harbin have failed to pay a total of 1.3 billion yuan of debts that are due, and still owe debts totalling 6.3 billion yuan. Some enterprises have been mired in a state of suspended or semi-suspended operation (p.1).

Whether the economic reform in China can be successful mainly depends upon enterprise reform. The transformation of the operation structure of state-owned enterprises and the reviving of state-owned enterprises are the key issues of economic reform.

Accounting Reforms Since 1979

The Promulgation of Accounting Law

The Accounting Law of the People's Republic of China was adopted on 21 January 1985 at the Ninth Session of the Standing Committee of the Sixth National People's Congress[1]. This was the first accounting law since the revolution of 1949. In the Chinese context, it has been proved time and again

---

[1] In China, the National People's Congress (NPC) enjoys great power: it amends the Constitution, makes laws, elects the Head of State, etc. The highest organ of state administration is the State Council, which is formed by the Premier, Vice Premiers, and Ministers.

that it is necessary to formalise the fundamental principles of accounting in a legal form in order to strengthen and improve accounting practice.

Since the promulgation of the Accounting Law, Chinese accounting legislation has three levels (Ji and Lu, 1992).

On the first level, there are laws promulgated by People's Congress such the *Accounting Law of the People's Republic of China*.

On the second level, there is accounting legislation promulgated by the State Council: *Regulations Concerning Certified Public Accountants of the People's Republic of China, Regulations Concerning Chief Accountants[2], Regulations on Accountants' Responsibilities*, and so on.

On the third level is legislation issued by Ministry of Finance or legislation which has been approved by the Ministry of Finance and promulgated by the relevant ministries. For example, the Ministry of Light Industry prepared *The Uniform Accounting System for Light Industry* which is employed only in light industry, the Ministry of Commercial Industry prepared *The Uniform Accounting System for Commercial Industry* which is employed in the commercial industry and so on.

The Reform of Financial Accounting

The reform of financial accounting is the most active part in the whole accounting reform. Every step in economic reform has involved great change in financial accounting. The uniform accounting system used by industrial enterprises has been revised and improved from 1980 under the impact of the economic reform and Western accounting development. In 1980, the new *Uniform Industrial Accounting System - Chart of Accounts and Financial Report* was published, and then in 1985 and 1989 some overall changes were made. From these changes, we can clearly see the impact of economic reform on accounting, particularly the reform of profit appropriation between the government and state-owned enterprises: from profit appropriation, to tax levying, and then to profit responsibility systems.

---

[2] In China the typical framework of management of a state enterprise can be described as "three levels of management and two levels of economic accounting". At the top management level are the directors, a chief accountant, a chief engineer and a chief economist. At the middle managerial level of the enterprise are the chief staff of the workshops, the engineers. At the third level are accounting clerks and workers. Normally, each state enterprise has an independent accounting department dealing with daily transactions and events, and in addition, each workshop has a few accounting staff measuring, recording and analysing costs and expenses incurred in the production process.

Since 1979, China has established several Special Economic Zones with special investment incentives, and has also provided favourable investment conditions in designated coastal cities, including the establishment within these cities of Economic and Technological Development Zones. *The Law of the People's Republic of China on Joint Ventures Using Chinese and Foreign Investment* was promulgated in 1979 by the State Council. Some accounting regulations regarding joint ventures have been published since then by the Ministry of Finance. For example, *the Accounting Regulation of People's Republic of China for Joint Ventures with Chinese and Foreign Investments, Classification of Accounts and Accounting Statements of Industrial Joint Ventures with Chinese and Foreign Investment,* which were published in 1985. This was the first time that accounting regulations departed from the fund-based accounting approach, and established the concept of accounting elements such as assets, liabilities, capital, revenue and expenses. The regulations were a first attempt to harmonise Chinese accounting practice with international practice.

The promulgation of *Accounting Regulations for Shared Enterprises* in 1992 was a turning point of Chinese accounting practice. Under these regulations the fund based accounting approach was abandoned and international practice was adopted.

Since the economic reform, many problems have arisen in financial accounting which Chinese accountants had never before encountered. These problems, which have been dealt with for many years in western countries, include: securities; leases; business combinations; bankruptcy; usage of land with compensation; intangible assets; operation under contract; corporation form of company, and so on. Every year new regulations regarding these problems are promulgated in China.

The Establishment of an Auditing System

On December 4, 1982, a new Constitution of China was drawn up by the fifth National People's Congress. For the first time in Chinese history, the Constitution required the government to establish an Audit Administration and to appoint an Auditor-General to take charge of it.

On September 15, 1983, China's State Audit Administration was officially established. Various audit departments were set up within the Administration. At the same time, audit departments were gradually established at all levels of provinces, cities and self-governing areas.

In 1985, the State Council and the State Auditing Office approved the *Tentative Regulations on Auditing Practice, Auditing Procedures* and *Regulations on Internal Auditing*. In June 1987, the State Council issued the *Tentative Regulations on Punishment for the Violation of Financial Laws and Disciplines*. In October 1988, a set of new *Audit Regulations of the PRC* was approved by the State Council. This new set of audit regulations replaced the 1985 *Tentative Regulations on Auditing Practice* and became effective on January 1, 1989.

Reintroducing the Certified Public Accountant System

The Certified Public Accountant system was restored in China in 1980, after being abandoned in 1960s. Since then, the growth of CPAs and CPA firms has been rapid. In 1993, The People's Congress promulgated the *Certified Public Accountants Act*. In 1995, the new Chinese Auditing Standards were issued by Ministry of Finance (MOF). By the end of 1993, there were more than 15,000 practitioners in the CPA profession in China. The certified public accountants system will be reviewed in Chapter 4.

Reform of Taxation System

The taxation system in China is probably the most ancient in the world. Records of land taxes go back almost 4000 years (Li, 1991). However, a comprehensive taxation system was not implemented until 1979. After 1949 and prior to 1978, all enterprises were owned by the people. Most income was turned over to the state legally in the form of profits, while only a small proportion was paid in taxes. The State kept tight control on revenues and expenditures. This was called the "big pot" financial system. Since the economic reform started in 1979, a comprehensive tax and fiscal system has gradually been installed in China. At the beginning of 1994, the central government overhauled the taxation system.

The Main Changes in the Taxation System

Reform of the enterprise income tax system The major element of this reform was the unification of income tax rates for domestic enterprises, by fixing pre-tax expense deductions and establishing a common tax base. The tax burden was reduced and a rational, unified proportional tax rate was implemented.

The central government had indicated the next task in the reform of enterprise income tax system was to unify the income tax rates for domestic enterprises with the income tax rates applied to foreign-funded enterprises.

Reform of the turnover tax system The main element in this reform was the establishment of a unified turnover tax system. The core tax in this system is a Value-Added Tax, and other supplementary taxes are Business Tax and Consumption Tax. Value-Added Tax was levied in most areas except some commodity operations. Meanwhile, the old Product Tax had been replaced by a Consumption Tax. The Consumption Tax is levied on some luxury consumption products and some restricted products such as tobaccos and liquid.

Introduction of new taxes In accordance with these developments and changes of tax sources some new taxes have been introduced, including a land appreciation tax, a resource tax, a securities trading tax, and an inheritance tax. The current tax system in China is illustrated in Figure 2-1.

Separation of the government functions as the owner of assets and as an administrator of operating of such assets Taxes and profits from state-owned enterprise profits have been separated. The State as the administrator of economic affairs will levy income taxes on all types of enterprises, which include state-owned enterprises. The State as the investor in the state-owned-enterprises will also be entitled to share the after-tax profits in these enterprises. The distribution rate of profits from a state-owned enterprise is no longer regulated by government.

Establishment of a tax-sharing system The significant change in 1994 tax reform was to establish a tax-sharing system by central and local authorities. The essential elements of the tax-sharing system are as follows: (a) The administrative authority of the central government and that of local governments was separated rationally. Then the revenue scope of governments at all levels was defined in accordance with the principle that financial power is subordinated to administrative authority, and tax categories were divided into central taxes, local taxes, and taxes shared by the central government and local governments. (b) Two sets of taxation administrative organisations, central taxation offices and local taxation offices, were established separately at the central and local levels. Central taxation offices were responsible for collecting central taxes and taxes shared by the state and local governments. Local taxation offices were responsible for collecting local taxes.

Those categories that are regarded as indispensable for protecting the interests and rights of the state and for effecting macro economic regulation and control are categorised as central taxes. Central taxes include Consumption Tax; Value-Added Tax levied by the customs on the import and export of products; income taxes on central government-owned enterprises; revenues collectively turned over by railways, banks, and insurance institutions (including Business Tax and Enterprise Income Tax); income tax of local and foreign-funded banks, as well as all non-banking financial institutions and enterprises, and all tax reimbursements on exports.

Those categorised as local categories of taxes are properly collected by local taxation offices, and can help arouse the enthusiasm of localities. These include:

- business tax (excluding railways, banks, and head offices of insurance companies);
- income tax on local enterprises;
- urban and rural land use tax;
- personal income tax;
- fixed-asset investment orientation tax;
- urban maintenance and construction tax;
- property tax.

Also available are:

- vehicle and vessel licence tax;
- stamp duty;
- animal slaughter tax;
- agriculture and animal husbandry tax;
- and farmland use tax.

Legally contract tax, inheritance and gifts taxes, value-added tax on property and real estate transfers, and tax on income from compensated sales of state land are in use. In order to ensure stable growth in the revenue of local governments, the Central government will constantly monitor tax categories in the future, according to local economic development and changes in tax resources (Yu, 1994).

Figure 2-1 The Current Tax System in China

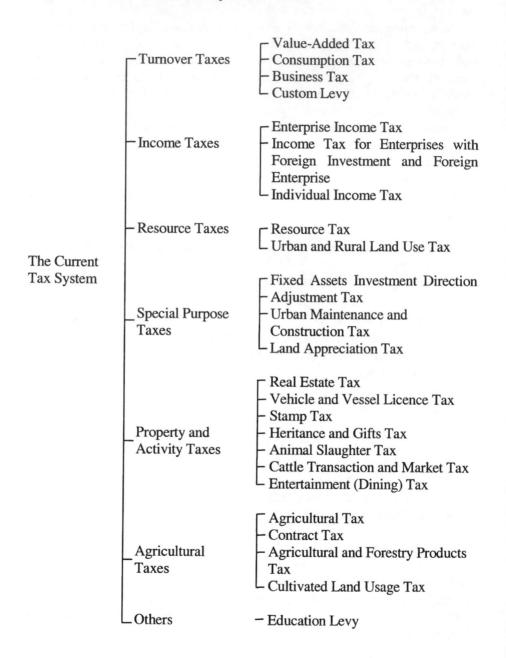

Turnover Taxes
- Value-Added Tax
- Consumption Tax
- Business Tax
- Custom Levy

Income Taxes
- Enterprise Income Tax
- Income Tax for Enterprises with Foreign Investment and Foreign Enterprise
- Individual Income Tax

Resource Taxes
- Resource Tax
- Urban and Rural Land Use Tax

Special Purpose Taxes
- Fixed Assets Investment Direction Adjustment Tax
- Urban Maintenance and Construction Tax
- Land Appreciation Tax

Property and Activity Taxes
- Real Estate Tax
- Vehicle and Vessel Licence Tax
- Stamp Tax
- Heritance and Gifts Tax
- Animal Slaughter Tax
- Cattle Transaction and Market Tax
- Entertainment (Dining) Tax

Agricultural Taxes
- Agricultural Tax
- Contract Tax
- Agricultural and Forestry Products Tax
- Cultivated Land Usage Tax

Others
- Education Levy

Tax categories that have a direct bearing on economic development are defined as taxes shared by both the central and local governments, including Valued-Added Tax, Securities Trading Tax, and Resources Tax. This was also proved to be one of the special characteristics of the current Chinese tax system of reform.

Reasons for the Reform of the Taxation System

Before this major reform in the financial area, China's income tax rates were fixed according to ownership. There was a rate of 55 per cent for state-owned enterprises, an eight-grade progressive rate for collective enterprises, and a proportional tax rate of 33 per cent for foreign funded enterprises (in addition to the preferential policy of "tax exemption in the first two years and tax reductions in the next three years"). Therefore different types of enterprises were loaded with different tax burdens and fair competition among them was out of the question.

As to turnover taxes, there was unequal treatment of domestic and foreign enterprises. While over 60 different rates of Product Tax and Value-Added Tax were applicable to domestic enterprises, foreign-funded enterprises paid only a Consolidated Industrial and Commercial Tax at the rate of 5 per cent; and as a consequence, the competitiveness of state-owned enterprises were adversely affected.

Another reason for tax reform was that the function of tax in the macro-economic administration changed. Before economic reform, tax was used as a tool to adjust prices. When cost, demand, and technical advance underwent inevitable changes, nothing but the tax rate could be employed to readjust prices. If products sold well and earned more income, the tax rate would be raised. On other hand, when the cost rose and market demand slackened, the tax rate would be reduced a little. In the end, there were more and more rates of tax. However, after economic reform the control on prices was gradually relaxed, and most products now have their price regulated by the market. Therefore tax was no longer treated mainly as a tool for adjusting prices of products, but has become an important fiscal tool in governmental macro fiscal and monetary policy and in decision-making.

43

3 Accounting Standards and Uniform Accounting Systems

For many years, China employed uniform accounting systems. The accounting reform that occurred in 1979 has focused attention on the relationship between uniform accounting and accounting standards. Questions have since been raised, including whether or not uniform accounting includes accounting standards. In other words, was it necessary to establish Chinese accounting standards beside uniform accounting systems. A special conference on accounting standards was held during the annual meeting of the Chinese Society of Accountants in January 1989, at which all Chinese accounting academics and practitioners agreed that it was indeed necessary to establish accounting standards.

In October 1988, a research group had been formed within the Accounting Section of the Ministry of Finance to be in charge of the establishment of Chinese accounting standards. After three years' preparation, the first draft of *Chinese Accounting Standards for Enterprises No 1 - Basic Standards* (The Ministry of Finance, 1991) was developed and sent to accounting academics and professionals for public hearing (Gang, 1992). An International Symposium on Chinese Accounting Standards was held in Shengzheng[3] in February 1992 (Yang, 1992). International experts were invited to join the discussion[4].

Finally, in December 1992, the *Chinese Accounting Standard for Enterprise* was formally promulgated by the Ministry of Finance in China (MOF, 1992a), effective from 1 July 1993. It was the landmark of Chinese accounting reforms, indicating that accounting practitioners and scholars in China had begun to use international accounting standards and Western experience to orient further accounting reforms. This chapter reviews the main contents of the Chinese Accounting Standard and examines the main

---

[3] Shengzheng is the first Chinese Special Economic Zone since China opened its doors in 1979, its success has surprised the world and has been the model of economic development in China.
[4] Mr Arthur Wyatt, Chairman of the International Accounting Standards Committee, and Mr David Cains, Secretary of the Committee attended the Symposium and gave speeches.

changes in accounting practices that ensued from the issue of the standards. This chapter also analyses the impact of economic development, foreign investment, reforms on the enterprise structure and the emergence of stock exchange markets on the setting of accounting standards. Conclusions are drawn about possible future developments of Chinese accounting standards and reforms after considering the experiences in Western countries.

Main Contents and Characteristics of the Chinese Accounting Standard

The Chinese Accounting Standard for Enterprise includes 10 chapters and 66 articles. These appertain general rules, basic principles, and the nature of asset, liability, owner's equity, revenue, expense, profit, financial statements and supplementary provisions.

The general rules include nine articles that explain the aim of setting accounting standards, the nature and scope of accounting standards, the relationship between accounting standards and the existing accounting regulations. Topics covered are accounting entity and objectives, going-concern concept, accounting periods, bookkeeping, recording currency and languages. It is clearly stated that this standard applies to all enterprises in China, including joint ventures, exclusively foreign-owned enterprises and those Chinese enterprises operating overseas.

The basic principles include 12 concepts that specify the basic criteria of accounting tasks: objectivity, relevance, comparability, timeliness, consistency, understandability, accrual basis, matching principle, conservatism, historical cost, separation of revenue expenditure and capital expenditure, and materiality.

Chapters 3 to 8 deal with so called accounting elements. There are six accounting elements: assets (chapter 3), liability (chapter 4), owner's equity (chapter 5), revenue (chapter 6), expenditure (chapter 7) and profit (chapter 8) in the Chinese Accounting Standard. In each chapter, the methods of ascertaining, measuring, recording, and reporting accounting elements are specified.

The major financial statements required are described in chapter 9 of the standard: the balance sheet, the income statement, and the statement of changes in financial position.

The Ministry of Finance of the People's Republic of China is responsible for formulating, explaining and amending Chinese Accounting Standards according to chapter 10.

Main Changes in Accounting Practices that were Initiated by the Issue of this Standard

China had not had its own accounting standards. The accounting practices were governed by uniform accounting systems and accounting regulations that contained major accounting assumptions and concepts. Comparing the uniform accounting systems and regulations with the accounting standard, they differ in many ways. And the promulgation of new accounting standards brought many changes in accounting practices.

Basic Accounting Equation

In the new Chinese accounting standards, "Assets = Liability + Owner's equity" is used as the basic accounting equation for the first time instead of the equation "Total Fund Application = Total Fund Source" and its subordinate equations: "Fixed Assets = Fixed Funds"; "Current Assets = Current Funds"; "Specific Assets = Specific Funds"[5]. For a long time, the accounting authorities insisted on use of the "Total Fund Application = Total Fund Source" to govern the classification of accounts and formation of balance sheet. They pointed out this was the crucial distinction between socialist accounting and capitalist accounting[6]. The reasons that Chinese accounting authorities gave up this Stalin ideology in accounting practices will be discussed later.

---

[5] In China, in most text-books, "fund" is defined as the monetary expression of property, goods and materials used in the process of the production. "Fund Source" is the channel for obtaining and forming funds, while "fund application" is the distribution, use and existing form of funds, property, food and material. Many accounting academics both in China and overseas recognise that the major differences between Chinese and Western accounting arise from the definition of financial source (see Lou, 1984, Bromwich and Wang, 1991). In Western accounting, capital structure includes Liabilities and Owner's Equity, but in China, financial sources are called funds. They are not allowed to be called "capital", due to political sensitivity.

[6] In 1951, an article outlining the nature of accounting was published in a major accounting journal (Xing and Huan, 1951). The debate on the nature of accounting had lasted for a long time. Does accounting bear a distinction of class, either socialist or capitalist, or is accounting mainly a discipline with a methodology of a technical nature? Obviously, the first opinion dominated.

Over three decades before economic reform, economic policy had generally followed the classic Soviet model. The government directly provided most investment funds and directly or indirectly administered all economic enterprises (Myers, 1980). It is explained in Chinese as *To Sou To Zhi*. The enterprises had no responsibility for financial management. Although this situation changed greatly after the economic reforms, we find that it remained unchanged to a certain degree in accounting regulations. When assets were depreciated, journal entries were required to reflect how the total depreciation fund was distributed between state and enterprise. For example: take an item of plant, cost $400,000 with nil residual value, which depreciates at 20 per cent per annum straight-line method.

(1)   Dr. Depreciation expense   80,000
                 Cr.   Accumulated depreciation   80,000
         Depreciation of plant at 20%

(2)   Dr.   Fixed fund - state   80,000
                 Cr.   Special fund   80,000
         Set aside special fund for fixed assets replacement

(3)   Dr.   Special deposit   40,000
                 Special fund   40,000
                 Cr.   Cash   80,000

50 per cent of this special fund is handed over to the state and the remaining 50 per cent is left to the enterprise in the form of special deposit.

The general entries above indicate that when enterprises depreciate assets they set up a special fund, 50 per cent of which would be submitted to the state and the remaining 50 per cent to be left in the enterprise to be used to replace the old plant. Obviously part of the fund generated by depreciating assets would be out of the operation. The problem here is that usually, when an enterprise needed money to replace old machinery, it did not have enough money; managers had to ask the bureaucracy for state funds. This is one of the reasons why some very old machines still keep running in state-owned enterprises in China.

In the new accounting standard, when an enterprise depreciates assets, only one journal entry is required, e.g., "Dr. Depreciation expense; Cr.

Accumulated depreciation". No part of funds will be out of operation. The enterprises will take full responsibility for financial management.

Manufacturing Cost Method

According to articles 48 and 49 of the Chinese accounting standard, the manufacturing cost includes direct materials, direct labour, and factory overheads. The administration expenses, financial expenses and sales expenses will be the operation expenses and will be deducted directly from the revenue. This means that China gave up the full-absorbing cost accounting method and adopted the manufacturing cost accounting method in practice. Before the promulgation of the standard, administration, financial and sales expenses had to be allocated to product. The reason that China adopted the manufacturing cost method is that the community needs to simplify cost calculation, distinguish cost responsibility and evaluate management performances under the reforms (Gang, 1993).

Conservatism

"The general constraint of uncertainty has served as a basis for the traditional accounting concept of conservatism" (Hendriksen, 1970). Conservatism is expressed in accounting: "to anticipate no profit, but to provide for all losses". This idea has had great influence in the setting of accounting standards in many countries.

Conservatism was never adopted as an accounting concept by Chinese accounting practitioners and scholars. This can be seen in the old system:

- Short term investment shall be stated in historical cost.
- Inventory shall be calculated in historical cost, i.e. FIFO, specific identification, weighted average, moving average method and averaged cost. Cost or market, whichever is lower basis, is not allowed to be used.
- No provision for doubtful debts is allowed.
- Non-current assets shall appear in historical cost. Non-current assets revaluation is allowed only when enterprises are in combination, bankruptcy and liquidation.

In contrast, under the influence of leftist ideas, people only talked about good things, they liked to anticipated profit. Even when a loss was actually made, surprisingly you still can read profit in the profit and loss statement.

Even in the draft of the Chinese accounting standard, conservatism was not considered as an accounting concept (Lou and Zhang, 1992). But when the standard was formally promulgated, it was written in article 18: "Accounting should calculate possible losses and expenses rationally according to the requirement of conservatism". One asks, what has led to this change? There are three possible reasons:

1. China does have inflation which is sometimes as high as two digits. For example, in 1993, the first-half economic statistics indicated that inflation was 17.4 per cent in the half, while GDP growth registered 13.9 per cent (Far Eastern Economic Review, 1993). If the government does not allow enterprises to use conservatism as a concept in accounting then notions such as accelerated depreciation, provision for doubtful debts, and the LIFO method in inventory calculation might not be able to be maintained.

2. Making the standard more rational. In the draft of the standard, Chinese scholars tried to avoid recognising the conservatism concept but some practice of conservatism was allowed. For example, "the method of accelerated depreciation can be used under the approval of government agencies", and "provision for doubtful debts can be calculated in some circumstances according to the amounts of accounts receivable". Obviously, this caused confusion. So when the accounting standard was promulgated, the concept of conservatism was recognised.

3. In the Western countries, there are many criticisms and arguments about conservatism (Thomas, 1966; Devine, 1963), but "unquestionably, conservatism holds an extremely important place in the ethos of the accountant. Indeed, it has even been called the dominant principle of accounting" (Wolk, Francis and Tearney, 1992). If China persists in not recognising conservatism as an accounting concept, and does not allow some application of conservatism in practice, there is no doubt that assets can be overstated. This could disadvantage international trade and investment.

Financial Reports

Article 57 states that "financial reports are the written documents that reflect financial situations and management performance of enterprises. They include the Balance Sheet, Profit and Loss Statement, Statement of Changes on Financial Position (or Cash Flow Statement), Supplementary Statements and Notes, and Statement of Financial Affairs"[7].

The financial reports are divided into two categories: external financial reports and internal financial reports. The external financial reports are: Balance Sheet, Profit and Loss Statement, Statement of Changes of Financial Position, and Supplementary Statements, Notes and Statement of Financial Affairs.

Internal reports, such as statements of product cost, can be designed according to enterprises' own needs. Before the release of the accounting standard enterprises had to submit many internal financial statements to government including a statement of product cost, and a statement of special fund applications. This change obviously gives enterprises more flexibility in preparing internal financial statements to suit management needs.

The second change in financial reporting is to the contents and structure of financial statements. As mentioned before, the basic accounting equation in China was "Total Fund Application = Total Fund Source" and its subordinate equations: "Fixed Assets = Fixed Funds"; "Current Assets = Current Funds" and "Specific Assets = Specific Funds". The major contents of the balance sheet were the fund application and fund source (see Figure 3-1: Format of the balance sheet used before the issue of accounting standards). In the new accounting standards, it is required that enterprises prepare and submit their financial statements using internationally accepted structures and contents, e.g., assets, liabilities and owner's equity.

Bookkeeping Method

The Chinese accounting authorities unified the bookkeeping method used in enterprises for the first time. Article 8 states "all enterprises should use the Debit-Credit double entry method".

The debit-credit double entry method was only used in medium and large manufacturing enterprises before this standard. There were two other bookkeeping methods used in small manufacturing enterprises, merchandising

---

[7] The Chinese Accounting Standards cited in this chapter were translated by the author from the Chinese version and not the official English publication.

enterprises and governmental agencies. The increase-decrease double entry method was used in small manufacturing enterprise and merchandising enterprises and the receipt-disbursement double entry method was used in government agencies (Wei, 1984). Those two methods emerged and were used in the mid of 1960s, during the period of the Great Cultural Revolution. They were the result of leftist ideology that debit-credit method is bourgeois and therefore was not in the interests of the proletariat. Therefore the proletariat should create the new socialism or communalism bookkeeping method (Lu, 1992). The different bookkeeping method created obstacles in accounting information and communication. Now it is certain that all manufacturing and merchandising enterprises will adopt the debit-credit method, but whether the governmental agencies will use the debit-credit method is still doubtful. Historically, "receipt" and "disbursement" were used as recording symbols in non-governmental accounting as far back as the *Han* Dynasty (206 B.C-A.D 220) (Aiken and Lu, 1993a).

The Impact of Economic Development, Foreign Investment, the Reform of Enterprise Structure and the Emergence of Stock Exchange Markets on the Setting of Chinese Accounting Standards

After a careful examination of the Chinese accounting standard, we notice that Chinese accounting practitioners and academics are attempting to demolish the influences of Stalinist ideology on accounting practices. In the initial period of accounting standards setting, some scholars and practitioners in China advocated establishing Chinese accounting standards with Chinese planned market economy characteristics (Ge, 1992). In the draft of Chinese accounting standards, some Chinese characteristics can be found such as the legality concept, and the uniformity concept. But when the accounting standard was formally issued, it seemed that some of these features had been discarded. These standards are more harmonised with the accounting standards of the West. One possible reason is that Chinese people have realised the need of moving towards the internationalisation of accounting in the world, but more importantly, economic and other developments in China itself are the major factors which caused this change. These factors are discussed below. They are also related to contemporary issues with a strong public interest and have significant implications for the future development of accounting standards in China.

Economic Development

With the development of this economy, new business activities have emerged, for example, leases, business combinations, bankruptcy, land compensation, intangible assets. Obviously, the old accounting regulations and central control (planned) administration systems that grew from Stalinist ideology were no longer appropriate. The new standard must eventually supersede them.

Foreign Investment

One of the most spectacular achievements since 1979, when China re-opened its doors to the outside world, has been the utilisation of foreign funds. By the end of 1991, the contracted amount of foreign investment had reached US $50 billion. Foreign investors participated in joint ventures, collaborations, exclusively-foreign-invested enterprises, and other areas (Lu, 1992). Several Special Economic Zones were established. The foreign accounting practices were brought in with increasing foreign investments. *The Accounting Regulation of People's Republic of China for Joint Ventures with Chinese and Foreign Investments* was promulgated by the Ministry of Finance in 1985 in order to match the special needs of foreign investment. This regulation was different from others used by state-owned enterprises at the time. It was written by using internationally recognised accounting rules. The introduction of western accounting thought and practice as well as accounting regulations for joint ventures were major challenges for the then existing accounting system.

Reform of the State-owned Enterprise Structure

Even after 20 years of economic reform in China, many large and medium-sized state-owned enterprises are still inefficient and uncompetitive. One reason for this is the lack of structural change in enterprise. Since 1979, the Chinese government has made many attempts to change the management of state-owned enterprises - from profit appropriation (*Li Run Liou Chun*) to tax levying (*Li Gai Sun*); from tax levying to operation responsibility (*Cheng Bao Jing Ying Zhe Ren Zhi*), in order to stimulate enterprises to greater efficiency and competitiveness. Those methods have not fundamentally changed the enterprise structures. So the results of these reforms were unsatisfactory. In 1991, the Chinese government decided to change the structure of state-owned enterprise. Most of the state-owned enterprises have been or will be transferred to share-holding corporations. Individuals and legal entities will be allowed to buy shares in state-owned enterprises. Considering the great significance of corporations in the history and development of accounting in western counties, it seems obvious that Chinese accounting must change.

The Diversity of Ownership and Emergence of Stock Exchange Markets

There are several kinds of enterprises – state-owned enterprises, collective enterprises, single proprietorship share-holding corporations, joint ventures, Chinese-Foreign collaborations, exclusively-foreign-investment type enterprises – in Chinese society. Until 1993, the Ministry of Finance issued individual accounting regulations for each type of enterprise. With increasing private ownership and joint ventures, this administrative method is no longer suitable for opportunity and competition. That seems to be the main reason that government urgently promulgated the Chinese accounting standards governing all kinds of enterprises in China.

In 1990, the Chinese government officially opened stock exchanges in Shanghai and Shenzhen. The demands on disclosure of accounting information of corporations accelerated the formulation of accounting standards.

Other Factors

It can be argued that accounting development in a certain country is strongly influenced by its culture and political, social, and economic environment. We have analysed the economic influence in the setting of the Chinese accounting standard. According to Mathews and Perera (1993): "Most accounting issues are politically sensitive because (a) the need for standards arises where there is controversy, and (b) accounting partitions wealth between different groups" (p.105). Are there some political or ideological influences in this standard-setting in China? We cannot know exactly. The old accounting systems originated in the former Soviet Union. With the collapse of the former Soviet Union, all Chinese accounting researchers and practitioners had to face this question: "the older brother has given up the Stalinist ideology in accounting practices, why should we still wear these old-fashioned clothes?". Perhaps this is another reason why Chinese accounting decision-makers reversed their attitude and adopted the western accounting theory and practice in order to set the new standard.

Comparison with Research Based on Western Experience

Compared with International Accounting Standards and the standards in Australia, the US, and the UK, the newly-issued Chinese Accounting Standard is more like a conceptual framework. Strictly speaking, the Chinese accounting standard is a guideline about how to set accounting standards and not a set of standards as in the west. This guideline can be seen to be a conceptual model (see Figure 3-1).

Comparison of the Chinese conceptual framework with others reveals significant differences (see Figure 3-2).

The Purposes of Developing Conceptual Frameworks

The purpose of setting the Chinese standard is to provide a guideline for developing further specific standards. The main purpose of setting a conceptual framework in Australia is to provide users, preparers and auditors of financial reports, and accounting standard-setters, with an explicit set of concepts (Henderson and Peirson, 1992). A conceptual framework in the US, according to the FASB, is: "... a coherent system of inter-related objectives and fundamentals that can lead to consistent standards. This prescribes the nature, function, and limits of financial accounting and financial statements" (FASB, 1978, p.1). There is an intention to use a conceptual framework as a structured theory of accounting to review and even re-write accounting standards in a more scientific and logical way in the USA and in Australia.

Procedures to Develop Conceptual Frameworks

The Chinese Accounting Standard was developed by firstly selecting the common accounting assumptions and principles in accounting practices, secondly using these assumptions and principles to recognise, measure, record, and report accounting elements and finally using accounting elements to formulate financial reports. In Australia, the conceptual framework is set by defining the scope and objective of financial reports and identifying and defining qualitative characteristics of financial reports. It also assists in selecting the basic elements of accounting reports and selecting the principles and rules of recognition and measurement of the basic elements and type of information to be displayed in financial reports in accordance with the restraints of the qualitative characteristics (Accounting Handbook, 1993).

Figure 3-1 The Structural Model of Chinese Accounting Standard

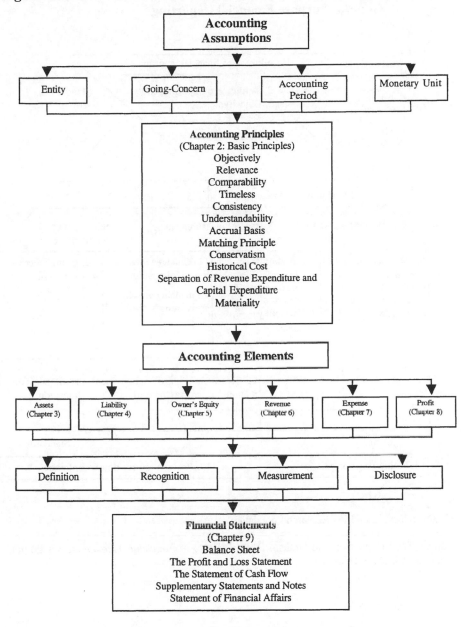

Accounting Assumptions

Entity | Going-Concern | Accounting Period | Monetary Unit

Accounting Principles
(Chapter 2: Basic Principles)
Objectively
Relevance
Comparability
Timeless
Consistency
Understandability
Accrual Basis
Matching Principle
Conservatism
Historical Cost
Separation of Revenue Expenditure and
Capital Expenditure
Materiality

Accounting Elements

Assets (Chapter 3) | Liability (Chapter 4) | Owner's Equity (Chapter 5) | Revenue (Chapter 6) | Expense (Chapter 7) | Profit (Chapter 8)

Definition | Recognition | Measurement | Disclosure

Financial Statements
(Chapter 9)
Balance Sheet
The Profit and Loss Statement
The Statement of Cash Flow
Supplementary Statements and Notes
Statement of Financial Affairs

Figure 3-2 Tentative Building Blocks of a Conceptual Framework for General Purpose Financial Reporting

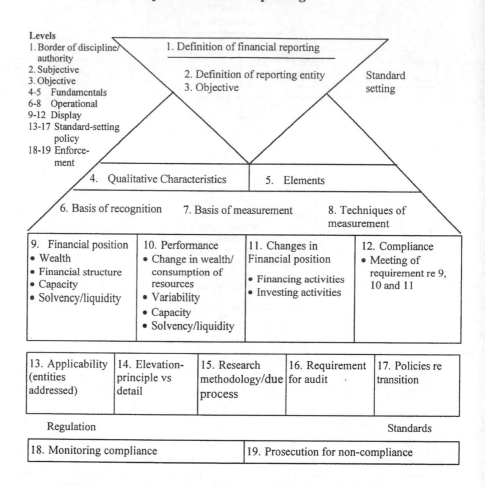

© Australian Accounting Research Foundation

Source: Scott Henderson and Graham Peirson, *Issues in Financial Accounting*, 5th Edition, Longman Cheshire, 1993, p.6.

Contents of a Conceptual Framework

In the US, there are six statements of financial accounting concepts (SFACs).

- SFAC1   Objectives of Financial Reporting by Business Enterprises
- SFAC2   Qualitative Characteristics of Accounting Information
- SFAC3   Element of Financial Statements of Business Enterprise
- SFAC4   Objectives of Financial Reporting by Non-business Enterprises
- SFAC5   Recognition and Measurement in Financial Statement of Business Enterprise
- SFAC6   Elements of Financial Statements: A Replacement of FASB Concepts Statement No.3 (incorporating an amendment of FASB Concept Statement No.2)

So far the Australian Accounting Research Foundation has published four statements of conceptual framework and other documents. These are:

- SAC1   Definition of the Reporting Entity
- SAC2   Objective of General Purpose Financial Reporting
- SAC3   Qualitative Characteristics of Financial Information
- SAC4   Definition and Recognition of Elements of Financial Statements

These conceptual frameworks are more comprehensive and concrete than the Chinese Accounting Standard. Each statement in the conceptual framework is inter-related. The definitions of financial elements are based on the same underpinning concepts advocated by the conceptual framework, that is the future economic benefits. The financial elements defined vary among different countries. For example, five financial elements – asset, liability, equity, revenue, expense – are defined in the Australian conceptual framework. There are five financial elements defined in the new Chinese accounting standard, asset, liability, equity, revenue, expense and profit. However, there is lack of a consistently theoretical basis behind these definitions. These definitions are simply descriptions of some characteristics of each element. The comparison of the definitions of financial elements in different countries is shown in Table 3-1.

57

Table 3-1 International Comparison: Conceptual Framework Definitions[2]

China: Basic Accounting Standard for Enterprises[1]	IASC Framework	United States: SFAC No. 6	United Kingdom Draft Framework: Chapter 3	Australia: SAC 4
ASSETS				
Assets are economic resources, which are measurable by money value, and which are owned or controlled by an enterprise, including all property, rights as a creditors to others, and other rights.	An asset is a resource controlled by the enterprise as a result of past events and from which future economic benefits are expected to flow to the enterprise. (para. 49(a))	Assets are probable future economic benefits obtained or controlled by a particular entity as a result of past transactions or events. (para. 25)	Assets are rights or other access to future economic benefits controlled by an entity as a result of past transactions or events. (para. 7)	Assets are future economic benefits controlled by the entity as a result of past transactions or other past events. (para. 14)
LIABILITIES				
A liability is debt borne by an enterprise, measurable by money value, which will b paid to a creditor using assets or services.	A liability is a present obligation of the enterprise arising from past events, the settlement of which is expected to result in an outflow from the enterprise of resources embodying economic benefits. (para. 49(b))	Liabilities are probable future sacrifices of economic benefits arising from present obligations of a particular entity to transfer assets or provide services to other entities in the future as a result of past transactions or events. (para. 35)	Liabilities are an entity's obligation to transfer economic benefits as a result of past transactions or events. (para. 24)	Liabilities are the future sacrifices of economic benefits that the entity is presently obliged to make to other entities as a result of past transaction or other past events. (para. 48)
EQUITY				
Owners' equity refers to the interest of the investors remaining in the net assets of an enterprise, including capital of the enterprise invested in by investors, capital reserve, surplus reserve, and undistributed profit retained in the enterprise ect.	Equity is the residual interest in the assets of the enterprise after deducting all its liabilities. (para. 49(c))	Equity or net assets is the residual interest in the assets of an entity that remains after deducting its liabilities. (para. 49)	Equity is the ownership interest in the entity: it is the residual amount found by deducting all liabilities of the entity from all of the entity's assets. (para. 44)	Equity is the residual interest in the assets of the entity after deduction of its liabilities. (para. 78)

China	IASC	United States	United Kingdom	Australia
REVENUES				
Revenue refers to the financial inflows to an enterprise as a result of the sale of goods and services, and other business activities of the enterprise, including basic operating revenue and other operating revenue.	Income is increases in economic benefits during the accounting period in the form of inflows or enhancements of assets or decreases of liabilities that result in increases in equity, other than those relating to contributions from equity participants. (para. 70(a))	Revenues are inflows or other enhancements of assets of an entity or settlements of its liabilities (or a combination of both) from delivering or producing goods, rendering services, or other activities that constitute the entity's ongoing major or central operations. (para. 78)	Gains are increases in equity, other than those relating to contributions from owners. (para. 52)	Revenues are inflows or other enhancements, or savings in outflows, of future economic benefits in the form of increases in assets or reductions in liabilities of the entity, other than those relating to contributions by owners, that result in an increase in equity during the reporting period. (para. 111)
Profit is the operating results of an enterprise in an accounting period, including operating profit, net investment profit and net non-operating income.		Gains are increases in equity (net assets) from peripheral or incidental transactions of an entity and from all other transactions and other events and circumstances affecting the entity except those that result from revenues or investments by owners. (para. 82)		
EXPENSES				
Expenses refer to the outlays incurred by an enterprise in the course of production and operation.	Expenses are decreases in economic benefits during the accounting period in the form of outflows or depletions of assets or incurrences of liabilities that result in decreases in equity, other than those relating to distributions to equity participants. (para. 70(b))	Expenses are outflows or other using up of assets or incurrences of liabilities (or a combination of both) from delivering or producing goods, rendering services, or carrying out other activities that constitute the entity's ongoing major or central operations. (para. 80) Losses are decreases in equity (net assets) from peripheral or incidental transactions of an entity and from all other transactions and other events and circumstances affecting the entity except those that result from expenses or distributions to owners. (para. 83)	Losses are decreases in equity, other than those relating to distributions to owners. (para. 52)	Expenses are consumptions or losses of future economic benefits in the form of reductions in assets or increases in liabilities of the entity, other than those relating to distributions to owners, that result in a decrease in equity during the reporting period. (para. 117)

Note:
(1) Definitions of accounting elements in Basic Accounting Standard for Enterprises are adopted from Tang, Y., Chow, L, and Cooper, B., *Accounting and Finance in China* (2nd Edition), Longman, 1994. (2) Definitions of accounting elements in other countries and in IASC are adopted from *Australian Accounting Handbook 2000*, Prentice Hall, 2000.

59

The Development of the Specific Accounting Standards

Since the promulgation of the first Chinese accounting standard in 1992, the Ministry of Finance has endeavoured to set up the new accounting regulation system by issuing the concrete accounting standards. However, this procedure is more complicated because of the coexistence of the unified accounting systems and accounting standards (Chen et al, 1997). So far 30 concrete accounting standards have been drafted and circulated for public comment. The major criticism of those drafts of accounting standards is that they are not suitable for the Chinese situation because they mainly copied the International Accounting Standards and the GAAP in the United States. The Ministry of Finance planned to establish the accounting standards system in three years with 32 concrete standards in 1993 (Aiken et al, 1995). However, so far only 8 concrete standards have been formally promulgated. They are: Changes of Accounting Policies, Estimations and Mistakes; Accounting for Revenues; Accounting for Investments; Accounting for Construction Contracts; Accounting for Reorganisation of Debt; After-balance Date Events; Cash Flow Statement; and Disclosure of Related-party Transactions. The main contents of these new accounting standards are explained as follows.

Changes of Accounting Policies, Estimations and Mistakes

This accounting standard sets the accounting and disclosure requirements for changes of accounting policies, estimations and mistakes (Ministry of Finance, 1998a). If changes of accounting policies are based on laws and administrative regulations and the impacts of such changes are material, financial reports shall be adjusted retroactively. Both current profits and retained profits have to be adjusted. However, previous financial reports need not be changed. In the notes of financial reports, the following information shall be disclosed: changes of accounting policies; the reasons and impact of such changes; reasons if those impacts cannot be assessed properly. If accounting estimations have been changed and these changes affect both current and future periods, the accounting estimate figures in both current and future periods have to be adjusted. If the mistakes discovered are associated with the current period, the related items in the current period shall be adjusted. If the mistakes belong to previous periods and are immaterial, adjustments are made to current profit/loss. If the mistakes in previous periods are material, both retained profit and current profit/loss are amended.

Accounting for Revenues

Revenues have three sources as defined in this standard: sale of commodities; provision of service; and utilisation of enterprise capital by other entities (Ministry of Finance, 1998b). Revenue from sale of commodities can only be recognised when the ownership as well as all benefits and risks associated with such commodities have passed from vendors to purchasers. Cash discount is regarded as current expense and trade discount and allowance are written off against the revenue. The revenue from provision of services shall be recognised by using the percentage completion method. The revenue from the utilisation of enterprise capital by other entities includes interest revenue and utilisation fee. In the financial reports the following information shall be disclosed: the accounting policies related to recognition of revenues and amounts of revenues from (1) sale of commodities; (2) provision of service; (3) interest revenue; and (4) utilisation fee.

After-balance Date Events

The after-balance date events refer to those events occurring between the financial reporting date (balance date) and the date when financial reports are officially approved and issued by the board of directors of the company. There are two types of after-balance date events: the adjusted events and unadjusted events. The adjusted events are those events which provide evidence of, or further elucidate, conditions which existed at balance date. The unadjusted events are those which create new conditions which are not associated with any things existing at the balance date. For these events, the standard is required to be disclosed in the notes to the financial statements. This accounting standard is similar to the AAS8 – Events Occurring After Balance Date in Australia.

Accounting for Construction Contracts

This standard sets out the recognition and disclosure requirements for construction contracts (Ministry of Finance, 1998d). According to this standard, the construction income includes initial income specified in the contracts and the income related to changing the contract, damage and rewards; the construction costs includes the direct and indirect costs occurred during construction period. Direct costs, which include direct labour, direct material, direct utilisation of machinery and other direct costs, should be

61

included in contract costs when they have occurred and indirect costs should be allocated into contract costs accordingly. Contract costs should match contract income based on percentage completion methods.

Debt Reorganisation

This standard is similar to the Australian accounting standard AASB 1014 Set-off and Extinguishment of Debt. However, the Chinese accounting standard is more complex than the Australian one. The Australian standard only deals with the issue of setting off the debt by assets. The Chinese standard includes three different methods in reorganisation of debt (Ministry of Finance, 1998e): (1) setting off debt by assets; (2) changing debt into equity; and (3) amending the clauses of the conditions of borrowing. The reason for issuing this accounting standard is that currently most state-owned enterprises have serious debt problems and have failed to repay principal and interest. The government encouraged banks to change their debt into equity and relieve the burden of debt in state-owned enterprises. According to this standard, the difference between the fair value of the debt set off and the fair value of shares acquired should be treated as profit or loss in the debtor's accounting. In creditor's accounting difference should firstly be off-set by the provision of bad debt if the company is making provisions, the remainder is charged to profit and loss.

Related Party Disclosures

This is the first specific Chinese accounting standard. It was issued in December 1996 and operated from 1st January 1997. The related parties refer to those entities in which one party has the capacity directly or indirectly to control, or has substantial influence on another party (Ministry of Finance, 1996). According to this standard, related parties include: (1) controlling or controlled entities; (2) joint ventures; (3) cooperate enterprises[8]; (4) major investors, key management staff and their close relatives; (5) other enterprises controlled directly by major investors, key management staff and their close

---

[8] The classification of enterprises in China is more confused in governmental legislation. There are many different classifications existing even in a single regulation. Here, joint ventures (*Heyin Qiyie*) refer to the enterprises in which business is regulated by contract and controlled by investors; cooperate enterprises (*Lianyin Qiyie*) refer to those enterprises which are not the subsidiaries or joint ventures of the entities involved. However these entities have strong influences on the enterprise.

relatives. The transactions between related parties have to be disclosed such as purchase or sale of products and other assets, provision or acceptance of services, and provision of finance. Compared to the Australian standard on related party disclosure, the disclosure requirements for the contents and scope of the transactions among the related parties in the Chinese accounting standard is much more substantial.

Accounting for Investment

According to this standard, investment can be classified as short-term and long-term investment in China (Ministry of Finance, 1998f). The long-term investment can also be sub-grouped into long-term debt investment and long-term equity investment. The long-term equity investment can be divided into four types according to the influences the investor has on investee: (1) control; (2) joint control; (3) significant influence; (4) no control, no joint control, no significant influence. According to the standard, if investors have control, joint control or significant influence on the investee, the investor should use the equity method to record their investment, otherwise they can use the cost method. This requirement is substantially different from that in Australia. In Australia, the equity method is only required when an investor has significant influence on an investee[9]. If an entity controls another entity the parent entity is required to prepare the consolidated accounts. So far there is no accounting standard on consolidated accounting in China. The Chinese might have not realised the complexity caused by using the equity method in the controlling entity and this may make the consolidating process more cumbersome because the initial goodwill or discount on acquisition has been buried in subsequent investment figures.

Cash Flow Statement

The format and content of the cash flow statement in China is similar to that in Australia. The cash flows are divided into: (1) cash flow from operating activities; (2) cash flow from investing activities and (3) cash flow from financing activities (Ministry of Finance, 1998g). One unique feature of preparing the Chinese cash flow statement is the treatment of the Value-Added-Tax (VAT), which is similar to the Goods and Service Tax (GST) in

---

[9] If the investor is a parent company and is required to prepare consolidated accounts, the equity methods are only used in consolidated accounts. The cost method is still required for use in the investor's accounts.

Australia. The credit of VAT is a cash inflow and payment of VAT is a cash outflow.

Further Reforms and Developments of Chinese Accounting Regulation Framework

Accounting development has progressed dependent on the developments in the economy and changes in social and political systems. With a growing economy and the improving legislative systems, Chinese accounting has changed rapidly.

Now accounting academics and practitioners are facing two major problems. The first is how to deal with the relationship of the *Accounting Law* and the accounting standards. The *Accounting Law of the People's Republic of China* was promulgated in 1985 and amended in 1993. There are six chapters:

- Chapter 1: General Provisions
- Chapter 2: Accounting Procedures and Bookkeeping
- Chapter 3: Supervision of Accounting
- Chapter 4: Accounting Organisations and Staff
- Chapter 5: Legal Responsibilities
- Chapter 6: Appendix

The *Accounting Law* is an accounting administrative framework and a code of professional conduct. It is concerned on the duties and rights of accountants. It is also a direct regulation on how the accounting organisation should be set up and how staff in an enterprise should be appointed and removed. There are few references to accounting standards. Therefore, the claim that Accounting Law is the highest regulation in the legislative structure[10] for accounting is not sustainable. The reason is the Accounting Law is not on how to set up accounting standards or the theoretical basis for setting up such standards e.g. the conceptual framework. The Accounting Law actually reflects many administrative control methods used under the traditional planned economy (Winkle et al, 1994).

---

[10] Some scholars argued that in China there exists a three tiers of regulation framework for accounting: the highest level is the Accounting Law, the middle level is Accounting Standards, the lowest level is the Uniform Accounting Systems.

The second problem is how to deal with the relationship between the new accounting standards system and the old uniform accounting regulations system. There are two views: the old uniform accounting regulations system should be abolished or else the new accounting standards and the old uniform accounting regulations should co-exist.

Uniform Accounting Systems have been implemented since the establishment of the People's Republic of China. The Revised Uniform Accounting Systems for thirteen industries were issued with the promulgation of Basic Accounting Standard in 1992. And more Uniform Accounting Systems for other industries have been issued since then. The details of the Uniform Accounting Systems used in China currently are shown in Table 3-2. There are four Sections in a Uniform Accounting System:

- Section 1: *General provisions.*
- Section 2: *Chart of accounts* – A detailed chart of accounts and explanations of usage of each account are provided.
- Section 3: *Financial Reports* – Formats and guidelines for the preparation of each financial statement are provided.
- Appendix: The illustrative double-journal entries for the economic events by using the accounts specified in the regulations.

The Chart of Accounts in *Accounting Regulations for Manufacturing Enterprises* and the explanations of usage of some accounts are illustrated in Table 3-3 and Table 3-4. As indicated in these illustrations, the uniform accounting systems are mainly focused on how to record the economic transactions.

When discussing the relationship between the accounting standard system and the uniform accounting regulation system, many scholars neglected the existence of another set of regulations, financial regulations (*Caiwu Zhidu*). Even under the planned economy, a uniform accounting system alone cannot be used to record an economic transaction, because the uniform accounting system only stipulates the recording rules for economic transactions. Most recognition and measurement rules were specified in the financial regulations. Accountants completed accounting records by reference to both the uniform accounting systems and the relevant financial regulations.

Table 3-2 Uniform Accounting Systems Used in China

Title of the Regulation:
Accounting Regulations for Manufacturing Enterprises
Accounting Regulations for Merchandising Enterprises
Accounting Regulations for Transportation Enterprises
Accounting Regulations for Railway Enterprises
Accounting Regulations for Aviation Enterprises
Accounting Regulations for Agriculture Enterprises
Accounting Regulations for Postage and Telecommunication Enterprises
Accounting Regulations for Real Estate Development Enterprises
Accounting Regulations for Construction Enterprises
Accounting Regulations for Banking and Finance Enterprises
Accounting Regulations for Insurance Enterprises
Accounting Regulations for Tourism and Catering Enterprises
Accounting Regulations for Foreign Economic Cooperation Enterprises

In 1992, while the first accounting standard was promulgated by the MOF, *A General Rules of Financial Management for Enterprises* was also issued. There are twelve chapters in the General Rules that stipulate the recognition and measurement rules for assets (chapter 3: circulating assets, chapter 4: fixed assets, chapter 5: intangible, deferred and other assets), investments (chapter 6: outside investment), costs and expenses (chapter 7), sales revenues, profits and distributions (chapter 8), foreign exchange activities (chapter 9) and finance (chapter 2). The General Rules also include regulations on liquidation of enterprises and regulations on the financial reporting and evaluation. Seven financial indicators have been chosen to evaluate the enterprise performance. They are asset/debts ratio, current ratio, quick ratio, accounts receivables turnover, inventory turnover, return on equity, return on sales and returns on total costs and expenses.

When comparing the accounting standard system used in western countries to the uniform accounting system and the financial regulation system (represented by the General Rules), it is found that the functions of western accounting standards are more similar to the functions of Chinese financial regulations: both are concerned about how to recognise and measure economic transactions and events. They are not concerned about how to record the economic transactions and events. Therefore, the relationship between accounting standards and uniform accounting systems are supplementary, they are not mutually exclusive. There is no argument that the

66

accounting standards should replace the uniform accounting systems. If something has to be replaced by the accounting standards in the future it is the set of financial regulations. The following figure shows the relationship between the accounting standards and uniform accounting systems.

Figure 3-3   The Relationship Between Accounting Standards and Uniform Accounting Systems

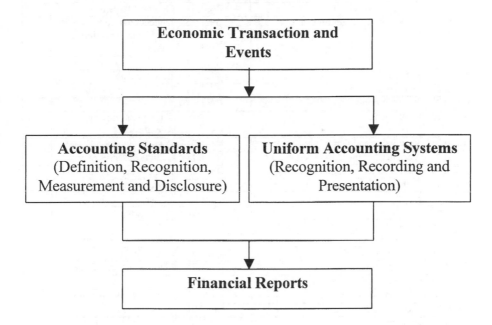

The issue of whether the uniform accounting systems should be abolished or not is not because the uniform accounting system contradicts to the accounting standard system. The issue is whether the recording of financial transactions should be regulated. An accounting procedure is to recognise, measure, record and present (disclose) economic transactions. In western countries, only the recognition, some of measurement rules and disclosure requirements are regulated by the means of accounting standards. The recording function is librated and vested to individual enterprise.

Table 3-3 List of Uniform Accounts

No	Code	Name	Page	No.	Code	Name	Page
		1. Assets Accounts		32.	209	Other Payables	
1.	101	Cash		33.	211	Salary Payables	
2.	102	Bank Deposit		34.	214	Welfare Payables	
3.	109	Other Monetary Funds		35.	221	Tax Payables	
4.	111	Short-term Investment		36.	223	Profit Payables	
5.	112	Bill Receivables		37.	229	Other Payables	
6.	113	Accounts Receivables		38.	231	Deferred Expenses	
7.	114	Provision for Doubtful Debts		39.	233	Undeducted Tax (Provision for Deferred Taxes)	
8.	115	Prepayments		40.	241	Long-term Loans	
9.	119	Other Receivables		41.	251	Bonds Payables	
10.	121	Materials Purchased		42.	261	Long-term Payables	
11.	123	Raw Materials					
12.	128	Containers				**3. Owners' Equity Accounts**	
13	129	Low-value and Perishable Articles		43.	301	Paid-up Capital	
14.	131	Variances of the Costs of Materials		44.	311	Capital Reserves (Surplus)	
15.	133	Materials for Outside Processing		45.	313	Profit Reserves (Surplus)	
16.	135	Self-manufactured Semi-finished Goods		46.	321	Current Year Profit	
17.	137	Finished Goods		47.	322	Profit Distribution	
18.	138	Goods Delivered on Instalments					
19.	139	Prepaid Expenses				**4. Expense Accounts**	
20.	151	Long-term Investment		48.	401	Production Costs	
21.	161	Fixed Assets		49.	405	Manufacturing Overheads	
22.	165	Accumulated Depreciation					
23.	166	Disposal of Fixed Assets				**5. Profit/Loss Accounts**	
24.	169	Projects under Construction		50.	501	Sales Revenue	
25.	171	Intangible Assets		51.	502	Costs of Goods Sold	
26.	181	Deferred Assets		52.	503	Sales Expenses	
27.	191	Undecided Gain/Loss from Assets		53.	504	Sales Tax and Other Levie	
				54.	511	Other Operating Income	
		2. Liability Accounts		55.	512	Other Operating Expenses	
28.	201	Short-term Loans		56.	521	Management Expenses	
29.	202	Bill Payables		57.	522	Financial Expenses	
30.	203	Accounts Payables		58.	531	Investment Income	
31.	204	Payments in Advance		59.	541	Non-operating Income	
				60.	542	Non-operating Expenses	

Notes:

Enterprises can add, delete and merge the accounts above according to the actual needs of enterprises

1. Specialised companies whose accounts are centralised, and companies that have subordinated units, can add a "Funds to Subordinates" account. The subordinated units may add a "Funds from Superordinates" account accordingly.

2. Companies, which have foreign exchange activities, can add a "Differences of Exchange Rate" account.

3. Enterprises, which have petty cash circulated among internal workshops and units, may add a "Petty Cash" account.

4. Enterprises that purchase products outside may set up a "Products Purchased Outside" account.

5. Enterprises, which receive special reserve funds from government, may add "Special Reserve Inventory" and "Special Reserve Funds" accounts.

6. Enterprises that receive deposits on containers or other deposits frequently, may add a "Deposits in Advance" account.

7. Enterprises that adopt the actual cost method in accounting for material, may not need to set up "Materials Purchased" and "Variances of Costs of Materials", they may instead set up a "Materials in Transition" account.

8. Enterprises that calculate the losses on spoilage and losses from stopping of manufacturing, may add "Losses on Spoilage" and "Losses from Stopping of Manufacturing" accounts.

9. Enterprises may not need to set up "Variances of Costs of Materials" account, and instead set up the sub-ledgers under "Raw Materials", "Lower Value and Perishable Articles" and "Containers" accounts to account for the variances.

10. Enterprises that have few lower value and perishable articles and containers, can merge these two accounts into "Raw Materials" accounts.

11. Enterprises that have few prepayments and payments in advance may not need to have separate "Prepayment" and "Payments in Advance" accounts, and account for these activities in the "Accounts Receivable" and "Accounts Payable" accounts respectively.

12. Enterprises that do not required to calculate separately the costs of self-manufactured semi-finished goods, may not need to have a "Self-manufactured Semi-finished Goods" account.

13. Enterprises, to whom the costs of raw materials consist of the large proportion of production costs, may divide the "Raw Materials" into several accounts as "Raw and Main Materials", "Auxiliary Materials", "Spare Parts for Repairs", "Fuel" and "Semifinished Products Purchased Outside" etc.

14. Enterprises can merge "Production Costs" and "Manufacturing Overheads" accounts into a "Production Expenses" account, or divide "Production Costs" into "Basic Production Costs" and "Auxiliary Production Costs" accounts according to the needs of management.

15. Enterprises using the planned cost method for accounting of finished goods, can set up a "Variances of Costs of Finished Products" account.

16. Enterprises that issue short-term bonds for less than one year,, can set up a "Short-term Bond Payable" account.

17. Enterprises that have a large scale of other operating activities, can separately account for these activities by setting up relevant accounts for assets, income, costs, expenses, and taxes according to the *Uniform Accounting Systems* for relevant business operations.

Table 3-4 The Illustration of Descriptions of Usage of Accounts in the Uniform Accounting System for Industrial Enterprises

111 Short-term Investments

1. This account accounts for securities and other investments purchased by enterprises that can be converted into cash at any time within one year. These securities include a variety of shares and bonds.

2. When purchasing securities, enterprises shall debit this account according to the actual price paid.

   The declared and unpaid dividends in the securities purchased shall be accounted as receivables. Enterprises shall debit this account according to the actual cost (the actual price paid minus the declared and unpaid dividends), debit "Other Receivables" account according to dividends accrued, and credit "Bank Deposit" account.

   When receiving dividends, enterprises shall debit "Bank Deposit", and credit "Gain/Loss on Investments", or "Other Receivables" accounts.

   When selling securities, enterprises shall debit "Bank Deposit" accounts according to the amounts received, credit this account according to actual cost, and credit "Other Receivable" for any unreceived dividend. The difference shall be debited/credited to "Gain/Loss on Investments" account.

   When receiving principals and interests on bonds on maturity date, enterprises shall debit "Bank Deposit" account and credit this account and "Gain/Loss on Investments" account.

3. Sub-ledgers shall be set up under this account according to the varieties of short-term investments.

171 Intangible Assets

1. This account accounts for the values of patents, non-patented techniques, trademarks, copyright, land utilising rights, goodwill and other intangibles.

2. When purchasing intangibles, or generating intangibles internally (internal generated intangibles shall be registered and certified according to the proper legal procedures), enterprises shall debit this account and credit "Bank Deposit" or other accounts according to the actual expenses.

    When receiving intangible assets as part of investments from other entities, enterprises shall debit this account and credit "Paid-up Capital" according to the agreed value.

    When enterprises are using intangibles as investment to other entities, they shall debit "Long-term Investments" account and credit this account.

    If enterprises sell or transfer intangible assets to other entities, the transferring income shall be debited to "Bank Deposit" account (or other relevant accounts), and credited to "Other Business Revenues". The costs of sale of intangibles shall be debited to "Management Costs" account and credited to this account.

3. Intangibles shall be amortised evenly and amortisation costs shall be debited to "Other Business Expenses" and credited to this account.

4. Sub-ledgers shall be set up under this account according to the types of intangibles.

5. The end balance of this account represents the value of unamortised intangibles.

209 Other Payables

1. This account accounts for payables and other money received temporarily from other entities and individuals, e.g. rent payable for leasing fixed assets and containers; deposits paid in advance by customers; and payables to retirement funds.

2. When occurring payables or receiving money temporarily, enterprises shall debit "Bank Deposit", "Management Costs" or other accounts and credit this account;

    When enterprises are paying these payables, they shall debit this account and credit "Bank Deposit" or other accounts.

3. Sub-ledgers shall be set up under this account according to the types of payables and money received on temporary base, and according to different entities and individuals.

71

In China, the whole accounting procedure is regulated by the uniform accounting systems and financial regulations (accounting standards in the future). Before abolishing the uniform accounting systems used in China, more empirical studies are needed to be urgently undertaken to study whether the Chinese system can provide more rigid, reliable and comparable financial information; whether uniform accounting systems are the plus or the minus for improvement of the quality of accounting information.

The last issue is how to reconcile the disclosure requirements in uniform accounting systems or accounting standards with that in *The Contents and Formats of Information Disclosure Requirements for Publicly Listed Companies* by the Chinese Securities and Exchanges Regulatory Commission. There are four disclosure requirements promulgated by the Commission. They are:

- No. 1: The Contents and Formats of Prospectus
- No. 2: The Contents and Formats of Annual Financial Reports
- No. 3: The Contents and Formats of Half-yearly Financial Reports
- No. 4: The Contents and Formats of Prospectus of Issuing Additional Shares to Existing Shareholders.

Of them No. 2 and No. 3 are overlapped with the requirements in uniform accounting systems and accounting standards. In order to save the time and cost for financial reports users and preparers, the contents and formats of financial reports should be kept consistent and comparable among three regulations.

Chinese Generally Accepted Accounting Principles

There is no a single document which is called Chinese Generally Accepted Accounting Principles. In fact, accounting principles in China are scattered among the Accounting Law, Accounting Standards, Uniform Accounting Systems and Disclosure Requirements for Listing Companies. There are two important documents neglected by many people when studying the Chinese accounting regulatory system. They are *General Rules of Financial Management for Enterprises* (1992c, MOF) and *Financial Management Regulations for Industrial (or Other Sectors) Enterprises* (1992d, MOF). They are actually the measurement and recognition rules for accounting elements. The scopes and norms for revenues and expenses are defined in these documents, such as the depreciation rates for non-current assets, and the percentages allowed for the provision for doubtful debts. Some measurement and recognition rules are also explained in accounting standards and uniform accounting systems, but the uniform accounting systems are mainly focused on the bookkeeping rules and procedures. In the following sections, the Chinese GAAPs are examined based on theses documents. In some circumstances, the detailed recorded rules – bookkeeping methods are also illustrated which shows how the Chinese GAAPs differ from the Western GAAPs.

Accounting for Receivables and Bad Debts

Receivables include Accounts Receivables and Bill Receivables. Two accounts have been prescribed respectively in the *Uniform Accounting System* for accounting receivables. Bill receivables can be sub-divided into bill receivables bearing interests and bill receivables without interests. Bill receivables bearing interests shall be accounted at their maturity value while bill receivables without interests are accounted at their costs. Interests on bill receivables shall be entered into accounts when they occur as financial revenues. Interests on bill receivables calculated in most banks in China are based on the simple interest method not on the compound interest method. Any cost from discounting bill receivables are treated as financial expenses.

Accounts receivables are accounted at cost. Volume discounts, returns of sales, outwards freights and bad debts expenses shall be deducted from accounts receivables. Cash discounts are regarded as financial expenses. In the past, the MOF (The Ministry of Finance) prohibited enterprises to estimate the doubtful debt expenses. The bad debt costs were only allowed to be written off when they occurred. With the promulgation of new accounting standards, enterprises in China now can estimate the doubtful debt expenses based on 0.3 - 0.5 per cent of the outstanding balance of accounts receivables at the end of year. The percentage varies among different industries. The criticism on the regulations for provision for doubtful debt is that the percentage is lower and arbitrary, and does not reflect the reality of business operations in China. It is argued that enterprises shall be allowed to set up their own estimates about the percentage of the provision for doubtful debt.

The classification of inventories is more detailed than that in western countries and each class of inventories has different accounting rules. According to the *Uniform Accounting System for Industrial Enterprises*, inventories are all goods owned by an enterprise and held for future sale or production in the normal course of the business. This includes merchandise, finished goods, semi-finished goods, materials, fuel, containers and low-value and perishable articles (MOF, 1992d). For the sake of convenience, these can be classified into merchandising inventory held for future sale, such as merchandise, finished goods, semi-finished goods; manufacturing inventory for further processing, including materials; low-value and perishable articles; containers, and materials for outside processing. As accounting for merchandising inventory and for manufacturing inventory is similar, this discussion will focus on the accounting for materials, accounting for low-value and perishable articles, accounting for containers, and accounting for materials outside processing.

Accounting for materials Materials are considered objects of production in the manufacturing process. Accordingly, as they are consumed or utilised, their costs become part of the cost of the products manufactured by an enterprise. The cost of materials is the largest component of production costs in many industrial enterprises.

Most enterprises in China have rigid regulations for materials control. The main requirements are: (a) that no materials should be purchased without proper authority and no more are to be purchased than is necessary; (b) that the quantity purchased is in fact received; (c) that the storage facilities permit physical control; (d) that no materials be issued from stores unless properly authorised and unless the purpose for which they are required is recorded; and (e) that the accounts provide a running balance of the value of materials on hand. In practice, however, the implementation of such regulations is in doubt because nobody, not even the director of an enterprise, is responsible for the enterprise's assets under the legal concept, and most enterprises suffer chronic shortages of critical materials. Stealing and inefficient use of materials are serious problems in many Chinese enterprises (Chen at al, 1993).

Materials can be divided into several groups according to their function in the production process: raw and main materials, auxiliary materials, spare parts for repairs, fuel, packing materials, semifinished products purchased outside (MOF, 1992b). The purchase price of materials is accounted at their actual cost to the enterprise. Actual cost is derived from the sum of purchase prices paid to suppliers plus additional purchasing and transport costs. These additional costs include the following: transport costs (delivery charges, loading and unloading charges, insurance charges, packing charges and storing charges); reasonable waste and loss during shipment; sorting expenses before storing; other expenses. The cost of issuing materials and the cost of materials on hand are more difficult to calculate. Issuing materials and materials on hand should be priced, in principle, at cost, but where the materials are purchased at varying prices some difficulty will occur in deciding the price to be allotted to any particular issue or material on hand. The methods allowed for deciding the cost of issuing materials and of materials on hand are as follows: (a) First-in First-out; (b) Average cost; (c) Last-in First-out; (d) Individual identification; and (e) Planned cost (MOF, 1992d).

If an enterprise adopts a planned cost system for materials accounting, the cost of issuing materials is based on planned cost. Planned cost is similar to standard cost used in the western concept. This is a predetermined cost established on the basis of planned production operations, efficiency levels, and expected capacity utilisation. However, even under a planned cost system, the cost of issuing materials has to be adjusted to actual cost. Therefore, there are two steps to be taken in calculating the costs of issuing materials: firstly, calculating the planned cost of issuing materials; secondly, adjusting the planned cost of issuing materials to actual costs. This is illustrated in Figure 3-4.

Obviously, there is a difference between the planned cost system and the standard cost system. Under the standard cost system a standard cost is predetermined and once determined is applied to all inventory movements, i.e. materials, inventories, goods available for sale, purchases and goods sold or materials placed in production (Hoggett and Edwards, 1992). However, under the planned cost system in China, the planned cost is only applied in the storage period. The cost of purchases of materials is based on actual costs and once materials are issued from storage to production, the planned cost of the materials has to be adjusted again to the actual cost [11].

---

[11] It is worth noting that the last-in, first-out method is not allowed in Australia, where the methods allowed to determine the costs of inventories are: (a) specific identification; (b) average cost (weighted); (c) first-in, first-out; (d) standard cost (Australian Accounting Research Foundation, 1994).

Figure 3-4 The Procedure of Materials Accounting Under the Planned Cost System

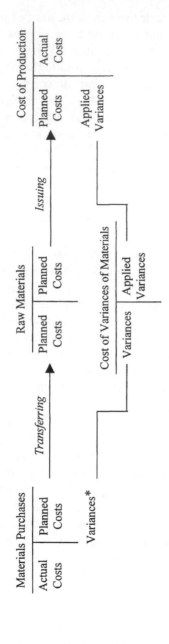

* Assumed that actual cost of materials exceeds the planned cost of materials

The applied variances of issuing materials = the planned costs of issuing materials × the variances of materials application rate

The variances of materials application rate = (the variances of materials at beginning + the variances of materials of purchasing) ÷ (the planned costs of materials at beginning + the planned costs of materials of purchasing)

Unlike the situation in the United States and Australia, the lower of cost and market rule is not allowed in determination of the cost of materials and inventories, which means that conservative doctrine has been only partly recognised in China[12].

Accounting for low-value and perishable articles Low-value and perishable articles are items which do not belong to either materials or fixed assets. The cost must be below certain fixed amounts (1,000 yuan, 1,500 yuan and 2,000 yuan) which arc determined by different enterprises, and their service-life must be less than one year (MOF, 1992b). Low-value and perishable articles are similar to materials in respect of their value and service-life. However, in respect of their nature, they can be used several times and keep their physical form unchanged, and are also similar to fixed assets. Based on this nature, accounting for purchasing and storing of low-value and perishable articles is similar to accounting for materials. However, amortisation is applied when low-value and perishable articles are issued and used. Usually, 50/50 amortisation is used. Fifty percent of the original cost is amortised at the time the articles are issued and the remaining 50 per cent is amortised when the items are removed from use due to deterioration or unfit condition. At that time, the amortisation is reduced by the value of scrap, which is charged to the appropriate materials accounts.

Accounting for containers Containers are the packing items, such as barrels, boxes, bottles, bags, which are used in products packing and are recycled in sales (MOF, 1992b). The containers are different to the packing materials which are assigned directly to cost of production. There are two catalogues of containers: (1) containers sold with the sales of products; (2) containers leased when products are sold. The accounting for containers sold is simple and the costs of containers can be treated as selling expenses or expenses for other operations. The accounting for containers leased is more complicated, involving accounting for lease income, amortisation of costs of containers and the treatment of scrap. The amortisation methods and the treatment of scrap are similar to those for low-value and perishable articles. The fifty-fifty amortisation method or the instalment amortisation method can be used.

---

[12] In the lower of cost and market rule, market, as the term is used in Australia, means the net realisable value of the inventory. In the United States, the lower of cost and market rule interprets "market" as replacement cost (Hoggett and Edwards, 1992).

Accounting for materials processing outside Sometimes due to limitations of manufacturing capacity, an enterprise has to send some materials to other enterprises for processing. The costs of materials for processing outside and the processing costs are calculated under "materials outside processing" account. When materials are transferred to outside processing, the costs of the materials are debited to the "materials outside processing" account, and when outside processing is finished, total costs including processing costs are written back to the relevant materials accounts.

At the end of the financial period, the ending balances for materials, low-value and perishable articles, containers and materials processing outside are integrated in the catalogue of inventories in the balance sheet.

Accounting for Employee Entitlements

The terminology of "the employee Entitlements" is borrowed from western countries. There is no accounting standard so far in China dealing with this issue. The employee entitlements in China may just include wages and other welfare benefits. The combined cost of wages and welfare benefits represents a major expense of operating for any business. However, compared with western countries, the cost of labour is cheaper in China and is a comparatively small part of overall industrial production costs. The total payments for labour include three components:

1. wages, including payments to employees for time worked or for work performed calculated according to tariff pay scales, or piece-work rates; additional payments; vocational payments; and overtime payments.
2. bonuses, the material awards to promote better performance: these may be productivity awards, calculated according to performance in production quantity, quality, time, safety, and efficiency; saving awards, based on saving on consumption of raw materials and energy; or competition awards.
3. allowances, including compensation for abnormal working conditions.

There are two major salary payment systems in China, the daily rate system and the piece rate system.

1. Calculation of salary payments under the daily rate system:

78

Total salary payments = Attendance payments + Overtime payments + Bonuses + Allowances + Sick leave payment.

Attendance payments = The days of attendance * Daily wage rate.

2. Calculation of salary payments under the piece rate system:

Total salary payments = (Qualified products + Spoilage not caused by workers) * Piece rate.

The original documents of attendance records and performance records have to be used in order to calculate employees' wages correctly. Usually, salary payments are made once a month in China.

Usually, Chinese workers do not need to pay personal income tax because only when taxable income exceeds 1000 Renminbi yuan per month, does one begin to pay five per cent personal income tax (National People's Congress, 1993). Most workers' salary payments are below this line. Also, concepts such as annual leave, public holiday pay, long-service leave, pay roll fringe benefits do not exist in China. Accounting for payroll is simpler than that in the Western countries. However, an enterprise in China has to consider workers' welfare because an enterprise is not only a economic unit but also a social and political unit. Usually, an enterprise has to make provision of about 11 – 14 per cent of total salary payment for workers' welfare, about 2 per cent of total salary payments for union fees, and about 1.5 per cent of total salary payments for employee education.

Other problems in accounting for employee entitlements in China are that only part of payments for labour costs are allowed to be deducted as expenses and another part of payments are deducted directly from equity – employee welfare reserves. Therefore, the cost of labour in the Chinese profit and loss statement cannot correctly reflect the total costs spent on labour because the part of expenses on labour are directly deducted from equity.

Accounting for Fixed Assets and Depreciation

Accounting for fixed assets and depreciation is influenced by governmental economic policy. Equipment and machinery usually have a longer period of use in China than in western countries because the government lacks funding to upgrade its industrial infrastructure. Another reason for the longer replacement period for equipment and machinery is that the cost of labour is cheaper in China than in other industrial countries and even cheaper than in some developing countries like Korea, Singapore and the Philippines. Most enterprises are labour-intensive and the demand for high technical equipment is still lower. However, this situation has been gradually changing with the huge investment from overseas.

Classification of fixed assets In China, assets can be treated as fixed assets when their useful life is more than one year and their unit value exceeds a certain amount. These amounts are 1,000 yuan, 1,500 yuan and 2,000 yuan according to the different types of enterprises, otherwise these assets can only be treated as lower value and perishable articles (MOF, 1992d). Fixed assets can be classified into seven primary groups on the basis of their status of usage and nature, according to a uniform industrial accounting system: productive assets, non-productive assets, leased out assets, unused assets, useless assets, land and financial leased assets (MOF, 1992b).

Productive fixed assets are those used to alter directly the objects of production during the manufacturing process. Assets such as buildings and other structures that provide the conditions necessary for the production process are also classified as productive fixed assets. Productive fixed assets are subdivided into the following groups on the basis of their function in the economic activity of the enterprise: (a) buildings; (b) construction such as roads, pipelines and platforms; (c) power-generating equipment; (d) output transmission mechanisms; (e) production machinery and equipment; (f) tools, measuring and regulating devices, and laboratory equipment; (g) transporting equipment such as trucks, vessels and cars; (h) management tools such as computers, typewriters and copy machines; (i) other productive fixed assets.

Non-productive fixed assets are those which are not utilised in the production process. They are usually utilised in performing social functions of an enterprise, such as cultural, medical, and social services. These assets include employees' dormitories, guest houses, canteens, hospitals, kindergartens and schools.

Leased out fixed assets are those lent to other units with the approval of the authorities.

Unused assets are those which have not yet been installed, are under reconstruction, or are temporarily out of production. However, assets which are under capital repair or are subject to a seasonal cessation of use are included as productive assets when calculating depreciation.

Useless assets are those which an enterprise no longer needs and which should be transferred to other enterprises or be disposed of.

Land is not included in the calculation of depreciation in China.

Leased assets include financially leased assets and operationally leased assets. Financially leased assets are treated as part of assets of an enterprise;

while operationally leased assets are not included in an enterprise's balance sheet, and enterprise can set up a separate off balance sheet account to account for operating lease. The treatment of leases is similar to the practice in western countries.

Accounting of assets evaluation Three concepts are used in the evaluation of fixed assets in China: original cost, replacement cost, and residual cost. Original cost, or historical cost is the basis of the evaluation of fixed assets.

The original cost of fixed assets is the cost derived from expenditures for their construction, manufacture, or acquisition. (a) For fixed assets from acquisition the original costs include the purchasing price or the book value of the fixed assets, packing and delivery expenses and installation expenses. (b) For fixed assets from self-manufacturing, the original costs included all expenditures of manufacture. (c) For assets as part of investment from other units, the original costs are the prices determined in the investment contract. (d) For fixed assets from financial lease agreements, the original costs include equipment prices, delivery charges, insurance charges and instalment charges. (e) For fixed assets from extension, reconstruction or renovation, the original costs are determined on the basis of the original costs of old fixed assets plus the costs of new parts, and minus the disposable income from discarded parts (MOF, 1992d).

Replacement cost is the cost of obtaining fixed assets in identical or similar condition and capacity to those currently in use. Replacement cost can only be used when evaluating the fixed assets donated or rediscovered after misplacement. It can also be used when fixed assets are reappraised by the government. Reappraisal of fixed assets has seldom been made by government and most fixed assets in China are undervalued (Yang, 1988)[13]. When fixed assets are reappraised, the difference between replacement cost and original cost is treated as an increase or decrease of paid up capital – governmental capital.

The difference between the original cost of fixed assets and the depreciation (the amount allowed for deterioration and obsolescence) is the asset's residual cost which decreases as the depreciation is gradually charged.

Accounting for acquisition and disposal of fixed assets Fixed assets usually increase as a result of capital investment. Capital investment can be made by outside bodies, such as government, other legal and personal entities, and

---

[13] Reappraisal of fixed assets has been undertaken by government four times: in 1951, 1972, 1986 and 1992; an enterprise is not allowed to re-appraise its assets individually in China.

through donations. Capital investment can also be carried out by an enterprise itself through acquisition, compensated conveyance, self-construction, manufacture and financial lease.

With the implementation of the new accounting standard and uniform accounting systems, two main changes have occurred. The previously separate accounting systems for capital investment and for the enterprise's principal activity have been integrated. Before reform, an enterprise had two separate accounting systems, construction unit accounting and industrial enterprise accounting. It had to prepare two sets of financial statements, one for its principal activity and the second for its capital investment transactions. Capital investment, including all transactions relating to asset cost and sources of financing, was previously calculated under the accounting system for the construction unit; then, when the process of construction, manufacture, or acquisition was completed the assets became subject to the enterprise accounting system for the enterprise's principal activity. Since the accounting reform, all capital investment activities are calculated using the account "Under Construction". This is an asset type account.

The other change that has occurred is that the gratuitous transfer of fixed assets from one enterprise to another has been abolished. Before reform, fixed assets could be transferred uncompensated from one enterprise to other enterprises under the order of government authorities. This was because the resources of all enterprises were the property of the state and the transfer of fixed assets between enterprises did not involve any payment. Since economic and accounting reforms, enterprises have been granted more responsibility for their own performance and are able to use cost benefit criteria to justify their behaviour. Thus, government authorised gratuitous transfers of fixed assets are now severely resisted by enterprises.

Fixed assets on financial leases are also required to be capitalised and accounting treatment of financial leases is similar to that in the United States and in Australia. The financial lease is disclosed under fixed assets and long-term liabilities in financial reports and the original cost is required to be disclosed separately in notes to financial reports.

Disposal of fixed assets results from one of the following actions: sale with permission of government authorities for assets no longer needed; investment in other enterprises; discarding due to deterioration or obsolescence; and destruction by natural disasters.

Fixed assets that have lost their productive value owing to physical deterioration as well as obsolescence are subject to disposal. The discarded asset is removed from the accounting records to settle with consideration of its original cost and depreciation, expenses incurred during disposal (dismantling, removal, etc), and the value of reusable materials remaining after disposal (supplies, fuel, spare parts, etc). The cost of any remaining materials is charged to appropriate inventory accounts.

Accounting for depreciation Fixed assets gradually wear out and/or become obsolete. In each month depreciation is calculated so that a portion of the cost of fixed assets corresponding to their deterioration and obsolescence may be included in the enterprise's cost of production. Depreciation is charged only for fixed assets in use, including productive, non-productive, leased out and financially leased fixed assets. However, unused and useless fixed assets except buildings and construction, fixed assets ceasing operation for more than one month but not for seasonal reasons, operational leased assets, and land are not to be included in the calculation of depreciation (MOF, 1992d). When fixed assets are received by an enterprise, the first depreciation is calculated and charged in the following month; for fixed assets leaving the enterprise depreciation ceases in the month following the removal of the assets. Usually the depreciation is calculated by using the straight-line method according to the asset's useful life. There is a uniform fixed asset depreciation scheme in China promulgated by the Ministry of Finance. The different types and groups of fixed assets have different depreciation rates. Every enterprise has to follow the regulations to calculate depreciation. The Industrial Enterprise Depreciation Scheme is shown in Table 3-5.

However, with the approval of the Ministry of Finance and the State Taxes Bureau, accelerated depreciation methods can be used by some enterprises. There are five depreciation methods allowed in the new accounting standard: Straight-Line (SL), Units-of-Production (UOP), Double-Declining-Balance, Sum-of-Years-Digits (SYD), and Shorted-Straight-Line (SSL) (MOF, 1992a).

The shorted-straight-line method is an accelerated depreciation method with unique Chinese characteristics. It is easy to apply because an asset's useful life can be shortened by 30 per cent on the basis of the *Uniform Fixed Assets Depreciation Scheme*. For example, the useful life of manufacturing machinery is 10-14 years, according to the scheme. However, under the SSL method, the useful life of manufacturing machinery will be 7-9.8 years (Chen et al, 1993).

The depreciation methods above are used for determining individual asset depreciation amounts. However, in practice in China most enterprises prefer to use a group depreciation rate or synthetic depreciation rate to compute annual or monthly depreciation amounts. This is for the sake of simplicity.

The calculation of the group or synthetic depreciation rate is based on the calculation of the individual asset's depreciation. The formulas are as follows:

1. Group depreciation rate = Σ Annual depreciation amount of each individual asset in the group ÷ Σ The original cost of each fixed asset in the group.
2. Annual depreciation amounts of the group = Σ Total of original cost of fixed assets in the group × group depreciation rate.
3. Synthetic depreciation rate = Σ Annual depreciation amount of each individual asset in an enterprise ÷ Σ The original cost of each fixed asset in the enterprise.
4. Annual depreciation amount for an enterprise = Σ Total original cost of fixed assets in an enterprise × Synthetic depreciation rate.

Accounting for Intangible Assets and Goodwill

The concepts of intangible assets and deferred assets are quite new for most accountants in China. According to the new accounting standard, intangible assets are those which are useful over a long time for an enterprise but have no physical substance, including patents, special technology, trademarks and brand names, copyrights, land use rights and goodwill (MOF, 1992b). Deferred assets are expenses which can not be included in the current year's profit and loss statement and have to be amortised in the future, including establishment fees and leasehold improvements. The costs of intangible assets and deferred assets are amortised on a straight-line basis in the benefit period. This is decided in the individual contract and is no less than ten years if the contract does not include a benefit period provision.

Accounting for Investments

The recognition and measurement requirements for accounting for investments are prescribed in the specific accounting standard: *Accounting for Investments* as well as in the *Uniform Accounting Systems* and *Financial Management Regulations for Industrial (or Other Sectors) Enterprises*. Some issues have been discussed in specific accounting standards before. The following discussions focus on the bookkeeping issues. The investments can be divided as short-term investments and long-term investment.

Table 3-5 Industrial Enterprise Depreciation Scheme

Classifications	Depreciating Years
A. General equipment	
1. Manufacturing machinery	10-14
2. Power-generating equipment	11-18
3. Transmission mechanisms	15-28
4. Transporting equipment	06-12
5. Automatic controlling equipment, instrument and meter	
(1) Automatic and semi-automatic controlling equipment	08-12
(2) Computer	04-10
(3) General measuring instrument	07-12
6. Industrial oven	07-13
7. Tools and other production accessories	09-14
8. Non-productive equipment and instrument	
(1) Equipment and tools	18-22
(2) Television, copy-machine and word processing machine	05-08
B. Special equipment	
9. Metallurgical industry special equipment	09-15
10. Electricity generating industry special equipment	
(1) Electricity generating and the heat suppling equipment	12-20
(2) Electricity transmission lines	30-35
(3) Electricity re-distribution lines	14-16
(4) Electivity re-distribution equipment	18-22
(5) Nuclear electricity generating equipment	20-25
11. Machinery industry special equipment	08-12
12. Oil industry special equipment	08-12
13. Chemical and medical industry special equipment	07-14
14. Electronic, instrumental and telecommunication industry special equipment	05-10
15. Construction materials industry special equipment	06-12
16. Textile and light industry special equipment	08-14
17. Mining, coal, and forestry industry special equipment	07-15
18. Ship construction industry special equipment	15-22
19. Nuclear industry special equipment	20-25
20. Public service industry equipment	
(1) Water suppling equipment	15-20
(2) Gas supplying equipment	16-25

Table 3-5 Continuing...

C. Buildings and constructions			
21. Buildings			
	(1)	General production buildings	30-40
	(2)	Production buildings in corrosive situation	20-25
	(3)	Production buildings in strongly corrosive situation	10-15
	(4)	Non-productive buildings	35-45
	(5)	Simple and crude buildings	08-10
22. Constructions			
	(1)	Dams of hydro-electric power stations	45-55
	(2)	Other constructions	15-25

There are two separate accounts "Short-term Investments" and "Long-term Investments" in the *Uniform Accounting Systems*. The short-term investment shall be accounted at cost. The detail bookkeeping method for recording the short-term investment has been illustrated in Table 3-4. It can be argued that bookkeeping methods for the usage of uniform accounts are very important parts in Chinese GAAPs.

Long-term investments include Equity Investments in Shares, Debt Investments in Bonds, and Other Investments. Equity investments in shares are accounted differently according the percentage of ownership the investor companies have in the investee companies and whether the investor companies control the investee companies. If the investor companies have less than 50% ownership in the investee companies, or investors do not control investees, then the investments shall be accounted by using the costs method. If the investor companies have more than 50% ownership interest in the investee companies, or investors control investees, their investments shall be accounted by using the equity methods. If the investor companies are the listing companies, they also required to prepare the consolidation accounts.

Debt investments in bonds shall be accounted at costs. The accrued interests on bonds shall be accounted separately in a sub-ledger called "Long-term Investment – Accrued Interests" in the Uniform Accounting Systems. The premiums and discounts on purchasing of bonds shall be amortised over the terms of the bonds by using straight-line method. It is a silence in the Chinese GAAPs on whether enterprises allowed to use the effective-interest method to amortise the discounts or to write-off the premiums.

Other long-term investments are direct investments in other enterprises by the means of fixed assets, cash, inventories, or intangible assets. They shall be accounted differently according to whether the investor companies use the cost method or the equity method: if the investor companies use the cost method to account for their investments, returns from investments shall be treated as investment revenues; while if the investor companies use the equity method, they shall increase/decrease proportionally the investments according to the increase/decrease of investee's profits/losses. When investor companies receive dividends from investees, they shall reduce the investment accounts.

Accounting for Liabilities

As the definitions of accounting elements in China depart significantly from those used in the Western countries, a liability is defined as "debt borne by an enterprise, measurable by money value, which will be paid to a creditor using assets, or services" (Tang et al, 1994). Liabilities then are divided into short-term liabilities and long-term liabilities. Short-term liabilities include short-term loan, accounts payable, bills payable, salary (payroll) and welfare payable, tax and profit payable, and other payable. In general, short-term liabilities shall be accounts at their book value (cost). The interests charged on short-term liabilities shall be regarded as financial expenses in the period as they occurred. Accounts payable shall be measured at costs (total payments due minus cash discounts available); bills payable shall be accounted at their book value, any interests associated with bills payable shall be charged to financial expenses and salary, and welfare payable shall be measured at total payments due to the employee.

Chinese enterprises pay many taxes based on sales volume (turnover), income, utilisation of certain resources (e.g. usage of land), transfer of property and other activities. The main turnover taxes in China are Value-Added Tax, Consumption Tax, and Business Tax[14]. The main income taxes are Domestic Enterprise Income Tax and Foreign Investment Enterprise and Foreign Enterprise Income Tax. The bookkeeping methods for accounting for

---

[14] The Value-Added Tax is a multistage tax imposed on business, which is measured by the value added at each stage to goods and services. It typically is imposed on sales of goods by businesses at each stage of production and distribution, and on services as they are rendered. The tax liability generally is equal to the difference between the tax charged on sales (output tax) and the tax payable on purchases from other businesses (input tax). Consumption Tax is a tax levied on consumption of some luxury goods, unhealthy goods and other goods. The purpose of this category of tax is to set up the correct signals for consumption, and adjust the demand and supply relationship of the market. Business Tax is levied on the business volume (sale volume) of activities carried out by taxpayers, and is mainly marked by its simple calculation and collection methods. It is the oldest tax in China and now its scope has been limited.

tax payable have been prescribed in the account, "Tax payable", in *The Uniform Accounting System*. Several sub-ledgers should also be set up by enterprises such as Value-Added Tax (VAT) payable, Consumption Tax payable, Business Tax payable, Income Tax payable. As most enterprises are levied on the Value-Added Tax, the accounting for Value-Added Tax is examined in the following details.

VAT payable is calculated as Sales Revenue multiplied by rate of VAT (VAT output tax) minus tax payable on purchases from other business (VAT input tax). When VAT output tax is greater than VAT input tax, enterprises shall credit "VAT payable" account according to the difference between VAT output tax and VAT input tax, and debit "sales taxes and additional levies" expense account. When VAT output tax is less than VAT input tax, the difference between them is negative. Enterprises shall debit "VAT payable" and credit "Provision for Deferred Taxes" accounts. In the subsequent periods, the "Provision for Deferred Taxes" should be reversed when VAT output tax is greater than VAT input tax.

Accounting for income tax payable will be discussed in accounting for tax-effect accounting.

There is a "Profit payable" account in *The Uniform Accounting System*. This account is accounting for the distributions of profits to investors, including payments to governments and private investors. The distribution of profits to investors does not depend on whether an enterprise makes profits or not in the current year. It depends on whether an enterprise has undistributed profit funds after making required profits reserves. The "Profits Payable" account is similar to "Dividend Payable" account under the Western concept.

Long-term liabilities include Long-term loans, Debentures, and Long-term payables. Long-term loans should be measured at present value of future payments (PV). The repayments on loans should be divided into principal payments and interest payments. The interest payments for the projects under construction shall be capitalised and be treated as part of the costs of the projects.

Debentures shall be accounted at their face value (nominal value). If debentures are issued at discounts or at premiums, these discounts or premiums shall be amortised by using straight-line methods over the term of debentures.

Accounting for Revenue and Expenses Recognition

The criteria for recognition of revenue and expense in China are similar to those used in Western countries. Revenue can be recognised in different points in the business cycle. They can be recognised at the point of sale for most economic transactions, or at the point of collection of cash, e.g. accounting for sales on instalment. Revenue can also be recognised even at the point of production. For example, the revenue from construction contract is required be recognised based on the percentage completion method. Matching principle is used to match expense that represents the effort against revenue generated. Expenses shall be either allocated over time or recognised immediately. Expenses which are required be allocated over time include depreciation expenses, amortisation expenses. Expenses which are required be written off immediately include management expenses and financial expenses. The costs of goods produced shall be appointed between costs of goods sold and inventory at the end of year.

Accounting for Profits Distribution and Owner's Equity

Profits in a typical Chinese enterprise include operation profits, other operation profits and non-operation profits. After paying tax on total profits, the profits after income tax then shall be divided into four accounts, compulsory profit reserve, which can be used to off-set previous losses or increase the capital; beneficial profit reserve, which is used to pay employees' welfare expenses or facilities; dividends; and undistributed profits. Accounting for distribution of profits highlights that the treatment of the total cost of employee entitlements in China is different from that in Western countries. In Western countries, all costs for employee entitlements, including wages, sick leave and other welfare benefits, are regarded as expenses and deducted before profits. In China, some employee entitlements, such as wages and sick pays are deducted as expenses. Other employee's benefits, such bonuses and expenses on recreation facilities for employees, shall be deducted from beneficial profit reserve after tax.

Owners' equity includes paid-up capital, capital reserve, profit reserve (including both compulsory profit reserve and beneficial profit reserve), and undistributed profits. The resources of capital reserve are from mainly four parts: the premium on issuing of shares; the donation of assets by others; the revaluation increase of assets; and exchange differences on capital received. Both capital reserve and profit reserve can be used to increase paid-up capital but normally the profit reserve should be kept at about 25 per cent of paid-up capital.

Accounting for Consolidation

Until 1995, when the Ministry of Finance issued the "Tentative Regulations on Consolidation of Financial Statements", Chinese enterprises were not required to consolidate their subsidiary's accounts with parent company's accounts. Currently, most companies are still not required to prepare the consolidated accounts because this regulation only applies to listing companies, selected experimental companies and foreign trade companies. However, although the consolidation concept is quite new to Chinese enterprises, the practice of adding-up different companies' financial reports together has existed for more than fifty years. Each year, financial departments and relevant industrial supervision departments are required to add-up individual enterprise financial reports according to different industries, different regions and different ownerships. In order to distinguish this practice from that of the consolidation, we may call this practice "Combination of financial reports". The inter-company transactions and interests are not eliminated during the combination process.

On the other hand, the inter-company transactions and interests shall be eliminated in the consolidation process. According to the tentative regulations, if a Chinese company owns more than fifty percent ownership interests in other companies or controls these companies by other means, then this company is regarded as a parent company and required to consolidate the accounts of its subsidiaries and its own accounts. There are some differences in the consolidation process between the Chinese version and the Australian version: (1) The investments of the parent company in the subsidiaries are accounted by using the equity method in China, rather than the cost method, which is used in Australia. (2) China uses the parent company concept for consolidation and regards the outside-equity interest as a liability and Australia uses the entity concept and regards outside-equity interest as part of equity. (3) In China, the consolidation process starts from elimination of parent company's investment at the reporting date with equity balances at the reporting date. The difference is regarded as "consolidation difference" in the balance sheet. This process then moves backward to eliminate the inter-company transactions in the current year and decomposes the ending balance of retained earning. In Australia, the consolidation process starts from the elimination of parent company's investment at acquisition day against the equities in subsidiary (net assets) at that date, the difference is regarded as "goodwill/discount" of acquisition. The consolidation process then moves forward to amortise goodwill and eliminate the inter-company transactions, and then calculates outside-equity interest in the post acquisition changes in subsidiary's equity.

If a subsidiary is a foreign company, the parent company shall translate the foreign company's financial reports into financial reports in the Chinese currency before consolidation.

Accounting for Tax-effect Accounting

In contrast to the situation in most western countries, such as the United States, the United Kingdom and Australia, the accounting system in China is closely linked with the taxation system and accounting regulations are tax oriented. As a general rule in western countries, there are accounting standards for book purposes, with guidance on the accounting treatment for tax purposes contained in the tax legislation. In the past however, Chinese accounting legislation has provided guidelines for both accounting and tax purposes. For example, there are no differences allowed for accounting and tax depreciation, and the accounting profit is equal to the taxable profit. The traditional agreement is that the State Taxes Administration Bureau is responsible for tax regulations and the Ministry of Finance is responsible for the regulating of accounting treatments for both accounting and tax purposes.

The situation has changed slowly. In 1994, the Ministry of Finance issued *The Tentative Regulation on Accounting Treatments for Enterprises' Income Tax*, which allows enterprises to use either the tax payable method or the tax allocation method. It was the first time that the Chinese financial authorities acknowledged that income tax is an expense not a distribution of profits. Enterprises only can choose one of the two methods; tax payable or tax allocation, allowed for accounting purposes. If an enterprise chooses the tax payable method, it should establish an "Income Tax" account. The amount of tax payable to the taxation authority is also the amount can be recognised as income tax expense in the "Income Tax" account. The amount of tax payable is calculated based on the accounting income, adjusted for some differences caused by governmental accounting and tax regulations. If an enterprise chooses the tax allocation (tax effect accounting) method, it should establish two accounts; "Income Tax" and "Deferred Tax". The income tax expense is calculated based on the accounting income and debited to the "Income Tax" account, the income tax payable is calculated based on taxable income and

91

credited to "Income Tax Payable" accounting. The taxes on timing differences caused by the differences between the accounting income and taxable income are debited (credited) to "Deferred Tax" account. "Deferred Tax" account also accounts for the changes of income tax rates under the liability method.

The tentative regulation for tax effect accounting in China is based on the "profit and loss statement" approach. However, the approach for tax effect accounting used the International Accounting Standard and Standards in other western countries has been changed from "profit and loss statement" approach to "balance sheet" approach. The reason for this change is to make the accounting standard for tax effect accounting consistent with the conceptual framework.

The Chinese GAAPs have been examined in details. The comparison of the Chinese GAAPs and the western GAAPs shows that there are some differences between two models, but the differences have been reduced gradually with more and more accounting standards and regulations promulgated by the Chinese government being internationally compatible.

4 The Accounting Profession in China

Compared with western accounting professions, which have existed for more than a century, the Chinese Certified Public Accountants (CPAs) profession is quite young. It is only 15 years since the CPA system was re-introduced officially in 1980. However, the growth of the accounting profession has been very rapid. There have been three big events during the fifteen years since 1980: firstly, *The Certified Public Accountants Act 1993* was promulgated by the Fourth Session of the Standing Committee of the Eighth National People's Congress. Secondly, the new Chinese Auditing Standards were issued in 1995. Finally, the two accounting professional bodies, the Chinese Institute of Certified Public Accountants (CICPA) and the Chinese Association of Certified Public Auditors (CACPA) were merged in June 1995. These events provide another significant step in China's effort to harmonise its accounting practices with the rest of the world after issuing the Chinese Accounting Standards (Aiken, Lu and Ji, 1995).

Historical Review of the Development of the Certified Public Accountants' System

Under the open door policy advocated by Deng Xiao-Ping, the system of CPAs which had been abandoned early in the post-revolutionary period was reactivated over a decade ago[15]. The Ministry of Finance promulgated temporary provisions for establishing accounting consulting offices in 1980. Since then CPA firms have been re-established in China. In 1985 an act entitled *Accounting Law 1985* was passed by the national congress. Under compliance with *Accounting Law 1985*, the State Council approved *"Provisions for Certified Public Accountants"* in July 1986. These provisions stipulated qualifications, ethics, and organizational edicts for CPAs.

---

[15] Deng Xiao-ping regained power at the Third Plenary Session of the Eleventh Central Committee of the Chinese Communist Party held in December 1978. After this conference, China began experimenting with economic reforms and re-opened the door to the outside world (Beijing Review, 1978).

With the further development of economic reforms and the widening of the open door policy, the CPA profession has made significant progress. By 1992 there were more than 10,000 Certified Public Accountants and more than 25,000 professionals performing CPA activities. By the end of 1993 the number of Certified Public Accountants increased to 15,000 and total practitioners increased in number to 40,000, there being 2,500 CPA firms at that time. However, these figures do not yet match the demand for CPAs, which, according to the estimates of the Ministry of Finance (MOF), is 100,000. According to the Vice-Minister of MOF, Zhang Youcai (Zhang, 1993):

> ... all business accounting should be verified by CPAs in a market economy. But this cannot be realized at present since China at the moment only has 15,000 people with CPA qualifications ... Our target is to produce over 60,000 CPAs in the next six years to bring the total number to some 100,000 by the end of this century ... (p.1)

Since the codification of '*Provisions for Certified Public Accountants*' by the State council in July, 1986, the economic system has changed significantly (Ji and Lu, 1992). The centrally planned economy is gradually being replaced by a socialist market economy. Functions of government in the administration of enterprises have been altered[16]. Enterprises now have more freedom when deciding how to make profits and how to survive in a competitive market.

Another pressure for change in the CPA regulations comes from the internationalisation of CPA practices. Comparable CPA systems are essential elements for international investment and economic transactions. With growing foreign investment there were complaints about the lack of a comparable CPA system in China. If China had not changed its CPA system, international investment in China could have been hampered and corporations with foreign associations would have been restricted in their activities, particularly with respect to finance. During 1990 China applied to re-join the General Agreement on Tariffs and Trade (GATT). Under negotiations with GATT, China was required to open six service markets including a CPA service. When the Uruguay GATT negotiation re-opened in March 1992,

---

[16] Company systems such as the limited liability company and the joint-stock limited company system have been introduced to reform state-owned enterprises. However, it will be a long time to complete this process, considering the current number of state-owned enterprises and political and economic conditions.

China promised to open six markets. There was an agreement that only foreign CPA firms whose annual incomes were more than US$20 million and whose staff numbers exceeded 200 could have access to the Chinese market. The total number of foreign CPA firms permitted to operate in China was restricted to fifteen (Ding, 1993).

Critical Assessment of the *Certified Public Accountants' Act 1993*

The *Certified Public Accountants' Act 1993* includes 7 chapters and 46 articles. The seven chapters cover: (1) general rules; (2) examination and registration; (3) scope of business and ethical rules; (4) CPA firms; (5) Institution of CPAs; (6) legal liabilities; and (7) supplementary provisions (*Certified Public Accountants' Act*, 1993). The comments on new Chinese CPA laws are now addressed.

Chinese Certified Public Accountants, an Independent Profession?

According to the *Certified Public Accountants' Act 1993*, Certified Public Accountants in China are persons who hold a certificate of the CPA and conduct CPA activities. The scope of CPA business includes:

1. Independent auditing: independent auditing, as elsewhere, is different from internal auditing and governmental auditing in that it includes the audit of an enterprise's accounting reports; appraising its assets; and auditing its consolidations, reorganisations, insolvencies and other relevant matters.
2. Accounting consulting: accounting consulting includes the design of accounting systems, accounting projects performed for management, taxation, business registration and staff training.

Therefore, the functions of Certified Public Accountants in China are classified to be appraisal and service provision. The basic function is appraising, or notarising. There is an argument in Australia about whether CPAs should provide consulting services because these may affect the independent statute of CPAs. However, providing consulting services is codified in the Chinese Act as one of the basic functions of CPAs. It seems that either the Chinese have not been aware of the potential conflicts between the auditing and consulting functions of CPAs, or they believe there is no material conflict.

Under the Act, CPA firms in China are those agencies which are established according to relevant laws to cover CPA responsibilities. CPAs can establish their own social organisations which are called Institutes of CPAs. The Chinese Institute of CPAs (CICPA) is the national organisation of CPAs and the Institutes of CPAs in provinces, autonomous regions and municipalities are the local organisations of CPAs. They can be regarded as the local branches of the CICPA.

Although CPA organisations are called social or professional organisations according to the CPA Law, the Chinese Institute of CPAs and local institutes of CPAs are all quasi-governmental agencies. CICPA has the power to organise CPA examinations, to grant registration, to promulgate CPA regulations, and to administer CPA affairs. However, the Ministry of Finance and the financial departments of local governments are responsible for the administration and instruction of CPAs, CPA firms and the   Institutes of CPAs. According to the Act:

> The Institutes of CPAs are the social organisations established by CPAs. The Chinese Institute of CPAs is a national organisation of CPAs and the Institutes of CPAs in provinces, autonomous regions and municipalities are the local organisations of CPAs.

> The Ministry of Finance of the State Council and the financial departments of local governments have rights to supervise and guide the CPAs, CPA firms and the Institutes of CPAs (Certified Public Accountants Act, 1993).

Therefore, CPAs do not comprise an independent profession in China. Government authorities have rights to interfere with a CPA business by the Act. In substance, most CPA firms are so-called 'institutional CPA firms' sponsored, supported and controlled by the financial departments of government. CICPA is a quasi-government agency of MOF. According to Richard Macve and Zhi Yu Liu (1995):

> The Chinese accounting firms have the Chinese Institute of Certified Public Accountants (CICPA) as their professional body, which is comparable with some Western counterparts. However, the MOF and local public finance departments are the real 'power behind the throne'; indeed all staff of the CICPA are governmental officers and officials ... (p. 54).

The Act clearly defines qualifications needed in order to become a CPA. It stipulates that only those candidates who have tertiary qualifications or have ranking as accountants or a medium ranking in cognate professions[17] can apply to sit the CPA examination. A candidate who has a high ranking in accounting or a relevant professional area can apply for exemption from certain subjects. After passing the uniform examinations and with two years working experience in accounting and auditing, one can apply to register with a local branch of the Chinese Institute of CPAs as a Certified Public Accountant. A certificate will be issued to that person.

The first CPA examination was held in China in December 1991 under the *Provision* of 1986. More than 23,700 practitioners in accounting and auditing took the examination. The subjects then included in the examination were: (1) Accounting; (2) Auditing; (3) Financial Management; and (4) Economic Law (Finance and Accounting, 1992). The second uniform examination was held in September 1993. Now the Taxation Law has been added in the CPA examination. Currently all the exams are taken in Chinese, so all those candidates are ethnic Chinese. Under the *Provisions of 1986*, accounting professors and associate professors, research fellows and those who have higher educational degrees and more than 20 years' experience could be exempted wholly from the examination. However, under the new Act, this no longer applies. Everyone has to pass the exam in order to obtain CPA status. This meets the criteria of fair competition and international requirements for practice.

In summary, if one wants to be a CPA in China, he or she should have a tertiary or equivalent qualification, pass the CPA examination and obtain at least two years' experience in the accounting and auditing area. Then they may register as a Chinese CPA and obtain a Certificate from a branch of the CICPA.

---

[17] There are uniform ranking systems in all professions, for example, the ranking of accountants' positions in China are: senior accountant, accountant, assistant accountant and accounts clerk. The obtaining of a higher ranking also requires certain qualification and work experience.

Auditors' duties are often complex and uncertain in the western world, where regulations about these duties have been changed frequently and have not yet been resolved satisfactorily. The pressure to place greater responsibilities upon auditors for fraud detection has increased (Tomasic, 1992). By professional agreement in the west, the main duties of auditors have been identified: (1) Auditors have a primary duty to audit, which encompasses a continuous duty to warn management promptly of any reasonable suspicion that fraud or error may exist. This duty is not constrained by the duty to report. (2) Auditors have a duty to pay due regard to the possibility of fraud and to actively investigate the possibility of fraud in circumstances in which suspicions are, or should be, aroused. However, auditors in the west claim they have no duty to detect fraud or error in the absence of circumstances which should arouse their suspicions, or because fraud or error has affected the financial statements. (3) Auditors have a duty to obtain sufficient, relevant and reliable evidence to satisfy themselves about the various matters necessary to form their opinion, and they are not entitled to rely purely on management submissions in this regard. (4) Auditors are not to be excused from negligent conduct on grounds that the client's directors or managers were also negligent, or even fraudulent. Reliance on independent sources of evidence is an aid to and not a substitute for an auditor's procedures. Professional standards and practices must reflect changes in the economic and business environment and are not limited to those practices adopted by a majority of the profession's members. Audit partners will be held liable for the consequences of any negligent conduct on the part of a subordinate (Godsell, 1993).

So far, issues of the duties of auditors have not caused severe problems in China[18]. There are no clear distinctions between an auditor's duties and ethical conduct in CPA regulations in China. The duties of auditors can be summarised according to the relevant laws:

1.   Auditors in China have a duty to audit and report. But they also have a duty to refuse to report in certain circumstances when clients request auditors to make an untrue or fraudulent report, when clients

---

[18] There have been two cases involving auditors providing fraudulent accounting information, one concerning the Zhong Cheng Accounting firm in Beijing, the other the Shenzhen Specific Zone Accounting firm in Shenzhen. The auditors in these two firms were disqualified from practising as CPAs (Ma, 1994).

refuse to supply relevant accounting information and documents, and when auditors cannot make a correct report because of unreasonable demands of clients.

2. Auditors have a duty to make a fair report according to relevant laws, ethics and working procedures. Auditors in China will be liable if they know and do not disclose material issues which would conflict with government regulations, where lack of disclosure would damage the interests of users of financial reports and other relevant groups, and could cause misunderstanding of financial reports.

3. Auditors have a duty not to act for their own self-interest. They cannot buy or sell a client's shares, debentures or other assets during an auditing period. Auditors cannot accept commissions and bribes. In addition, advertising by CPAs or their firms is not permitted and CPAs in public practice are prohibited from seeking clients by soliciting.

4. Auditors have a duty to keep a client's business information confidential.

5. Auditors have a duty not to audit an enterprise's financial activities if he/she has a near relative in that enterprise as a director or other senior decision-maker.

Comparing the auditors' duties in China with those in western countries, one may find issues regarded as ethical problems in the west which are codified into the Chinese CPA Act. For example, to keep a client's business information confidential, not to advertise CPA's services, and not to work at the same time in two or more than two CPA firms, are all legal responsibilities of CPAs in China. In Australia, these have been tied also to ethical rules. Furthermore, why does China need a separate CPA law, when Australia does not? The reasons are: (1) China has a different legal system. The Chinese legal system is a code law system alone while the Australian legal system is also a case law system. There are numerous cases, as well as the regulations in Corporations Law, about the duties of auditors in Australia on which judges can rely. However, there are no precedents which can be relied upon by judges in the Chinese court. The promulgation of CPA law is regarded by the Chinese as a very important step to improve its overall legal system. (2) There is no clear cut line between legal liabilities and ethics in China. Putting many ethical issues into the Chinese CPA law seems to make the legal position of CPAs in China more harsh than what it would be in Australia. However, it might be helpful because the CICPA is quite young. Greater awareness of professional ethics and potential disciplinary sanctions upon Chinese CPAs is important.

Limited Partnership: A Unique Innovation for Chinese CPAs?

There is neither Partnership Law nor limited liability Corporation Law in China. Therefore, the establishment of CPA firms can only rely on the relevant articles about partnership relationships in the General Civil Law, although this Law itself needs to be improved. Based on the General Civil Law, two methods of establishing a CPA firm have been stipulated by the Act: firstly, a CPA firm can be set up by certified public accountants. The legal position for this kind of CPA firm is as a partnership in which members jointly bear unlimited liabilities. Secondly, a CPA firm can be promoted by a government agency which bears limited liability. Thus, from a legal aspect there are different types of CPA firms in China: the pure private CPA firms established by individual CPAs are unlimited partnerships, while the CPA firms sponsored by institutional agencies are limited partnerships. This situation is more complex because not all institutional agencies can promote CPA firms.

The Main Features of the New Chinese Auditing Standards

Three years after the first Chinese Accounting Standard issued in 1993, the first batch of Chinese Independent Auditing Standards was issued and became effective on 1 January 1996. To 1999, three batches of independent auditing standards had been issued and a relatively comprehensive auditing standard system established. This auditing standard system includes four different kinds of standards: Independent Auditing Standards; Professional Conduct Standards; Quality Control Standards; and Continuing Professional Education Standards. The details of Independent Auditing Standards are illustrated in Table 4-1.

Table 4-1 Independent Auditing Standards

Independent Auditing Standards

Independent Auditing Standard Preface

Independent General Auditing Standard

Independent Specific Auditing Standards (1-24)
1. Financial Statement Auditing
2. Auditing Business Engagement Letters
3. Auditing Planning
4. Auditing Sampling
5. Auditing Evidence
6. Auditing Worksheet
7. Auditing Reports
8. Errors and Cheating
9. Internal Control and Auditing Risk
10. Materiality of Auditing
11. Analytical Check
12. Use of Expert's Work
13. Use of Other CPA's Work
14. Opening Balance
15. Events After Balance Date
16. Related-Party transactions
17. Going Concern
18. Activities Which Violate Laws and Regulations
19. Other Information Disclosed with Financial and Auditing Reports
20. Auditing in EDP Environments
21. Understanding of the Situation in Client Companies
22. Consideration of Internal Auditing
23. Statement from Management Authorities
24. Communication with Management Authorities

Independent Auditing Practical Statements
1. Capital Evaluation
2. Suggestions towards Management
3. Auditing of Small Enterprises
4. Check the Forecast of Earnings
5. Special Considerations for Auditing of Consolidated Financial Statements
6. Auditing Reports for the Special Purpose Businesses.

The Main features of the new Chinese Auditing System are explained briefly as follows:

1. The Chinese Auditing Standard System consists of Independent Auditing Standards, Professional Conduct Standards, Quality Control Standards, and Continuing Professional Education Standards. Independent Auditing Standards include: General Standard, Specific Standards and Practical Statements, and Practical Guidance Releases.

2. The Independent Auditing Standards have been and will be promulgated by MOF rather than CICPA. CICPA only has rights to draft and explain the Independent Auditing Standards. Therefore, Independent Auditing Standards are government regulations rather than professional standards. In the west, auditing standards are drafted, issued and revised by the accounting professions themselves and government regulative bodies such as the Securities and Exchange Commission (SEC) in the United States and Australian Securities and Investment Commission (ASIC), have rarely intervened. Other standards such as Professional Conduct Standards, Quality Control Standards and Continuing Professional Education Standards are to be published by CICPA itself.

3. The objectives of public auditing are different in the west. The United States only requires auditors to give an opinion whether a client's financial statements provides a "fair view" of the financial position of the company. In United Kingdom and Australia, auditors are asked to form a conclusion whether a client's financial statements provide a "true and fair view". However, in European countries, such as France and Germany, auditors are required to examine the legality of a client's financial statements. According to the Chinese Independent Auditing General Standard:

> The objective of Independent Auditing is to provide opinions on the legality, fairness and the consistency of using accounting methods of the financial statements of the entities audited (Article 4, Independent Auditing General Standards).

Thus, the objectives of Chinese auditing are to assess the legality, fairness and consistency of a client's financial statements, which mix the objectives of the United States, the United Kingdom, and the European countries.

4. There are other unique features in the Independent Auditing Standards: (a) Capital evaluation is regarded as a main business of CPAs in China and an Auditing Practical Statement has been included in the Independent Auditing Standards; (b) The format of the Chinese auditing reports is divided into scope section and opinion section. If a qualified report is given, an explanation section should be inserted between the scope and opinion sections; (c) Auditing business engagement letter should be written in line with the Chinese Business Contract Law.

The Merger of two Accounting Professional Bodies: CICPA and CACPA

The coexistence of two accounting professional bodies, CICPA and CACPA, in China and the vicious attack from each other have been well documented by some scholars (Macve and Liu, 1995, Aiken, Ji and Lu, 1996). In fact, almost all accounting professional firms are institutional firms backed up by financial departments or auditing departments. CICPA is controlled by the Ministry of Finance (MOF) and CACPA is backed up by Audit Administration Department (AAD). The fundamental issue is not about how many accounting professional bodies should exist in a country. For example, there are also two accounting professional bodies in Australia: Australian Society of Certified Practising Accountants (ASCPA) and Institute of Chartered Accountants in Australia (ICAA). The real concern here for Chinese authorities, MOF and AAD, is who should have the power to regulate and control the public auditing market. In China, power means authority, therefore every governmental agency seeks as much power as they can in order to enhance their importance in macro-economic management and controlling. CICPA and CACPA are all quasi-governmental organisations and used by MOF and AAD as the battle vehicles to try to control or monopolise the public auditing market.

The battle between MOF and AAD in controlling the financial supervisory functions and powers in public sector as well as within governmental or non-public sector has existed for a long time. In the centrally-planned economy, the financial supervisory functions were carried out exclusively by MOF and its subordinate financial departments on different levels. On December 4, 1982, a new Constitution of China was promulgated by the fifth National People's Congress. For the first time in Chinese history, the Constitution required the government to establish an independent Audit Administration

Department and to appoint an Auditor-General to take charge of it. China's *Constitution* stipulates that:

> The State Council will establish an auditing body to supervise through auditing the revenue and expenditure of all departments under the State Council and of the local governments at different levels, and those of the state financial and monetary organizations and of enterprises and undertakings[19].

> Under the direction of the Premier of the State Council, the auditing body independently executes its power to supervise through auditing in accordance with the law, and is subject to no interference from any other administrative organ or any public organization or individual (Article 91).

On October 21 1988, *The Audit Regulations of the People's Republic of China* was approved by the State Council and the new auditing system was finally set up. However, this auditing system suffered many criticisms because it confused the functions of government auditing, independent auditing, and internal auditing. Auditing departments were empowered to perform these three functions and to authorise agents in enterprises to perform internal auditing and then separate agencies to perform social auditing (Lau and Yang, 1991). Social auditing firms are quasi-governmental agencies managed by the auditing departments.

The *Auditing Law of People's Republic of China* was issued in August 1994 and became effective on 1 January 1995. This law reinforces the functions of auditing in three areas: government auditing, independent auditing and internal auditing. The law stipulates that the auditing departments still have the power to audit state-owned enterprises and share-holding corporations in which the State owns the majority of shares. *Auditing Law* states:

> All departments of the State Council and local governments, state-owned financial institutions, enterprises and non-profit organizations should establish sound internal auditing systems. These internal auditing departments should be supervised and directed by the state auditing authorities (Article 29).

---

[19] On September 15, 1983, China's State Audit Administration was officially established. Various audit departments were set up within the Administration. At the same time, audit departments were gradually established at all levels for provinces, cities and self-governing areas.

According to the relevant laws and regulations, social auditing firms should be supervised, directed and managed by the state auditing authorities (Article 30).

Thus, the functions of government auditing, independent auditing and internal auditing have not yet been clarified. Here, we cannot only criticise the AAD for mixing up the three functions of auditing. MOF has also been under blame as it still performs some government auditing through its own financial supervisory departments throughout the country, controls independent auditing through its quasi-government agency, CICPA, exerts influences on internal auditing through exercising its strong financial muscles, e.g: subsidies and taxes. Therefore, if the three functions of auditing should be separated clearly and the accounting profession becomes a real independent profession, both AAD and MOF may not need to interfere in CPA business.

Because of the power battle between MOF and AAD, enterprises have suffered from endless inspections by government and quasi-government agencies. There are at least four types of departments empowered to inspect a state-owned enterprise's financial reports and accounting records. They are: (1) auditing administration departments; (2) auditing firms under the control of the AAD; (3) the MOF and Financial Departments which have their own financial supervisory departments; and (4) CPA firms under the control of the MOF. A private enterprise and joint venture can be audited by: (1) taxation authorities; (2) auditing firms under the control of the AAD; and (3) CPA firms under the control of the MOF. Each of these audits enterprises according to their vested interests. As the Chinese maxim has it, "Everyone wants to eat Monk Tong's body"[20]. Departments often fight over the sharing of clients and finally have to compromise or reach a gentleman's agreement. In past years, many complaints have arisen from endless inspections by powerful government agencies and finally, the central government decided to put two barking dogs into one cage.

Under the criticism both from public and the State Council, the Auditing Administration Department (AAD) and the Ministry of Finance (MOF) announced jointly that CICPA and CACPA merged from June 1995. The special representative congress of new CICPA was held in Beijing on 5, June 1996. Although two accounting profession bodies, CICPA and CACPA have been merged into the new CICPA, the battle between AAD and MOF, CPA firms and former auditing firms (which can change their name into CPA firms

---

[20] Monk Tong was a hero in an ancient Chinese novel, Travelling in the West. It was alleged anyone who ate his body would become a supernatural being (Wu, 1993).

if they wish) will continue as long as their business nature is still the institutional firms and they cannot get the fully independent status.

The Impact of the Chinese CPA System on Foreign CPAs Seeking to Enter the Chinese CPA Service Market

Foreign CPA firms have explored Chinese markets since the early 1980s. Ernest & Whinney established the first representative office in Beijing in January 1981. So far the "big six" international accounting firms of Arthur Anderson, Coopers & Lybrand, Deloitte Rose Tohmatsu, Ernst & Young, KPMG Peat Marwick and Price Waterhouse have all established representative offices in China. There are approximately 20 foreign accounting firms' offices in Beijing, Shanghai, Shenzhen, Guangzhou and Fuzhou. Registration of these offices is administered by the Ministry of Finance (MOF).

Usually, foreign accounting firms do not carry on business on their own and the common approach is to establish a joint arrangement with a Chinese CPA firm. So far seven joint venture accounting firms have been established in China. These include Arthur Anderson/Hua Qiang, Coopers & Lybrand/Zhong Xin, Price Waterhouse/Da Hua, KGMP Peak Marwick/Hua Zheng, Ernst and Young/Hua Ming, Deloitte Rose Tohmatsu/Hu Jiang and DBO/Xin De. A joint venture accounting firm is a Chinese legal entity. Chinese CPAs and foreign CPAs cooperate in the procedures of auditing and in consultant businesses (Tang et al, 1994). Auditing reports are valid within the territory of China only when they are signed by Chinese counterparts; the foreign counterpart's signature is only allowed for the foreign clients.

Foreign accounting firms are prohibited to carry on their own business in China. For example, they cannot audit Chinese listed companies which only issue domestic shares (A Shares) in the Shanghai and Shenzhen Stock Exchange. However, if a company issues B shares, which are only available for overseas investors and listed in Shanghai and Shenzhen Stock Exchange, or wants to list abroad, by issuing H shares in Hong Kong Stock Exchange or N shares in New York Stock Exchange, foreign CPAs are allowed and invited to perform listing requirement tasks and audit the company's financial reports with the Chinese CPAs. Their reports are valid only for their foreign clients and not for the Chinese. If foreign CPAs want to conduct temporary audit activities in China for their foreign clients, they should apply for a licence from financial departments above the provincial level and accept the supervision from Chinese CPA associations and financial departments. The licence lasts for only half year and CPAs should re-apply when it expires.

In the new CPA Act, according to the principle of mutual benefit, foreigners can apply to take the uniform CPA examination organised by the Chinese Institute of CPA's (CICPA). This indicates that if a country or territory allows the citizens of the People's Republic of China to take its CPA examination and to obtain CPA registration there, then China also allows the citizens of the relevant country or territory to take the Chinese CPA examination and to register as a CPA in China. The first CPA examination for foreigners was held in Tianjing in September 1994 (People's Daily, 1994). More than 480 candidates from the USA, England, Malaysia, Canada, Singapore, Taiwan and Hong Kong were enrolled for the examination. Thus, there will be foreign citizens who are registered CPAs in China.

Although all big six firms have established joint-ventures with Chinese accounting firms, they have found themselves to be strictly restricted with respect to the main business activities in China. There may be two reasons for this. Firstly, perceptions of the function of foreign CPA firms in Chinese markets are different. Foreigners intend to share the CPA market with the Chinese, while the main purpose of Chinese authorities in allowing foreigners to enter this market is to train Chinese CPAs and to enhance the operational capacity of domestic firms. According to Fisher (1994):

> The Chinese authorities recognise that western firms are the key to training. They are, however, reluctant to allow the firms to spirit their profits out of the country. As a result, the controls on western firms operating in the country are exceptionally strict. The government has announced that it will grant just 15 licences for western auditing firms operating in China, all of which can only exist through a joint venture with an existing Chinese accounting firm (p.45).

On the other hand, big six firms might have made a strategic mistake in establishing joint-ventures in China. To be successful in China, the most important factor is to find a good partner. In China, the accounting firms can be classified into three levels: (1) sponsored and controlled by the financial departments and auditing departments, which are so called "institutional firms"; (2) promoted by other governmental departments or non-governmental organisations, such as universities, which may be called "public firms", and (3) promoted by individual CPAs, which are "private firms". The Chinese auditing market is shared by these three types of firms based on their unique powers and relationships (*Guan Xi*). Therefore, the biggest accounting firms in China are usually institutional firms, being the accounting firms of financial departments and the auditing firms of the government auditing departments. There is a continuing battle between these two giants. Most enterprises and listed companies are willing to choose government auditors as their auditors, even though this is not mandatory. However, these institutional audit firms have strong links with the financial departments and taxation authorities. Companies can establish good relationships with government authorities through the institutional firms, hoping that they may get some financial and tax benefits. So far none of the Chinese partners of the big six is an institutional government firm. For example, the partner of Price Waterhouse is the Da Hua accounting firm which is promoted by professors from Shanghai University of Economics and Finance; the partner of Coopers & Lybrand is China International Trust and Investment Corporation. The position of these Chinese partners restricts their ability to help the big six firms to expand business in China.

The Impacts of Chinese CPA System on Foreign Investment

China has attracted huge foreign investment since it opened the door to the outsiders in 1979. From 1979-1994, the total foreign direct investment accounted for 9.56 $US billion or 638 $US million per year. By the end of 1994, there were 206,096 foreign investment enterprises, which included Chinese and foreign equity joint ventures; Chinese and foreign cooperative joint ventures and wholly foreign-owned enterprises. Total investment in these enterprises were 4.90 $US billion, and the registered capital were 3.12 $US billion. In 1995, China became the second largest country, next only to the United States, in terms of the volume of foreign capital introduced.

Instead of setting up joint ventures or wholly-foreign owned enterprises directly in China, more and more foreign investors show interest in buying shares in listed Chinese companies in the stock exchange market in Shanghai, Shenzhen, New York and Hong Kong[21]. Currently, overseas investors are not

---

[21] On December 19, 1990, Shanghai Stock Exchange, the first in the People's Republic of China, was established. In the following year, the Shenzhen Stock Exchange officially went into operation. Currently, there are over 400 enterprises listed in two Exchanges and the total market value is 380 billion yuan. Chinese stock consist of four kinds of shares: (1) Personal shares (A shares), which are held by domestic investors and listed in Shanghai and Shenzhen Stock Exchange; (2) Foreign capital shares which are held by overseas investors, including B shares (listed in the Shanghai and Shenzhen Stock Exchange); H shares (listed in the Hong Kong Stock Exchange); and N shares (list in New York Stock Exchange); (3) State shares, which are unmarketable; and (4) Corporate shares, which are basically non-transferable.

allowed to buy A shares, they can buy B shares in Shanghai and Shenzhen Stock Exchange, N shares in New York Stock Exchange, H shares in Hong Kong Stock Exchange. When companies are listed in Chinese stock exchange markets, they should meet the Chinese stock listing rules and the financial statements should comply with Chinese accounting standards and regulations for stock limited companies. Currently, foreign accounting firms are not allowed to audit or provide service to the listing companies which are only issuing A shares in both Shanghai and Shenzhen Stock Exchange by themselves because their reports are not valid in the territory of the People's Republic of China (PRC). The joint venture accounting firms are allowed to perform auditing and other service tasks as long as the reports are signed by Chinese CPAs. However, if a company issues B shares, or wants to be listed aboard, e.g. in Hong Kong Stock Exchange and New York Stock Exchange, foreign CPAs are allowed and invited to perform listing requirement tasks and audit the company's financial reports with the Chinese CPAs. Their reports are regarded as valid only for their foreign investors. If a company wants to list abroad, its financial statements of the company should comply to overseas listing rules and General Acceptable Accounting Practice (GAAP) or International Standards. Usually, overseas stock exchange markets require their auditors rather than Chinese auditors to perform the listing requirement tasks and audit the financial statements of listed Chinese companies. When a Chinese company issues both domestic and overseas shares (A and B or H, N shares), Chinese CPAs and foreign CPAs are both required to perform auditing tasks. Sometimes, the opinions given by Chinese CPAs and foreign CPAs regarding the listing Chinese companies are quite different. The main differences are as following (Xing De, 1995):

1. Bad debts allowance. According to the Chinese Accounting Standard, bad debts allowance should be 0.3 – 0.5 per cent of the total amount of accounts receivable. However, foreign CPAs calculate the bad debts allowance according to the ages of the accounts receivable and the possibility of recouping the debts.

2. Inventory evaluation. If a company issues both A shares and H shares, its inventory can be valued using cost and market value whichever is the lower method. If a company issues both A shares and B shares, according to Chinese regulations, inventory only can be priced using the historical method. Foreign CPAs may disagree and adjust the inventory value in line with the market value.

3. Depreciation. Fixed assets are depreciated according to the Uniform Depreciation Scheme issued by MOF in China, in which the depreciating years of equipment and buildings are fixed from 5 years to 55 years. According to the International Accounting Standards the depreciating years should be calculated based on the estimated useful life and the outputs produced. There is a huge difference between Chinese CPAs and foreign CPAs regarding the calculation of depreciation expenses.

4. Long-term investment. Chinese CPAs use cost method and foreign CPAs prefer the equity method if the joint control exists in the investee.

5. Staff welfare payable and reserve. According to Chinese regulations, staff welfare payable is regarded as cost and the staff welfare reserve which is transferred from the post-tax profit is not regarded as expenses. However, foreign CPAs treat both staff welfare payable and reserve as expenses.

6. Revenue recognition. Chinese CPAs recognise the revenue as long as the ownership right of the property has been transferred. Foreign CPAs are more concerned about whether the risk has really been transferred when the ownership title is passed.

7. Consolidation. The main argument focuses on when the control exists. For example, A has 40 per cent shares in B, A's Workers Union also has 40 per cent in B. The Chinese CPAs' opinion is A and B should be consolidated, while foreign CPAs disagree and treat A and A's Workers Union as two separate entities.

Future Developments and Conclusion

The future development of the CPA profession in China depends not only on its own innovations but also on influences from outside. Unlike the United States, the UK and Australia, the government in China has a direct and dominant influence on accounting practices from which the CPA profession has not been exempt[22]. Although it is alleged that the influence of the government is too weak in Western countries, government influence in China may be too strong. The CPA profession becomes a rule-follower. This could be made worse by the power struggles between different government departments, as mentioned previously.

Independence and Government Control

The development of powerful government agencies has a long history. Before the economic reforms of 1978, China had a centrally planned economy in which government granted all powers of administration. With economic reforms and a wider-open door policy, China has imported some practices from Western countries to modify its Soviet-style government administration. However, transplanted experience has not been solely from one ideology. Some of it comes from Eastern European countries while other elements originated in Japan, Germany and the United States. Conflicts and power struggles have occurred because new departments were established while old ones still existed. This was the case with respect to the Auditing Administration Department which the Ministry of Finance overviews to administer CPA activities. The most recent body is the Securities Commission of the State Council, which has power to regulate the financial disclosure requirements for listed corporations. The Securities Commission of the State Council is similar to its counterparts, the Securities and Exchange Commission (SEC) in the United States and the Australian Investment and Securities Commission (AISC), which are the representatives of government for administering disclosure issues.

Other powerful departments which have strong influences on the CPA profession are the People's Bank of China (Central Bank), the State Commission for Economic Restructuring, the State Planning Commission, the State Economic and Trade Commission, the State Taxation Bureau, and the State Government Assets Management Bureau.

Obviously, the authority of these government agencies in accounting and auditing will have to be clarified. Throughout the world there are three main patterns of administration of the CPA profession: (a) the administering power

---

[22] There is a trend towards government intervention in accounting standards setting and the accounting profession in the United States and Australia. For example, the Metcalf Report charged that the "big eight" accounting firms monopolise the auditing of large corporations and control the standard-setting process (Belkaoui, 1985).

may belong to the Ministry of Finance, as in Japan, Singapore, Korea, Peru; (b) economic administrative departments may be responsible as in Germany and Switzerland; and (c) the CPA profession itself, as partly in the United States and Australia. The continuing pattern for China is most likely to be the first.

The Competence of CPAs

The development of CPA business depends upon the numbers of skilful, competent, qualified CPAs. There are several suggestions for the future development of CPA's in China. Firstly, the Chinese profession may need to set up continuing professional development programmes (CPD). Such continuing professional development programmes in the West are designed to ensure that accountants are kept abreast of the changes in skills and knowledge that are required in a dynamic business environment. These programmes are emphasised by the American and Australian professions. For example, the Australian Society of Certified Practicing Accountants (ASCPAs) has stipulated that a person advancing to the status of CPA has to complete 20 hours of continuing professional development per year. Recently, MOF set up three CPA training centres in Beijing, Shanghai and Guanzhong to conduct CPA training programme and has authorised seven universities to establish CPA courses. Secondly, Chinese CICPAs may need to set up a hierarchical structure for the CPA profession – associate CPA; CPA; and CPA specialist. Thirdly, the Certified Public Accountants Act 1993 stipulated regulations only for public sector accountants. However, most accountants in China are non-public sector, as in enterprises, government agencies, and research institutions. The MOF is empowered to administer these accountants[23]. One suggestion is to establish a second accounting

---

[23] In September 1978, the State Council of the Peoples' Republic of China promulgated the Accounting Staff Authorities Regulation 1978. This was the first time that all accounting staff could hold a professional title. The hierarchy is as follows: senior accountant, accountant, assistant accountant, accounting clerk. The Department of Accounting Affairs Administration of the Ministry of Finance is responsible for the evaluation of professional titles. In 1988 there were 10,719 senior accountants, 785,022 assistant accountants and 1,135,714 accounting clerks in China. Each professional title was awarded under an honour system according to one's qualification, the duration one had been engaged in the accounting profession and one's contribution to the profession. However, the regulations were changed in 1990 when an examination system was introduced. Now the titles of accountant, assistant accountant, and accounting clerk are awarded mainly on examination results. "Senior accountant" as a title is still an honorary title which will be given to persons who make great contributions to the accounting profession.

professional body. This may be achieved by simply changing the Accounting Society of China (ASC) as an academic body to the Accountants' Society of China (ASC) as a professional body[24]. It would be similar to the Institute of Certified Management Accountants (ICMA) in the United States. The Department of Accounting Affairs Administration of MOF could transfer its powers to ASC and allow it to become a self-regulating professional body. A suggested model is attached in Figure 4-1.

The Legal Position of CPA Firms

The regulations expressing the legal position of CPA firms may have to be revised. There are two types of CPA firms according to the *Certified Public Accountant Act 1993.* One bears limited liability and is promoted by government agencies. The other bears unlimited liability and is set up by CPAs. This regulation may be challenged on the grounds of equity and fairness. Also there is no reason why these two types of CPA firms should be treated differently. The establishment of CPA firms should be according to relevant law such as the civil law, company law, and administrative regulations.

In the future, the Chinese CPA profession should become more important and the auditing services market will be one of the biggest in the world. However, the development of the CPA profession may not allow an independent professional body to exist like its counterparts in western countries; it may still be a quasi governmental agency and its influence will be limited by statute.

In this case government will continue to dominate accounting practices in China, a tradition which has lasted over time. Perhaps this is the most likely scenario for future development under existing cultural preferences. The examination of change in this paper indicates that there is still a long way to go if the influence of Western countries is to prevail throughout the Chinese economy and in public administration. As mentioned at the outset, time alone will tell whether the modern structure for professionalism in public

---

[24] Besides the Chinese Institute of Certified Public Accountants (CICPA), there is another quasi-governmental agency, the Accounting Society of China (ASC). This is not a professional body, but is an academic research body. However, it has great influence on the setting of accounting regulations. Some of the senior financial officials in government also hold important positions in the ASC. It is an advisory agency of the Ministry of Finance (MOF) and carries out most research tasks of the MOF. For example, the ASC participated in the setting of the Chinese Accounting Standards. But, ultimately the Ministry of Finance bears the power to issue accounting standards.

accounting and auditing in China will prevail against traditional forms of accountability which have evolved over thousands of years.

Figure 4-1 A Model for Chinese Accounting Profession

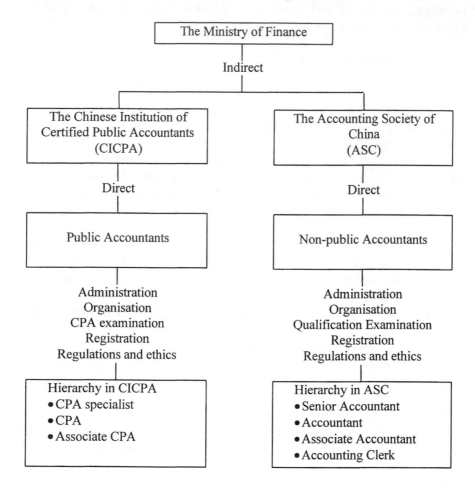

This being so it behoves practitioners to become familiar with accounting controls and legislative requirements which can reflect traditional attitudes to commerce and administration. Also, clients entering China to do business may need to become aware of cultural influences, patronages and financial conventions. Otherwise misunderstandings may occur leading to consequences which need not be foreseen in the business environment of western countries.

5   Accounting Education in China

Accounting education has a long history in China. It is said that Confucius was an accountant some 2000 years ago. He was a great Chinese philosopher and educator, and accounting was one of the main subjects taught in his classes. Some of his students found good accounting positions in government and in rich family businesses after graduating from Confucius' school (Gao, 1991). However, in the following centuries, accounting was regarded as a technical skill which only needed to be learned by the master-apprentice method. It was not taught again in schools until early this century.

The Structure of Accounting Education

Modern Chinese accounting education systems have all been introduced from overseas (Lu and Ji, 1994). During the 1920s, some scholars, for example Xie Lin and Dr. Pang Xurun, who had received their education abroad, returned to China and established the first modern accounting and accounting education systems based mainly on their experience of United States and Japanese models.

During the 1950s China completely adopted the Soviet accounting and accounting education systems. Soviet accounting experts were invited to China to conduct lectures and train accounting teachers. Soviet accounting textbooks were translated and taught in classrooms. The important thing was that the Soviet ideology was brought into China. That is the main reason why the accounting education catastrophe occurred in the 1960s and why accounting scholars indulged in qualitative explanation and ideological debate rather than quantitative analysis. Lin and Deng (1992) described the situation as follows:

> ... for political and economic reasons, China completely adopted the Soviet-style accounting systems and accounting educational program. During 1950-1957, the curriculum for accounting majors in all Chinese universities was simply modeled after that of the Soviet Union. Some Soviet accounting scholars and experts were invited to China to conduct special training programs for accounting instructors across the country. Accounting research concentrated on the translation of Soviet accounting literature and textbooks or the interpretation of Soviet accounting regulations and standards...

After 1979, China re-opened its door to the outside and carried out a series of economic reforms. The west began to influence China. The accounting education system has been gradually changed. At present there are three systems of accounting education in China: (1) higher education; (2) secondary vocational and technical education; and (3) adult education.

In higher accounting education, there are about 150 universities, institutes and colleges. Horizontally, these universities and colleges are operated by different ministries. Vertically, these institutions are operated by the central government and local governments. For example, the Ministry of Finance (MOF) has five universities: Shanghai University of Finance and Economics, Central-South University of Finance and Economics, North-East University of Finance and Economics, Central University of Finance and Banking, and Jiangxi University of Finance and Economics. The People's Bank of China (Central Bank) controls three universities: West-South University of Finance and Economics, Hunan Institute of Finance and Economics, and Sanxi Institute of Finance and Economics.

Shanghai University of Finance and Economics (SUFE) is currently funded and managed by the MOF and the Municipality of Shanghai. The university has 23 specialties within 13 colleges or faculties. The total enrolment is over 9,000, in which more than 4,800 students are undergraduates and 700 students are postgraduates. The university offers 7 doctoral programmes and 28 master programmes. The structure of SUFE is in Table 5-1.

The current accounting education system in China is still a hybrid of the Soviet model. The former Soviet Union has had a profound impact on the education system in China, not only on accounting education but also in other disciplines. The major criticism of the Soviet model of education is its orientation of technical training and over-specialisation. Tang, Chow and Cooper (1996) said:

In contrast to many Western universities, finance, economics and accounting programs in Chinese universities are highly specialized, often industry oriented. It was found by the State Education Commission that the total number of different kinds of specialties in economics and finance increased from 37 in 1982 to roughly 80 in 1986. The major factor behind this increase is the proliferation of finely divided specialties in the same sub-disciplines. An example is the ten different kinds of specialties in the accounting sub-discipline which existed in 1985. These include accounting, financial accounting, industrial accounting, agricultural accounting, commercial accounting, material accounting,

117

management accounting, banking accounting, tourism accounting and petroleum accounting ...

In 1997, China started another educational reform with the main objective being to reduce the specialties. However, how far China can achieve this goal depends on how they can reduce the special institutions controlled by different governmental ministries.

The Curriculum of Accounting Education

Since the economic reform was carried out eighteen years ago, the curriculum of accounting education has changed gradually in China. Until the early 1990s, the Soviet style curriculum pattern which dominated in accounting education at the tertiary level (Watne and Baldwin, 1988, Lin and Deng, 1992) emphasised specialised training and loyalty to socialism. The core courses were: (1) Principles of Accounting; (2) Industrial Accounting; (3) Financial Management for Industrial Enterprise; and (4) Analysis of Economic Activities. This curriculum still exists in some universities and colleges and especially in professional training colleges.

From the late 1980s to the early 1990s, with the increase in western influence on education, a new accounting education curriculum has been introduced. This sprang initially from Professor Lou Er-Ying's proposal in Shanghai University of Finance and Economics (Lu, 1992). The core courses in the new curriculum are: (1) Principles of Accounting; (2) Financial Accounting; (3) Cost Accounting; (4) Management Accounting; and (5) Auditing.

The major difference between the two curricula is in classification, while the contents of the principles of accounting, financial accounting and cost accounting in the new curriculum remain similar to the principles of accounting and industrial accounting of the old. The reason is that accounting education has been restricted by the Uniform Accounting System in China. Most accounting courses are actually used to interpret and digest that system. Theoretical reasoning has rarely been attempted (Tang et al, 1996).

The *Directive Teaching Program* of International Accounting Specialty in the Faculty of Accounting in SUFE (Table 5-2) shows that the basic courses of accounting discipline in China are still basic accounting, intermediate financial accounting, cost accounting, management accounting and auditing.

The Pedagogy of Accounting Education

A class in accounting at tertiary level is smaller than that in western countries. Normally, a class has about 40 students with a given specialty, e.g. industrial accounting or international accounting. The lecture-tutorial teaching model is rarely used in the university and, in fact, the teaching model in China is much like the one used in TAFE colleges in Australia. The main teaching method in China is the so-called "Passive teaching" method, or instructor-dominated teaching. Tang et al (1996) described it as follows:

> Most undergraduate courses consist of one-way delivery of lectures and test paper examinations at the end of each semester. Teachers confine themselves to elaborating on details of textbooks and students are used to taking notes and memorizing what is said in textbooks. Few courses are found to include much two-way communication between teachers and students such as discussions in small groups, tutorials, or presentations by students in the classroom. The case study approach is not popular in class teaching.

The main drawback of this method is that it restricts the students' creative capacity to analyse and solve problems. In recent years, some western pedagogues have tried to introduce, in the leading universities, approaches to accounting education such as case studies, classroom discussion and research projects (Lin and Deng, 1992). However, it is doubtful how these western methods can be integrated with Chinese traditions. Changes in pedagogy are not only related to education, but also influenced by culture, tradition and people's thinking. For example, in Australia overseas students from south-east Asia have found some difficulties in adapting to Australian education methods, e.g. they are less active in participating classroom discussion, confining themselves only to memorising textbooks and lecture notes.

Accounting Research

Compared to western universities, the accounting research in China is more subject to criticism. The teachers and accountants indulge in qualitative explanations and ideological debate on topics such as whether accounting bears a class nature.

Table 5-1 The Structure of Shanghai University of Finance and Economics

ID No.	Colleges, Faculties, Departments, Divisions and Centres	Specialties
01	Faculty of Economics	Economics
02	Faculty of Economic Law	Economic Law, International Economic Law
03	Faculty of International Economics	International Finance, International Trade
06	Faculty of Public Finance	Public Finance, Taxation, Asset Appraisal and Management Specialty
08	Faculty of Accounting	Accounting, Auditing, International Accounting Specialty, Certified Public Accountants Specialty, Electronic Accounting Specialty
09	Faculty of Statistics	Statistics
10	Faculty of Economic Information Management	Economic Information Management, Management Information System (MIS)
11	Faculty of Foreign Languages for Economics and Trade	English (for Economics and Trade)
12	Nande College of International Economy and Management	International Finance, International Trade
14	College of Securities and Futures	Securities and Futures Specialty
33	College of Management and Business Administration	Industrial Economy, Enterprise Management, International Enterprise Management, Marketing, Trade
27	Wantai College of International Investment	Investment, Real Estate Operation and Management, International Investment Specialty
26	College of Finance and Banking	Money and Banking, Finance, Insurance, Insurance and Calculation Specialty
16	Ideological Education Centre	
19	Basic Course Education Centre	
21	Computer Centre	
32	The Division of Econometric Research	

Table 5-2 Directive Teaching Programme in International Accounting Specialty

Classification	Subjects	Credits	Hours
Common Ordinary Courses	Philosophy	4	84
	Chinese Revolution and Socialist Construction	2	42
	International Politics and Relationships	2	42
	Life Philosophy	1	21
	Ethics	1	21
	University English	22	462
	University Chinese	3	63
	Economic Writings	2	42
	Physics	4	168
	Military Theory	2	42
	Health Protection	1	21
Common Restrictive Electives	Restrictive Electives I	2	42
	Restrictive Electives II	2	42
	Restrictive Electives III	3	63
	Restrictive Electives IV	2	42
Common Subject Courses	Marxist Economics	4	84
	Western Economics	4	84
	Socialist Economics	2	42
	Calculus I	4	84
	Calculus II	4	84
	Linear Arithmetic	3	63
	Probability	2	42
	Statistics	4	84
	Public Finance	2	42
	International Finance	2	42
	International Trade	2	42
	Money and Banking	2	42
	Marketing	2	42
	Management	2	42
	Outline of Economic Law	2	42
	Applied Computer I	3	63
	Applied Computer II	3	63

Specialties	Basic Specialties		
	Basic Accounting	3	63
	Intermediate Financial Accounting	6	126
	Cost Accounting	3	63
	Management Accounting	3	63
	Auditing	3	63
	Directive Specialties		
	Advanced Financial Accounting	6	126
	Financial Management	3	63
	Electronic Accounting	4	84
	Electronic Auditing	2	42
	Elective Specialties (at least 9 Credits)	9	189
	Accounting Theory	3	
	Accounting for Foreign Investment Enterprises	2	
	Accounting for International Transaction	2	
	International Taxation	2	
	International Business Letters	2	
	Accounting for Securities Companies	2	
	Chinese Accounting and Auditing	2	
Sub Total		142	3,108
Electives		14	219
Social Practice		6	
Graduation Thesis		8	
Total		170	3,327

Note:
a. **Restrictive Electives I:** Outline of Sociality, Outline of Politics, Governmental Administration, and Scientific Research Methodology in Social Science, Public Relationships, Population Research, and Public Media.
b. **Restrictive Electives II:** Outline of Chinese Culture, Outline of Chinese Literature, Outline of Chinese History of Philosophy, Traditional Religions in China, Communication Skills, Psychology for University Students, Outline Modern Western Culture, Outline of Foreign Literature, Outline Western History of Philosophy.
c. **Restrictive Electives III:** Operations Research, Outline of the Development of New Technologies, History of Science and Technology, Outline of Life Science, Environmental Science, Systemic Science, Informational Science, Economic Control Theory
d. **Restrictive Electives IV:** Outline of Aesthetics, Music Appreciation, Calligraphy and Paintings, Visional Arts, Physics.

122

Tang and Fang's (1987) summary of China's achievements in accounting research until the late 1980s might help us to understand what kind of research has been undertaken by the Chinese. They said:

> Following closely in the footsteps of the reform of economic structure ... Chinese accounting researchers and professionals realized a pressing need for a tenable theoretical framework to govern and guide accounting practice ... many people engaged in the field of accounting ... have written and published widely, either before or after 1983, on various topics, in form of articles, textbooks and monographs, thus contributing a great deal towards the establishment of such a framework. Some of the major achievements deal with (1) the essence of accounting, (2) objective of accounting, (3) the function and role of accounting, (4) the nature of accounting, (5) basic concepts, assumptions and principles of accounting, and (6) accounting based on historical cost vs. other alternatives (p. 142).

There has been research on the nature of accounting. For example, after considerable debate among accounting academics and professionals a consensus has been reached that accounting has a "dual nature": both a class nature and technical nature.

The reasons that Chinese accounting research has an ideological orientation are: (1) most accounting academics and accountants, having been educated under the Soviet-style accounting education system, have little knowledge of western accounting. They find western accounting thought and research methodology hard to grasp and need in-service training. (2) Western accounting was only introduced into China in the early 1980s. Western research methodology has not been understood by most researchers. Accounting staff with a western higher education degree are rare in China. In the future, more students will be educated in western countries and have postgraduate qualifications. They will come back to the motherland and the quality of accounting research in China will be lifted.

Accounting Staff

The lack of highly qualified accounting staff is a constant and serious problem in accounting education in China. There are some historical and economic reasons. Firstly, since most senior accounting staff have been trained under the Soviet model, their knowledge and skills need to be improved. Secondly, a generation of accounting staff has been lost because of the closure of accounting departments for more than ten years during the Cultural Revolution. Thirdly, the salary of accounting staff is lower than for those who have a job in the professional or governmental sectors. This problem has become more serious because more and more joint ventures and foreign companies use higher salaries to attract the postgraduates to their sectors. Finally, cooperation with the foreign universities in the accounting discipline has not gone as quickly as in other disciplines. China has sent a few accounting students overseas to undertake PhD and masters' studies and most of them have never come back.

Comparative Research on Accounting Education Systems in China and Australia

Two universities have been chosen for this study. They are Shanghai University of Finance and Economics in China and La Trobe University in Australia. The differences between these two accounting education systems are identified. The results will have significance because the accounting education systems in these two universities represent the patterns of their respective cultures. The period of completing a Bachelor degree of accounting in China is four years but it is three years in Australia. Students completing four years of study will get a Bachelor with Honours in Australia. Therefore, the Bachelor programme in China is compared to the Bachelor with Honours programme in Australia. The curricula of the two universities have been broken into the following categories: (1) Ideological subjects. In China, these subjects are compulsory, and include Marxist economics, philosophy, Chinese revolution and socialist construction, international politics and relationships, life philosophy, physical education, military theory, health protection, and ethics. Such subjects are not required in Australia. (2) General knowledge and skills subjects. English and Chinese languages, economic writing plus about eight elective subjects in the Chinese curriculum have been placed in this group. The reason for including English and Chinese in this group is that these subjects enhance students' language skills. In Australia, business communication skills and research methodology subjects and three other elective subjects have been included in this group. Recently, more emphasis has been put on enhancing students' skills and broadening general knowledge in Australia. (3) Basic knowledge subjects related to accounting. These cover subjects of mathematics, statistics, computing, economics, business law, taxation, management, and marketing. (4) Accounting subjects. These include topics on elemental accounting, financial accounting, management accounting, finance, and accounting theories and practices. (5) Social survey and thesis. In Australia, only the Honours students are required to write a thesis, which equals two subjects. On the other hand, each student is required to complete a social survey or a mini thesis to obtain a Bachelor degree in China. The comparison of results is shown in Table 5-3.

Comparing the accounting education curricula in China and Australia, it is easy to see there are great differences between these two systems. (1) Ideological education is an important part of accounting education in China. 18.37 per cent of courses or 12.35 per cent credits are allocated to ideological education. (2) Students in China are required to take more courses on general knowledge and skills than students in Australia. Students in China are required to take 22.45 per cent of the courses or 29.41 per cent of the total credits from general knowledge and skills courses. In Australia, students are required to earn about 15.63 per cent credits on general knowledge and skills courses. (3) Australian students concentrate on accounting subjects. They take about 46.87 per cent of total courses from accounting courses and it is implied that accounting education in Australia is more professionally oriented. On the other hand, Chinese students are required to take about 24.71 per cent of total credits from accounting subjects. (4) Australian students are required to study more basic knowledge courses related to accounting, eg. economics, management, organisational behaviour. On average, an Australian student needs to earn 31.25 per cent credits for basic knowledge courses. In China, a student is only required to earn 25.29 per cent credits in this category.

There are also other differences between the accounting education systems in Australian and China. An academic year consists of two semesters in both China and Australia. However, the coverage of a semester is longer in China, being 21 weeks rather than 13 weeks. On average, a student in China needs to take 6-7 subjects in each semester and spends 24-28 hours in class per week. On the other hand, an Australian student is required to take 4 subjects in a semester and spend 12 hours in class per week.

Normally, a subject can be completed within a semester in Australia. However, a subject may be studied for more than one year in China. For example, students need to study English for three years. In order to obtain a Bachelor degree, a Chinese student needs to complete 40 subjects and an Australian student only needs to complete 24 subjects. An Australian student finishing 32 subjects can get the Bachelor degree with Honours.

Table 5-3 Comparison of Accounting Curriculum in China and Australia

Category of subjects	No.	%	Credits	%	No.	%	Credits	%
	China (SUFE)				Australia (La Trobe)			
Ideological subjects	9	18.37	21	12.35				
General knowledge and skill subjects	11	22.45	50	29.41	5	15.63	75	15.63
Basic knowledge subjects related to accounting	16	32.65	43	25.29	10	31.25	150	31.25
Accounting subjects	13	26.53	42	24.71	15	46.87	225	46.87
Social Survey and Thesis			14	8.24	2	6.25	30	6.25
Total number:	49	100	170	100	32	100	480	100

Source: Shanghai University of Finance and Economics, *Directive Teaching Program*, 1997
La Trobe University Handbook, 1997

Apparently, students in China have much heavier studying burdens than those in Australia. However, how efficient and effective these two accounting education systems are cannot be compared without further investigation.

Australian accounting education emphasises professional skills. This characteristic is reflected not only in the tertiary education curriculum but also in post-tertiary education. The Institute of Chartered Accountants in Australia (ICAA) offers the Professional Year programme to students completing an accredited Australian degree. Candidates are also required to be employed in an organisation accredited by the ICAA and have at least 52 weeks of relevant accounting experience. The Professional Year Programme comprises five modules, three core technical modules, an Ethics module and an elective. Students are required to prepare research projects and problems, attend workshops and an exam to complete each module.

Discussion and Suggestions on Reform of the Chinese Accounting Education System

Reform of the Chinese accounting education system has been advocated for many years (Watne and Baldwin, 1988, Lin and Deng, 1992, Lu and Ji, 1994 and Tang, et al, 1996). However, the pace of the reform is relatively slow. For example, some universities include capitalist accounting or joint-venture accounting subjects to reform the curriculum, but this does not mean that western accounting theory and practice have been integrated into the mainstream of core courses. The core courses in Chinese accounting education are still mainly about explaining and interpreting the Uniform Accounting System. Therefore, some academics have suggested that the Chinese accounting education system should be radically changed. Lu and Ji (1994) have suggested:

> Just as American experts were invited to build the first accounting education system in China and Soviet experts helped to build the second, so it should be possible to invite international accounting experts to build a third modern accounting education system. Western accounting theory and practice should be fully imported in accounting education. Only after that, can western accounting be digested and assimilated into Chinese accounting as a whole. Deng Xiao-ping said: "A good cat is one which can catch mice, no matter which colour it is, white or black". It is not necessary to check what is ideologically suitable and what is not, what is capitalist and what is socialist.

More practical suggestions on reform of the Chinese accounting education system are as follows:

The Objectives of Tertiary Accounting Education

The objectives of tertiary accounting education in China are to train students morally, intellectually, and physically suitable for the needs of socialist reforms and construction (Watne and Baldwin, 1988). Therefore, there are dual objectives in Chinese education: one is to ensure each student is loyal to the Communist party, the country and its people; the other is to train students with certain specific skills and knowledge to serve the economic reforms and construction. Thus, ideological subjects are compulsory in the Chinese education system and these subjects cannot be omitted regardless of how far the education reforms have gone.

The political objectives of accounting education cannot be changed in China. However, the academic objectives of accounting education in China may be changed. Birkett (1987) identified four perspectives on accounting education: technical, disciplinary, professional, and research perspectives. The current accounting education model in China is more like a technical perspective on accounting education, which emphasises the development of a level of mastery in calculation, communication and a range of accounting routines and procedures. Therefore, the aim of Chinese accounting education reform is to integrate disciplinary, professional and research perspectives into its programmes. Tertiary accounting education should not only monitor the practice in China currently, but should also monitor the development of accounting in the world.

Accounting Curriculum

In the future, the accounting education curriculum needs to be written according to Chinese accounting standards and regulations as well as the International Accounting Standards. The accounting topics need to be chosen carefully, for example, the issues of leasing, foreign transactions, and construction accounting need to be included in financial accounting. Then, both Chinese and international measuring and disclosing requirements of those issues should be taught. If the topics do not exist in China, for example accounting for employee entitlement and financial instruments, they should be taught according to the International Accounting Standard because these topics are not practicable in China today but may be possible in the future. Also these topics will expand students' knowledge.

The core courses in tertiary accounting education may consist of: (a) Accounting principles; (b) Financial accounting; (c) Cost accounting; (d) Management accounting; (e) Auditing; (f) Accounting theory. The topics and contents of each course should be comparable to those in western accounting courses.

As Political Economics is an ideological course in China, several basic courses need to be added in accounting education: (a) Micro-economics; (b) Macro-economics; and (c) Management; and (d) Statistics. These courses provide basic economic theory and the tools used in analysing accounting problems.

International accounting needs to be added to the accounting courses to focus on: (a) basic international accounting topics such as foreign exchange accounting, consolidation of international financial statements and inflation accounting theory; and (b) accounting theories and practices in countries other than Anglo-Saxon countries.

Another course which may be added is accounting research methodology. After graduation, a student should have knowledge about contemporary accounting issues, current research undertaken by top accounting academics, and the ability to conduct a research project. Quantitative research methods should be emphasised in accounting education.

Staff Training

As mentioned before, the shortage of qualified accounting staff is a drawback in the development of accounting education. The most feasible way to accelerate accounting education reform in China is to invite a large number of western academics and practitioners who can conduct lectures to retrain the teachers in Chinese universities. The experience of introducing Soviet accounting experts in the 1950s can be used again.

There are many overseas Chinese accounting scholars in western universities and colleges. They are potential human resources which can accelerate accounting education reform in China. Most of them are bilingual, in English and Chinese. They can easily deliver western accounting lectures in Chinese.

Some people may think there are considerable differences between Chinese and Western accounting. However, nobody asked the same question when Soviet accounting was introduced in the early 1950s. Only after its introduction, were some changes and modifications made by the Chinese. Obviously, in the future, Chinese accounting and accounting education systems may not be identical to any one western accounting model. The characteristics of future Chinese accounting may include concrete measuring and disclosure methods which are Anglo-Saxon oriented and accounting administration which is German-Japanese oriented. This means that China's own uniform accounting system may be kept and that the government will maintain its authority and influence in promulgating accounting standards and regulations.

Accounting Textbooks

Currently, accounting textbooks in China mix Soviet and western ideas and terminologies. Some include China's own inventions, such as with responsibility accounting. During recent years, more and more western accounting textbooks have been translated into Chinese, however, because the translators lack background knowledge of western society and accounting, the textbooks have been translated word for word and are hard to understand. Also the terminology of accounting used in China and in the West is very different. The best way is for western scholars who understand Chinese and their Chinese counterparts to collaborate to produce some textbooks that are suitable for Chinese students.

Pedagogy

As mentioned before, some western teaching methods, e.g. case studies, classroom discussion and research projects, have been tried in universities (Lin and Deng, 1992). However, the success of these methods has not been reported. In China teachers are highly respected even though on average they are poorer than those in western countries. What teachers say is correct and unchallenged by students. Therefore, changes of pedagogy from passive learning to fostering a positive approach depends on how quickly people's attitudes can change. China may need to find a suitable pedagogy which complies with its culture and tradition.

Conclusion

The Chinese education system has experienced slow changes and has lagged behind the economic reforms. There are still substantial differences between the accounting education system in China and western countries. Some differences can be narrowed in the near future. However, some of them may remain for a long time because they reflect the different objectives of the two systems. The Chinese accounting education system can be reformed and changed from the technical perspective but not from the political perspective. Ideological education remains as a core in the curriculum. Some scholars consider this is an accounting education system with Chinese socialist characteristics. Western accounting may increase its influences on Chinese accounting and education. China may then adopt more and more international accounting standards and methods in its own systems and make China more comparable, but not identical, in an international business environment.

6   Cost Accounting Systems in China

The current Chinese cost accounting system originated from the Soviet Union. In the early 1950s, when China was under Russian political and economic influence, the Soviet cost accounting system was introduced. Subsequently a few changes were made. Then, in 1993 the first accounting standard was promulgated by the Ministry of Finance, in which full absorption cost accounting was replaced by manufacturing cost accounting. However, the direction of the cost accounting system has not changed greatly; being still used mainly for cost determination, not for decision-making purposes. Descriptions of western methods may at times seem to be mundane but are useful for comparisons with Chinese methods.

The Objectives of Cost Accounting

In China the objective of cost accounting is to monitor and report fund movements. This concept originated in the planned economy under which enterprises had to report all funds sources and applications, and systematically calculated the money to be returned to the government. There are three periods in the funds movement: the supply period, production period and selling period. The main sources of funding are government, legal entities individuals, foreign investments and borrowing. In the supply period, monetary funds are used by enterprises to buy materials. These become inventory funds. In the production period when enterprises use labour and equipment to transform materials into product and thus pay labour costs and allocate depreciation on fixed assets, inventory funds become production funds. In the selling period when enterprises sell products and receive money in return, the production funds become monetary funds again. This is the cycle of funds movement. Specifically, the objectives of cost accounting are to calculate: (1) the increase and decrease of funds caused by funds inflow, outflow and turnover; (2) manufacturing expenses; (3) operating income and net profit; (4) tax commitments and dividends.

The tasks of cost accounting can be summarised as follows:

- calculating product costs correctly and providing timely cost information;
- establishing cost budgets and enhancing the control of costs; and
- assigning cost management responsibilities.

The Organisation of Cost Accounting

Every enterprise should have an accounting department to take charge of accounting matters according to the *General Accountant Regulation 1990*. Large-medium size enterprises should set up a General Accountant position which is similar to treasurer, financial controller, or financial manager in the western concept. A General Accountant should have either an accountant or a senior accountant qualification. Usually there are several sub-groups in the accounting department in charge of specific tasks. The structure may be as shown in Figure 6-1.

The Principles of Cost Accounting

Cost accounting has been regulated by the governmental authorities, specially the Ministry of Finance (MOF) in China. The MOF has promulgated a series of regulations: *Cost Management Regulations for State-owned Enterprises* (1984), *Accounting Standards for Enterprises* (1992a), *Uniform Accounting System for Industrial Enterprises* (1992b), *General Rules of Financial Management for Enterprises* (1992c), *Financial Management Regulations for Industrial Enterprises* (1992d). Therefore, cost accounting in China would follow rigid rules and allow little room for professional adjustments.

According to the regulations set up by the governmental authorities, cost accounting should adhere to the following principles: (1) to divide properly the accounting periods; (2) to follow the accrual basis; (3) to adhere to the revenue and expenditure matching principle; (4) to separate revenue expenditure and capital expenditure; (5) to observe the legality principle; (6) to observe the consistency principle; (7) to adhere to historical cost; and (8) to adhere to the materiality principle.

132

Figure 6-1 Structure of Accounting Organisation in an Enterprise

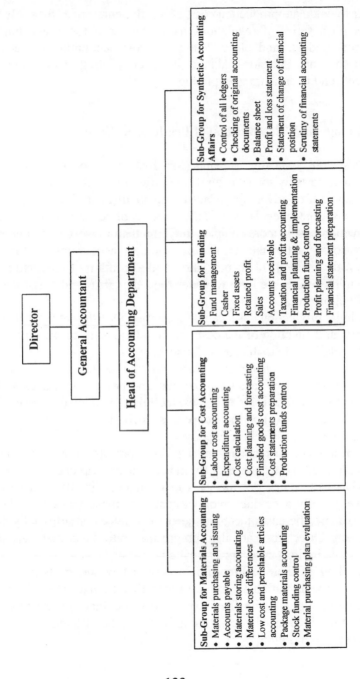

In order to calculate production costs correctly, enterprises themselves should also set up a series of regulations including those for establishing normal costs, cost budgets and plans. These are cost accounting procedures, cost forecasting and decision-making; cost controlling and analysis; cost statements and internal transfer pricing.

Terminology and Classification of Production Costs

A cost system typically accounts for costs in two broad stages: (1) it accumulates costs by some "natural" classification such as raw materials used, fuel consumed, or advertising placed; and then (2) it allocates (traces) these costs to cost objectives. However, this process of accumulation and allocation of production cost is more complex in China than in western countries for two main reasons: firstly, the terminology of cost accounting is different; and secondly, the methods of accumulation and allocation of production costs are different. Therefore, we have to understand the terms and classification used for production costs.

In China, production costs can be classified in different ways according to the nature and function of the costs, their relationship to the cost objectives, and their relationship to the cost behaviour.

Considering their nature and function, the costs of production can be grouped under (a) raw materials; (b) fuel and power; (c) wages and welfare expenses; (d) manufacturing expenses, including depreciation expenses, repair expenses and so on; (e) periodic expenses, including administrative expenses, financial expenses and selling expenses.

According to their relationship to the cost objectives, production costs can be classified as (a) direct costs or (b) indirect costs. Direct costs are those that, on the basis of source documents, can be traced directly to a specific cost objective, usually a product. Indirect costs are those that cannot be directly traced to a specific cost object and need to be allocated artificially among all cost objects. Direct costs are also sub-grouped into direct materials and direct labour, while indirect costs are also called overheads.

According to their relationship to cost behaviour, costs are considered variable or fixed. Variable costs are those that change when the volume of production changes, while fixed costs are those that are not related to the volume of production. The relationship between the different types of costs in China is shown in Figure 6-2:

134

Figure 6-2 Relationship Between Different Types of Costs

Nature of costs	Cost objectives	Cost behaviour
Raw materials	Direct materials	
Fuel and power	Variable costs	
Wages and welfare	Direct labour	
Manufacturing expenses	Overhead	Fixed costs
Administration expense	Period expense	Fixed costs
Selling expenses	Period expense	Variable costs

Procedure for the Calculation of Product Costs

There are six steps for the calculation of the cost of a product:

Step 1: Accumulating and allocating cost elements to the cost objectives. The cost elements are raw materials, fuel and power, wages and welfare expenses, depreciation expenses, and other manufacturing expenses. The cost objectives in this step will be: (a) the main production departments, or main products if the costs are traceable directly to products; (b) auxiliary departments; and (c) factory overheads. Direct materials and direct labour are traced to the main production department, and indirect manufacturing costs are traced to the relevant factory overhead accounts. However, all costs related to auxiliary departments are accumulated and applied in the auxiliary department accounts, no matter whether they are direct or indirect costs.

Step 2: Accumulating accrued expenses under the deferred or prepaid expense account, and allocating those costs to costs objects which are similar to those in step 1.

Step 3: Allocating auxiliary department costs to production departments or main products in relevant factory overhead accounts.

Step 4:   Allocating factory overheads to the main production departments or main products.

Step 5:   Allocating production costs between finished goods and work in process.

Step 6:   Calculating and determining the cost of a product.

The procedure for calculation of the cost of a product is as in Figure 6-3. As the procedures for accumulation and allocation of raw material expenses, labour expenses and depreciation expenses are similar to those in the western countries.   The following discussions focus on the accumulation and allocation of deferred or prepaid expenses, auxiliary department expenses and factory overheads.

Accumulation and Allocation of Deferred or Prepaid Expenses

As the accrual principle is adopted in cost accounting, some cost adjustments have to be made to reflect costs incurred and paid in different accounting periods. There are two accounts used in cost adjustments: "deferred expenses" and "prepaid expenses". Deferred expenses are those which have been charged to the cost of production but have not yet been paid, such as provision for fixed-assets repair expenses and provision for interest on loans. Prepaid expenses are those which have been paid but should be charged to current and further accounting periods, such as prepaid insurance and rent.

Accumulation and Allocation of Expenses of Auxiliary Departments

Auxiliary departments are production support departments, which are called service departments in western countries. The expenses of each auxiliary department are accumulated in the "Auxiliary production" ledger which includes a subsidiary ledger for each auxiliary department. All the expenses, including direct and indirect costs and the overheads of each auxiliary department are calculated under the relevant subsidiary ledger. The methods of allocating auxiliary department expenses are similar to those in western countries, including (1) the direct allocation method; (2) the step-down allocation method; (3) the reciprocal allocation method; (4) the once-only reciprocal allocation method; and (5) the planned cost allocation method.

136

Figure 6-3 Procedure for Calculation of Product Costs

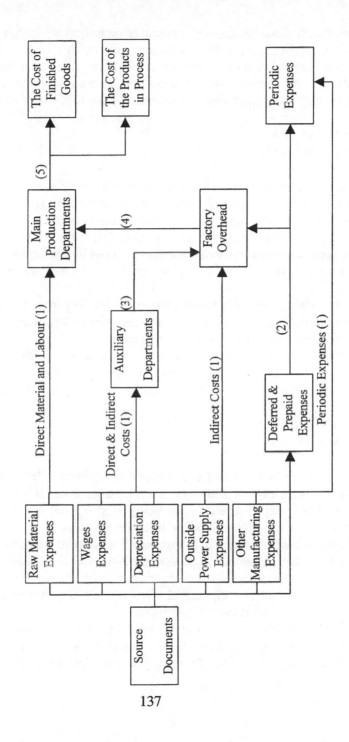

The direct allocation method, once-only reciprocal allocation method and planned cost allocation method are more popular in China. The reciprocal allocation method and the once only reciprocal allocation method differ slightly. In the former, the complete reciprocated costs of each service department are calculated first, as illustrated by the following formulas:

$$\{\ A = A' + a * B\ (1)$$
$$\{\ B = B' + b * A\ (2)$$

A – the complete reciprocated costs of service department A
B – the complete reciprocated costs of service department B
A' – the costs of department A before being reciprocated
B' – the costs of department b before being reciprocated
a – the percentage of service of department B used by department A
b – the percentage of service of department A used by department B

Next, these costs are allocated to production departments based on the percentage of usage of services by each department. From the mathematical viewpoint, this method is correct and accurate.

In the once-only reciprocal allocation method, there are still two steps: the first being the calculation of complete reciprocated costs of each auxiliary department. However, the formulas used are different, as follows:

$$\{\ A = A' + a * B'\ (1)$$
$$\{\ B = B' + b * A'\ (2)$$

A – the complete reciprocated costs of service department A
B – the complete reciprocated costs of service department B
A' – the costs of department A before being reciprocated
B' – the costs of department b before being reciprocated
a – the percentage of service of department B used by department A
b – the percentage of service of department A used by department B

Then, the complete reciprocated costs of each department are allocated directly among the production departments.

In the planned cost allocation method, the expenses of auxiliary departments are allocated to each user based on the amount of usage and planned cost per unit. The difference between actual costs incurred and

138

planned costs allocated will be charged directly to the administrative expenses of the enterprise. Most state-owned enterprises in China use this method because the variance can reflect the performance of each unit in the enterprise.

Accumulation and Allocation of Factory Overheads

Factory overhead expenses are also called manufacturing expenses in China. There is only one factory overhead ledger in some small businesses and all indirect costs incurred in the enterprise are firstly accumulated in this account. Then the factory overhead is allocated to each production department, and sequentially to the products. However, in most enterprises, the factory overhead ledger consists of several subsidiary ledgers in line with each production department. The indirect expenses of each production department are accumulated in its own factory overhead subsidiary ledger and then applied to the products. Whether a single overhead pool or multiple overhead pools are used, the principle of accumulation and allocation of overhead is the same. The application bases of overhead include: (1) direct labour costs; (2) direct labour hours; (3) machine hours; (4) units produced, and (5) material costs or material quantities. Therefore, the application methods used in overhead allocation in China are identical to those used in western countries.

Allocation of Production Costs between Finished Goods and Work in Process

Using proper methods to allocate production costs between finished goods and work in process is critical for cost accounting. There are four methods used in determining the costs of work in process in China.

1. Direct material method. The costs of work in process only include direct materials. Labour costs and manufacturing costs are fully charged to finished goods.

2. Normative cost method. The costs of work in process are determined by normative or standard cost. The total costs of working in process can be calculated by using the following formulas:
   The normative direct material costs = Quantities of work in process × normative cost per unit
   The normative direct labour costs = Quantities of work in process × normative labour hours * normative cost per labour hour

The normative overhead costs = Quantities of work in process × normative machine hours * normative cost per machine hour

Total normative costs of work in process = the normative direct material costs + the normative direct labour costs + the normative overhead costs

3. Normative cost proportion method. In this method, the allocation of production costs between finished goods and work in process is based on the normative costs of both. The costs of work in process and finished goods can be calculated using the following formulas:

Allocation rate = (Actual costs of work in process, beginning + actual costs started during current period) ÷ (normative costs or quantities of work in process, beginning + normative costs or quantities started during current period).

The costs of finished goods = normative costs or quantities of finished goods × allocation rate.

The costs of work in process = normative costs or quantities of work in process × allocation rate

The normative cost method is different from the normative cost proportion method. In the former, the work in process is calculated on normative cost and the difference between the actual cost and normative cost is charged to finished goods. In the normative cost proportion method, the difference is shared by work in process and finished goods.

4. Equivalent units method. This method is more popular in western countries. The costs of work in process can be determined by the following steps: (a) summarise the flow of physical units; (b) compute output in terms of equivalent units; (c) summarise the total costs to be accounted for, which are the total debts of work in process (basic production costs, in the Chinese concept); (d) compute equivalent unit costs; and (e) apply the costs to units completed and to units in the ending work in process.

These can be calculated as follows:

Equivalent units = work in process * the degree of processing (%)

Allocation rate = (costs of work in process, beginning + costs started in current period) / (finished units + equivalent units)

The costs of finished goods = finished units × allocation rate

The costs of work in process, ending = equivalent units × allocation rate.

Costing Methods

There are several costing methods used in China. On the surface, these methods appear different from those used in western countries. Actually, Chinese cost accounting methods can be classified into two groups which are similar to the western concepts of job-order costing and process costing (Figure 6-4).

Figure 6-4 Comparison of Costing Methods

Western Countries	China
Job-order costing	Variety or Assortment costing
	Group costing
	Batch costing
Process costing	Parallel process costing
	Sequential process costing

Job-order Costing Methods

The Chinese costing methods used which fall into this group include the variety costing method, the group costing method and the batch costing method. The difference between these costing methods is that the cost objectives are different; being a variety of products, a batch of products, a group of products or a single product. The costs of a variety, a batch or a group are calculated first and then the costs are applied to each individual product. The cost of products can be calculated as follows:

$$P = M * R_m + L * R_l + O * R_o$$

Suppose $R_m = R_l = R_o = R$

$P = (M + L + O) * R$

P – cost of product
M – material
L – labour
O – overhead
R – the rate of finished goods, equals units of finished goods / (units of finished goods + equivalent units in work-in-process), for M, L, O. The job-order costing system can be illustrated as in Figure 6-5.

Process Costing Methods

The process costing method used in China is quite different to the western concept. If a bridge of understanding is to be built between job-order costing methods used in China and those in western countries, we need to examine Chinese process costing methods in detail. There are two main process costing methods used in China: sequential process costing and parallel process costing.

1. Sequential Process Costing

The objectives of sequential process costing are the semi-finished goods in each step. Sequential process costing is usually used in enterprises which have multiple production steps. Semi-finished goods are manufactured in each step and then transferred to the next step for further production. The procedure is as in Figure 6-6 and the formula for calculation of the costs of finished goods and the semi-finished goods in each step is as follows:

$S_i = S_{i-1} * R_{si} + M_i * R_{mi} + L_i * R_{li} + O_i * R_{oi}$

Suppose $R_{si} = R_{mi} = R_{li} = R_{oi} = R_i$

$S_i = (S_{i-1} + M_i + L_i + O_i) * R_i$

$WIP_i = (S_{i-1} + M_i + L_i + O_i) * (1 - R_i)$

$F = S_n = (S_{n-1} + M_n + L_n + O_n) * R_n$

142

Figure 6-5 Job-order Costing System

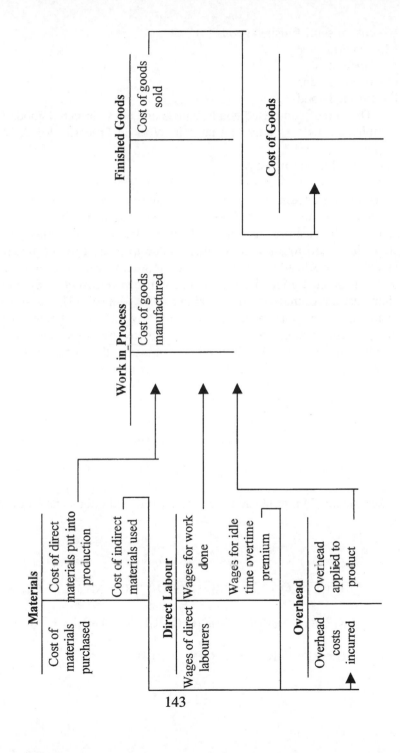

143

S – cost of semi-finished goods
M – material cost
L – labour cost
O – overhead cost
F – finished goods
R – The rate of completed goods, equals units of completed goods / (units of completed goods + equivalent units in Work-in-Process), for S, M, L, O in step i
WIP – working-in-process

Because semi-finished goods are transferred from one process to another, the cost elements in finished goods are the cost of semi-finished goods in last step, and the cost of direct materials, direct labour and overhead in the final step. It is hard to know how much is due to overall direct material, direct labour and overhead in finished goods. In order to get these figures, the costs of semi-finished goods have to be decomposed retrospectively into the cost elements, direct material, direct labour and overhead. This is so-called cost restored. It is mandatory, under government regulations, if enterprises choose the process costing method. Suppose there are three steps involved in production and the procedure of decomposing the costs of semi-finished goods into cost elements can be illustrated as follows:

$$S_1 = (M_1 + L_1 + O_1) * R_1 \qquad\qquad (1)$$

$$S2 = (S_1 + M_2 + L_2 + O_2) * R_2 \qquad\qquad (2)$$

$$F = S_3 = (S_2 + M_3 + L_3 + O_3) R_3 \qquad\qquad (3)$$

Take (1) and (2) into (3) and the costs of finished goods can be decomposed as:

$$F = S_3$$

$$= \{[(M_1 + L_1 + O_1) * R_1 + M_2 + L_2 + O_2] * R_2 + M_3 + L_3 + O_3\} R_3$$

$$= (M_1 R_1 R_2 R_3 + M_2 R_2 R_3 + M_3 R_3) + (L_1 R_1 R_2 R_3 + L_2 R_2 R_3 + L_3 R_3)$$

$$+ (O_1 R_1 R_2 R_3 + O_2 R_2 R_3 + O_3 R_3) \qquad\qquad (4)$$

The sequential process costing system is more complicated than the process costing system used in western countries. Accounting academics and practitioners in China are of the same opinion, and several methods for improvement have been proposed. One which is now popularly used involves transferring the normative costs sequentially and normative variances in parallel. The features of this method are that the cost of semi-finished goods is calculated under normative costs and the normative variances of semi-finished goods are transferred firstly to the account of semi-finished goods cost variance and then applied to the cost of finished goods. The reason why this method is so popular in China is that it builds a bridge between responsibility accounting and cost accounting for products. Management can use the variances to measure the performance of each cost centre and the actual costs for finished goods for financial reporting purposes. The procedure is as in Figure 6-7. The details of responsibility accounting will be discussed in the next chapter.

Figure 6-6 Sequential Process Costing

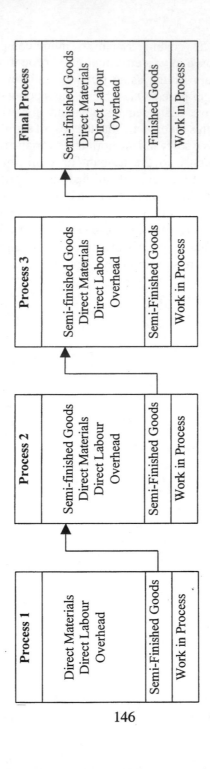

Figure 6-7 Sequential Transfer Normative Costs and Parallel Transfer Normative Variances

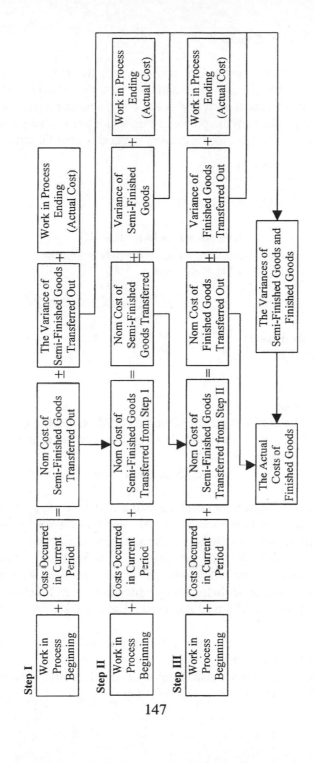

147

2. Parallel Process Costing

Under parallel process costing, in each step only that step's proportion of the cost of finished goods is calculated and then transferred to finished goods. The cost of work in process in each step is not computed separately and the cost of semi-finished goods from the previous step is not transferred to the next step. The procedure of parallel process costing method is as in Figure 6-8:

$$F = S_n = R_n * \sum_{i=1}^{n} (M_i + L_i + O_i)$$

$$BWIP_i = (M_i + L_i + O_i) * (1 - R_n) = (M_i + L_i + O_i) * [(1 - R_i) + (R_i - R_n)]$$

$$= (M_i + L_i + O_i) * (1 - R_i) + (M_i + L_i + O_i) * (R_i - R_n)$$

$$= WIP_i + (M_i + L_i + O_i) * (R_i - R_n)$$

$$R_i > R_n$$

S – semi-finished goods
M – material cost
L – labour cost
O – overhead cost
F – finished goods
R – the rate of completed goods, equals units of completed goods / (units of completed goods + equivalent units in work-in-process), in step i
WIP – work-in-process, in step i
BWIP – work-in-process in broad concept, in step i

The features of parallel process costing are: (1) the expenses of each step only include the expenses incurred in that step and do not include expenses transferred from previous steps; (2) finished goods in each step means the final finished goods in the final step and not semi-finished goods in each step; (3) work in process in the broad concept not only includes work in process in each step itself, but also includes goods which have been finished in each step, but have not yet been fully manufactured. These are known as semi-finished goods.

The amount of costs transferred to the finished goods can be computed using the following formula:

    (1) Equivalent units = finished units + equivalent units of work in process in the broad concept.

(2) Costs per equivalent unit = (cost of work in process in the broad concept, beginning + cost incurred in the current period) ÷ the equivalent units.

(3) The cost transferred to finished goods = the cost per equivalent unit × the finished units.

(4) Cost of work in process in the broad concept, ending = cost of work in process in the broad concept, beginning + cost incurred in the current period − cost transferred to finished goods.

Figure 6-8 Parallel Process Costing

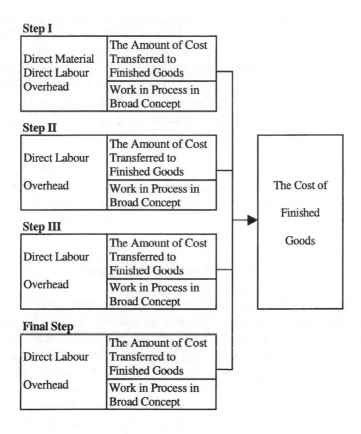

Accounting for Spoilage, Joint Products and By-products

Accounting for spoilage is simpler in China than in western countries. In most western countries, spoilage is classified into normal spoilage and abnormal spoilage. The costs of normal spoilage are treated as inventoriable costs which are borne by finished goods and work in process, and the costs of abnormal spoilage are treated as period costs which are written off in the current period (Horngren and Foster, 1991). In China, on the other hand, spoilage is classified into repairable and unrepairable spoilage. All costs of spoilage, including the costs of repairable spoilage, and unrepairable spoilage, are charged to the finished goods. Therefore, it is not necessary to calculate the costs of spoilage separately, although some enterprises do for the sake of cost control (Chen et al, 1993).

There are three basic approaches to calculating the cost of joint products in western countries: (1) to allocate costs using market selling price data. Three common methods are used in applying this approach: the sale value at split-off; the estimated net realisable value (NRV); and constant gross-margin percentage of NRV (2) to allocate costs using a physical measure (3) not to allocate costs (Horngren and Foster, 1991). Some of these approaches have been used in China, for example the market selling price method and the physical amount method. However, the more common method used is the artificial fraction method.

In China, the treatment for by-products is similar to that for joint products and is different from the treatment in western countries, where by-product is treated as a cost deduction for main or joint products, or as separate revenue or as other income item.

Standard Costing System and Normative Costing System

It is difficult to identify the person or persons who were responsible for the introduction of standard cost as a western accounting technique. David Solomons (1952) pointed out that while one or two nineteenth century writers had indicated the possibility of setting up norms of cost with which actual product and process costs might be compared, credit for the earliest detailed description of a system of standard costing was given to the American, G. Charter Harrison, who designed and installed the first standard costing system known to exist. In 1918 Harrison published the first set of equations for analysis of cost variances. From then on, the literature relating to standard

150

costing grew in volume, and today the standard costing system is used popularly across many industries.

Standard costing was introduced to the Soviet Union in 1929 but at the same time the normative costing system was initiated in an agricultural machinery factory in the Soviet city of Harkefu. In the early stages the two systems were implemented slowly in Soviet factories because of the instability of the centrally planned economy. However, from 1932 the standard costing system came under serious criticism in the Soviet Union because of the ideological differences between socialism and capitalism. The normative costing system was then promoted by the government under the assumption that it carried socialist characteristics (Dai, 1984).

The normative costing system was brought to China in the 1950s with the establishment of a Soviet-style centrally planned economy. However, the implementation of normative costing experienced difficulties in both China and the Soviet Union. For example, in 1974 only one-third of manufacturing enterprises in the Soviet Union and only a few Chinese enterprises were using normative costing.

It is important to understand that while the standard costing system is substantially different from the normative costing system, the meaning of standard cost, normative cost and planned cost is similar. All are a scientifically predetermined cost and the procedure for setting each is also similar. All can be based on historical records and engineering studies.

The main difference between the two systems is their purposes. The fundamental purposes of a costing system are cost control and product cost determination. Horngren and Foster (1991) summarises the major purposes for using standard costing as follows:

(1) to assist in setting budgets and evaluating managerial performance; (2) to act as a control device by highlighting those activities that do not conform to plan, and thus to alarm decision-makers to those situations which may be "out of control" and in need of corrective action; (3) to provide a prediction of future costs that can be used for decision-making purposes; (4) to simplify the task of tracing costs to products for inventory valuation purposes; (5) to provide a challenging target that individuals are motivated to achieve (p.222).

Therefore, the main purpose of using standard costing is to evaluate managerial performance. Because standard costs can be used in inventory valuation, the determination of actual costs of products becomes less important. Although it is possible to proportion the standard variances to get the actual costs, few companies do these calculations and prefer to charge

151

standard variances directly to profit and loss accounts. Management focuses on the analysis and investigation of variances and the evaluation of the performance of each department, rather than on the calculation of actual costs of products. The standard costing system is illustrated in Figure 6-9.

In contrast to standard costing, the main purpose of the normative costing system is the determination of actual cost of products rather than cost control. Some scholars argue that normative costing is capable of cost control (Li, 1988). However, this purpose became secondary to the determination of actual costs and was overshadowed by the complicated calculation of the actual cost of products. In Soviet-style planned economies, the implementation of normative costing system was under the mandate of central governmental authorities and the financial statements mainly served the purposes of central governmental planning and administration. The central government authorities were logically concerned about information of actual costs of products in order to make price and resources allocation decision and were less interested in enterprises' need for internal control and performance evaluation.

In normative costing systems, variances are to be proportioned between work in process, semifinished goods, and finished goods, in order to calculate the actual costs of semifinished goods and finished goods. Less attention is given to analysis of variances and evaluation of performance. The normative costing system is illustrated in Figure 6-10.

Standard Cost System

$$SS_i = (SS_{i-1} + SM_i + SL_i + SO_i) * R_i$$

$$SWIP_i = (SS_{i-1} + SM_i + SL_i + SO_i) * (1 - R_i)$$

$$F = SS_n = (SS_{n-1} + SM_n + SL_n + SO_n) * R_n$$

$$V = \sum_{i=1}^{n} VS_{i-1} + VM_i + VL_i + VO_i$$

Variances are normally charged directly to the Profit and Loss Accounts

Normative Cost System

$$AS_i = (SS_{i-1} + SM_i + SL_i + SO_i) * R_i + Vi * R_i$$

$$\text{AWIP}_i = (\text{SS}_{i-1} + \text{SM}_i + \text{SL}_i + \text{SO}_i) * (1 - R_i) + V_i * (1 - R_i)$$

$$F = \text{AS}_n = (\text{SS}_{n-1} + \text{SM}_n + \text{SL}_n + \text{SO}_n) * R_n + V_i * R_n$$

SS – standard or normative cost of semi-finished goods
AS – actual cost of semi-finished goods
SM – standard or normative cost of material cost
SL – standard or normative cost of labour cost
SO – standard or normative cost of overhead cost
F – finished goods
R – The rate of completed goods, equals units of finished goods / (units of completed goods + equivalent units in work-in-process), for S, M, L, O in step i
SWIP – standard cost of work-in-process
AWIP – actual cost of work-in-process
V – Variance for M, L, O in step i

The second difference between standard costing and normative costing is the classification of variances. In standard costing, the variances are classified as: (1) material price variance; (2) material quantity variance; (3) labour rate variance; (4) labour efficiency variance; (5) variable overhead variance; (6) fixed overhead variance, which includes budget variance and application variance. This classification is in line with the cost control purpose. On the other hand, in normative costing, the variances are classified as: (1) normative variances; which include normative variances in material, labour and overhead, (2) change-of-norms variances; which is the difference in work in process in the beginning, before and after changing of norms. These variances are applied to finished goods and work in process in order to get the actual cost of products.

Actual cost of products = Normative cost of products ± Normative variances ± Change-of-norms variances

The third difference between standard costing and normative costing is in the treatment of variances. In standard costing variances are usually treated as period costs, while in normative costing they are treated as inventoriable costs.

Conclusion

The current Chinese cost accounting system is derived from the old Soviet model. Little change has been made since the 1950s. The purpose of the cost accounting system in China is for the determination of the product cost, not for decision-making. It is the central government planning and not the ordinary users of financial statements which has been important. The cost accounting system used in China is more complicated than that used in the western countries. Costs are categorised into much more detailed formal groups and calculated separately. China has its unique cost accumulation and allocation procedures, such as parallel process costing and sequential process costing. These methods cause much difficulty for westerners wishing to understand Chinese cost accounting. These problems have been explained in detail in this thesis. Finally, the Chinese normative costing system is compared to the standard cost system. It is concluded that the standard cost system is simpler than the normative cost system and more easily adopted in practice.

Figure 6-9 Standard Costing System

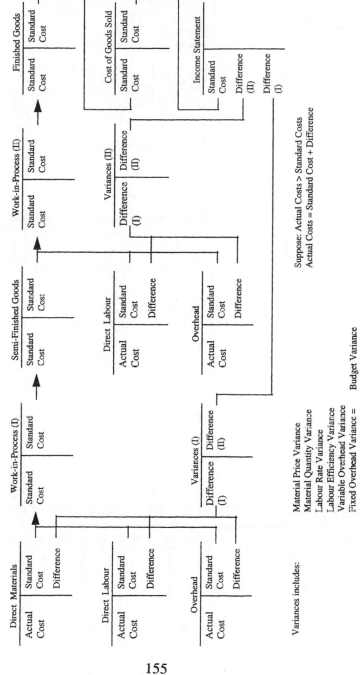

155

Figure 6-10 Normative Costing System

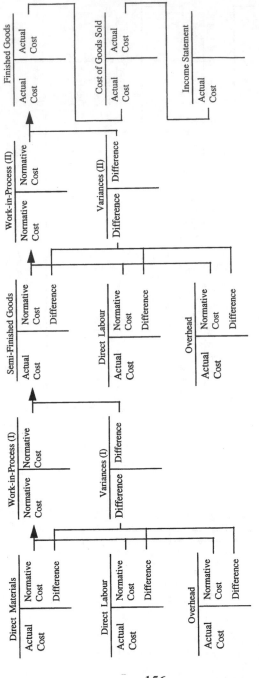

7　The Development of Management Accounting in China

According to Johnson and Kaplan (1991), the history of modern management accounting started in the early nineteenth century. At that time, the factory accounting system, standard costing, the concept of return on investment (ROI) which measures the performance of multidivision forms of organisation had been invented and used in western countries, especially in the United States and the United Kingdom. The development of management accounting was often subordinated by the development of financial accounting. Since the Second World War, management accounting research has flourished and many decision models have been innovated. However, those models have hardly been used in practice. It became apparent in the 1980s that there was a significant gap between the theory and practice of management accounting. In the 1990s, with the rapid development of new technology and the successful Japanese experience, management accounting became focused on useful and simpler cost methods, such as activity-based cost accounting, and the emphasis shifted from internal to external, from past to future, from quantitative analysis to quality control.

On the other hand, the development of management accounting in China was limited to responsibility accounting. This mainly imitated the Soviet model which was introduced into China after the revolution in 1949. Although management accounting existed in China in the 1950s, the term "management accounting" did not appear until the late 1970s. Western management accounting began its influence on China in the early 1980s. Many management accounting techniques, such as cost-volume-profit analysis, standard costing, fixed and variable costs, variances analysis, and long-term and short-term decision methods, have been introduced into China. However, the application and adoption of western ideas, models and methods have often been slow and difficult.

The Developments in Management Accounting Practice in Western Countries

Modern management accounting emerged in the early nineteenth century (Johnson and Kaplan, 1987). Prior to this, all transactions among entities occurred in the market, and the owner could easily measure the success of each order by comparing the cash collected from customers with the cash paid out to the suppliers of production inputs. Johnson and Kaplan (1991) state:

> The origins of modern management accounting can be traced to the emergence of managed, hierarchical enterprises in the early nineteenth century, such as armories and textile mills. These enterprises were formed to conduct an entire multistage production process within a single organisation. The organisations took advantage of economies of scale from relatively capital intensive processes to hire groups of workers who manufactured the firm's output ... Information was needed to replace information formerly available from market transactions so that the efficiency of internal production processes could be measured ... Thus, for a textile mill, internal measures were developed on cost per yard or cost per pound in the separate processes of carding, spinning, weaving, and blanching fabrics (p.5).

Following the emergence and rapid growth of railways in the mid-nineteenth century, management accounting systems were advanced. New measures such as cost per ton mile, cost per passenger mile and the ratio of operating expenses to revenues were created and reported on a segmental and regional basis. Many of the innovative management accounting measures developed by railway companies were subsequently adopted and extended to other business sectors, such as in Woolworth in retailing. Here, gross profits and stock turnover ratios were used to measure the profitability and efficiency of the different departments.

At that time there were two accounting systems: the management accounting system which both motivated and measured the efficiency of internal processes; and the financial accounting system which recorded transactions for preparing annual financial statements for the owners and creditors. Thus, the two systems; management and financial accounting, operated independently of each other.

Further advances in management accounting were associated with the scientific management movement, whose most famous advocate was Frederick Taylor. The aim of the scientific management movement was to improve the efficiency of the production process by simplifying and

158

standardising operations. There were three purposes of information about standards:

- to analyse the potential efficiency of tasks or processes;
- to compare the actual efficiency with this potential;
- to simplify the task of valuing stock and work-in-process for the yearly financial report (Loft, 1991).

According to Johnson and Kaplan, (1) and (2) in the list were crucial to the drive behind the setting up of cost accounting systems; (3) was merely a by-product. In 1911, Charter G. Harrison, designed and installed the first standard costing system. In 1918, Harrison published the first set of equations for the analysis of cost variances (Johnson and Kaplan, 1987).

With the merger emphasised in the United States in the early decades of the twentieth century, a centralised unitary organisational structure was developed in which the firm's operations were broken down into separate divisions, each with highly specialised activities. Each division was run by its own manager. The role of top management was to coordinate the diverse activities, direct strategy and decide on the most profitable allocation of capital to a variety of different activities. New management accounting techniques were devised to support multi-activity, diversified organisations. Budgetary planning and control systems were developed to ensure that the diverse activities of different divisions were in harmony with overall corporate goals. In addition, a measure of return on investment (ROI) was devised to measure the success of each division and the entire organisation. Top management used the ROI measure to focus on the productivity of capital and to help allocate capital to the most profitable divisions (Drury, 1992).

Most of the management accounting practices used today had been developed by 1925, and for next 60 years there was a trend to stagnation. Johnson and Kaplan (1991) say:

> The next sixty years, from 1925 to 1985, were not nearly as productive in the development of management accounting procedures. The exact reasons for the slowdown, even halt, of management accounting innovation are still being debated. But at least part of the reason appears to lie on in the demand for product cost information for financial accounting reports (p.6).

Before the Second World War, the practitioners were the main innovators of management accounting techniques. Management accounting became an academic subject in universities in the 1950s. At that time, researchers

159

focused on developing decision models for managers based on applying ideas derived from micro-economic theory. An early contribution to this economic-based literature was the concept of 'relevant cost'. It was demonstrated that a single concept of cost could not be unique for all purposes, and the expression 'different costs for different purposes' become a fundamental part of the management accounting literature in the 1950s.

During the 1960s and 1970s, management accounting research flourished and two schools; economic perspective and organisational and behavioural perspective, emerged. Economic perspective research concentrated on the application of neoclassical economic theory to problems of business decision-making and control. Organisational and behavioural research focused on enhancing the economic performance arising from the use of existing management accounting techniques. Their motivational impact was emphasised (Drury, 1992).

During the 1980s it became apparent that there was a significant gap between the theory and practice of management accounting. The evidence from the various empirical studies suggest that simple techniques rather than the approaches outlined in textbooks were used in practice (Drury et al, 1992). Horngren provided an explanation for the unpopularity of economic decision-making models (Horngren, 1986):

> The cost-benefit theme is the foundation for judging whether cost accounting systems should be revised. Many academicians are frustrated and disappointed when they discover that most organisations, including some successful giants, do not use multiple overhead rates, discounted cash flow, regression analysis. In my opinion the cost-benefit rationale helps explain why: there is a cost of keeping the costs. Many managers perceive, rightly or wrongly, that costs of more elaborate systems exceed prospective benefits. Moreover, the costs of implementing changes are seldom trivial (p.35).

The recognition of a gap between theory and practice has resulted in a change of emphasis from normative to positive research. In particular, current research is placing greater emphasis on understanding practice, whereas previous research was more concerned with developing normative economic decision-making models.

Not only has the management accounting theory suffered criticism but management accounting practices have also. Kaplan has argued that most companies still use the same management accounting systems that were developed decades ago for an environment very different from that of today

(Kaplan, 1984). The principle criticisms of current management accounting practices were summarised by Drury (1992):

(1) Conventional management accounting does not meet the needs of today's manufacturing and competitive environment. (2) Traditional product costing systems provide misleading information for decision-making purposes. (3) Management accounting practices follow, and have become subservient to, financial accounting requirements. (4) Management accounting focuses almost entirely on internal activities, and relatively little attention is given to the external environment in which the business operates (p.803).

Although the management accounting practice had suffered severe criticisms from academicians in 1980s, no overall changes in management accounting seem to have occurred in 1990s. According to an investigation provided by Bromwich and Bhimani (1989) significant changes in management accounting are slow in developing:

The evidence and arguments advanced by advocates of wholesale changes in management accounting are not yet sufficient to justify the wholesale revision of management accounting.

Evidence of the benefits of new accounting techniques and continued benefits of some conventional techniques is only beginning to emerge. No general crisis has been identified within the management accounting profession vis-a-vis a changing manufacturing environment and therefore no radical reforms are recommended at this stage (p. 97)

Nevertheless, changes in management accounting practices are taking place, and during the next decade it is likely that firms will experiment with new techniques. The likely developments in management accounting occurring in 1990s include:

- the growth of activity-based costing system;
- less emphasis on variance analysis for operational control; greater emphasis on quality measurement;
- life-cycle reporting;
- strategic management accounting; and
- customer profitability analysis (Drury, 1992).

161

Production calculations were used in China as early as the first century before Christ. Fan Sheng-chih used production calculations as the basis on which to calculate the amount of profit that would be derived from a given acreage by growing gourds and converting them into ladles (Scorgie and Ji, 1996). In the centuries that followed other writers set down production measurements for agricultural activities and indicated how they could be used for evaluation of investments in technology and for planning. In the seventeenth century the works of Song Ying-hsing stand out. In his treatise entitled *T'ian Kung K'ai Wu*, Sung Ying-hsing showed that production calculations were used by Chinese to justify investments in technology. Both agricultural and manufacturing activities were explained.

However, with a long lasting feudal system, the development of commerce and the capitalist embryo was very slow. A complete costing system did not exist in factories in China until the 1940s (Guo, 1988). It was even hard to find any management techniques used at that time. Therefore, the modern history of Chinese management accounting started only from the 1950s when China brought in the management systems from the Soviet Union.

The word "management accounting" did not appear in China until 1979. Some scholars argue whether management accounting existed before the late of the 1970s. Management accounting can be defined as the area of accounting dealing with the provision of information to all levels of management in an organisation to facilitate decision-making for planning and control (Horngren, 1986). According to this definition, we may argue that management accounting has existed in China since the 1950s and the purpose was mainly to provide information for planning and control, both for the governmental authorities and for enterprises themselves.

In 1950s, work-team accounting flourished in China. The work-team was a bottom unit in the management hierarchy and a cost centre at the lowest level. Workers in the team were responsible for achieving planned production tasks, including production quantity, quality and cost savings. Under the socialist planned economy, the fulfilling of planned production targets was more important than making profit, and financial measurement was subordinated to the material measurement. Production tasks were assigned to teams of workers rather than individuals because individualism was discouraged in the socialist ideology.

During the 1960s, a target stratification management system was used in many enterprises. It served a custodial function and ensured the designated use of funds. Prior to that, there was no clear accountability. However, free access to goods and services from other enterprises or departments was common under the misguided notion that all resources belonged to the nation. Therefore the target management system could not achieve its goals and misuse of resources was a serious problem at that time (Yu, 1988).

During the 1970s, an economic accounting system, which was also called the internal economic accounting system replaced the old system, providing accountability for transactions between enterprises, and ensuring proper allocation of resources in order to improve the overall efficiency of enterprises.

All these methods belonged to the area of responsibility accounting and were influenced by the Soviet accounting techniques. Not only were these management accounting techniques used in practice, but they were also taught in colleges and universities from the 1950s.

The term "management accounting" first appeared in Chinese accounting literature at the end of the 1970s. With the implementation of reform and the "open-door" policy, western management accounting methods were introduced into China. Chinese accounting academics and practitioners showed their enthusiasm in absorbing and digesting western management accounting theories and techniques. They tried to apply these techniques in Chinese enterprises. As a result, the internal responsibility accounting system was innovated and implemented in many large-medium enterprises in China. However, the Chinese found gradually that western management accounting techniques were not suitable for Chinese enterprises. Consequently, the process of application of these methods has been slowed (Bromwich and Wang, 1991).

Workshop and Work-team Accounting

Workshop and work-team accounting was the basic form of the Internal Economic Accounting System which originated in the Soviet Union[25]. The

[25] Economic Accounting System was firstly used in the Soviet Union. After the success of the communist revolution in 1918, the centralised supply and distribution system was implemented in all the state-owned enterprises in the Soviet Union. Under this system, production was according to central government planning. All materials were supplied by the government agencies free of charge and all products were distributed by the government. Nobody was

system was introduced into Chinese enterprises from the early 1950s. During the "recovery" period (1949-1951), a uniform accounting system was established in China in line with the planned economy. In most state-owned enterprises, a planned management system was established, including planned costing, budgeting and inventory control. From 1952, the main task of accounting in an enterprise began to shift to further strengthening internal control and finding some effective methods of managerial accounting applicable in a socialist country (Yang, 1981). The workshop and work-team system was initiated based on the "mass line" philosophy, which means that the management of enterprises should rely upon the ordinary workers. The main contents of the workshop and work-team accounting system were: each workshop or work-team calculates product quantity and quality, cost and fund usage individually; the enterprise evaluates each workshop and work-team's performance by comparing planned targets and actual results. Finally the enterprise rewarded or punished each workshop or work-team according to an incentive scheme.

Accounting is a highly comprehensive reflection of the result of production and management. It is extremely difficult for an ordinary individual worker who does physical work in a team to see how his routine work is connected with the profit or loss of the whole enterprise. Therefore a simplified system had to be implemented to meet the needs of workshop or work-team management. This simplified system included:

1. the targets of each workshop and work-team, which could include product quantity, product quality, cost of production, fund usage, and savings on materials;
2. measurement of each target;
3. the cost of each item saved or wasted;
4. an incentive scheme.

The workshop or work-team only calculated the product quantity, product quality, cost of production, funds usage, and savings on materials. A part-time ordinary worker was responsible for calculating the result each day or week. The head of the workshop and the accountants from the

responsible for the achievement of production therefore it was found this system was inefficient. It wasted materials, human resources and money. From 1921, the new system called Economic Accounting System was introduced to replace the centralised supply and distribution system. All the state-owned enterprises had to be responsible for their own performance.

accounting department checked the results regularly and evaluated the performance of each workshop and work-team. The table below shows the work-team accounting system used by a shift group in the extrusion department of a medium plate mill operated by An-Shen Steel Corporation (Yang, 1981). Here, total output is the quantity variable; output of prime product is the quality variable, and bloom consumption is the cost variable. The calculation of one shift's performance is as shown in Table 7-1.

The workshop or work-team accounting system was a very useful tool for on-floor management. The targets and the calculations were quite simple and straightforward. Even ordinary workers could understand the content and meaning and know the effects of their work on the total performance of the enterprise. The other advantage was that the results could be calculated quickly and managers could get feedback rapidly because the figures were available at the end of each shift or day. They could then use these figures to monitor and evaluate performance and to make necessary adjustments. The workshop or work-team accounting system was also used to promote competition among workshops or work-teams where the environmental conditions were the same, and therefore promote efficiencies in the overall performance of the enterprises. There is much evidence showing that the workshop and work-team accounting system was a very useful tool in management, especially in the 1950s. A case study (Yang, 1981) about the work-team accounting system used in Ai-Shen Iron & Steel Co. in 1955, showed that about 280,000 tons a year in the usage of bloom was saved and that costs decreased about 4 million Renminbi Yuan a year after implementation of the work-team accounting system.

Table 7-1 The Calculation of One Shift's Performance in Work-team Accounting System

	Norm	Actual	Variance	Unit price	Gain or loss
(1) Total output (tons)	105	100	(5)	10	(50)
(2) Output of prime product	95%	97%	2%	20	40
(3) Bloom consumption (tons)	105	104	1	200	200
(4) Total					190
(5) Accumulated to date					1880

Source: Yang.C.L (1981) "'Mass Line' Accounting in China", *Management Accounting*, May 1981.

Target Stratification Management System

Target stratification management was used regularly in enterprises in the 1960s. At first, the targets only included the funds and costs but, with the development of the system, profit and other targets were included later. Target stratification management assigns overall targets such as funds, cost, and profit targets to workshops and work-teams vertically. Simultaneously the system assigns overall targets to functional management departments such as the supply department, production department, sales department and accounting department horizontally.

Fund Target Stratification Management System

The Concept of Funds

The funds management concept had been used for 45 years when the first accounting standard was issued by the Ministry of Finance in 1992. In it, the basic accounting equation is: Total funds application = Total funds source. This is contrary to the basic accounting equation in western countries: Assets = Liabilities + Owner's equity.

The term of "funds" is the monetary expression of property, goods and materials used in the process of production (Wang and Qian, 1987). It refers in general both to funds source and funds application. Funds application is the physical form of the funds and funds source is the monetary form of funds. Therefore funds application and funds source are two different sides of the same thing. From the physical view, funds application can be classified as fixed assets, current assets and specific assets. From the monetary view, funds source can be classified as (1) fixed funds, which means the funds applied to fixed assets; (2) current funds, which means the funds applied to current assets; (3) specific funds, which means the funds applied to specific assets.

Current funds can be sub-classified as follows: storage funds, which are applied to procurement items such as raw materials, fuel, and spare parts; production funds, which are applied to the producing of work in process, self-manufactured semi-finished products and deferred charges; finished product funds, which are applied to finished products; monetary funds such as cash and bank deposits; and settlement funds, which include sales receivable and other receivables.

Establishing Overall Fund Targets

The Chinese funds stratification management system focused mainly on current funds management. Current funds management was similar to the western concept of working capital management. In operation, it was the core of funds management because it covered a great proportion of total funds and its turnover affected the operation of the enterprise. There were two methods to set overall current funds targets:

1. Based on last year's actual current funds:
   Overall current funds target in this year =
   (Current funds in last year − unreasonable usage) ×
   (1+ the increase rate in production) ×
   (1 − the accelerated or decelerated rate in current fund turnover)

2. Based on the sales budget and the current fund/sales ratio:
   Overall current funds target in this year =
   sales budget × current funds/sales ratio

Horizontally Assigning of Overall Funds Targets to Functional Departments

When the overall funds targets are set up, they are broken down into several sub-targets, such as storage funds target, production funds target and finished product funds target. These targets are assigned to relevant functional departments. For example, the storage fund target is assigned to the supply department and the maintenance department; the production funds target is assigned to the production department, and the finished product funds target is assigned to the sales department.

Vertically Assigning Targets to Individual Workshops or Divisions

Every functional department assigns the departmental funds target to individual workshops or divisions. The heads of workshops and divisions have the responsibility for funds usage within their management scope. The following Figure 7-1 shows the Globe Light Industry Company's funds stratification management system.

Cost Targets Stratification Management System

Cost control is very important in management accounting. The cost targets stratification management system is designed to control costs in different levels and places. Every department and centre, and every worker in the enterprise, is involved in cost control. Cost control is not only the management's or accounting department's job but also it is part of the job for all staff in the enterprise. An enterprise sets up the overall cost target and then assigns the target vertically and horizontally to all departments, workshops, work-teams and individuals. Every person in the enterprise is responsible for the reduction of cost. The procedure of implementation of cost targets stratification is as follows (see Figure 7-2):

1. set up overall cost targets;
2. analyse the components of costs and expenses;
3. identify departments and centres for controlling these costs and expenses;
4. assign the cost targets to responsible departments and centres;
5. assign departmental costs to workshops, work-teams and individuals.

Economic Activity Analysis

Financial reports reveal the enterprise's operational performance. These figures give little help to management in decision-making if they are not analysed. Analysis of financial reports, including external and internal reports, is very important for management when making economic choices. The objectives of economic activity analysis are to compare an enterprise's current financial position with other comparable enterprises, or with its own performance in previous years, or with the budget. This is to identify the strengths and weaknesses of enterprise operations, analyse the factors affecting the performance of the company and predict the future development of the enterprise. Four kinds of analytical methods are still used in China: (1) horizontal analysis (2) vertical analysis (3) ratio analysis and (4) effect-chain analysis. This has similarities with the diagnostic analysis of financial statements as on a periodic basis.

Figure 7-1 Globe Light Industry Company's Fund Stratification Management System

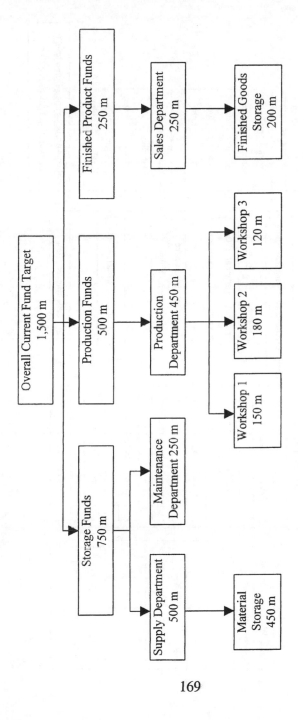

Figure 7-2   Globe Light Industry Company's Cost Stratification Management System

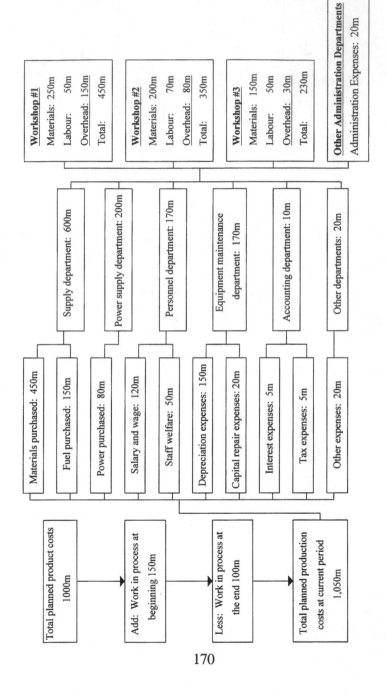

Horizontal Analysis

Many business decisions hinge on whether the numbers in sales, income, expenses and costs are increasing or decreasing over time. The study of percentage changes in comparative statements is called horizontal analysis. For example, trend percentage analysis indicates the direction a business is taking. In China the horizontal analysis is focused on comparing actual cost planned cost and the previous year's cost.

Vertical Analysis

Vertical analysis of a financial statement reveals the relationship of each statement item to a specified base, which is the 100 percent figure. For example, when an income statement is subjected to vertical analysis, net sales are usually the base, and cost of goods sold, gross profit, income from operations and other items are explained in the proportion of sales.

Ratio Analysis

Ratios are important tools for financial analysis. Eight ratios are officially required by government to analyse the performance of enterprises (Ministry of Finance, 1992c). They are:

1. Debt-assets ratio. The Debt-assets ratio highlights the proportion of a company's assets that it has financed with debt. It indicates the security of debt financed operations.
   Debt-assets ratio = Total liabilities / Total assets

2. Current ratio. This measures the ability of a company to pay its liabilities.
   Current ratio = Current assets/ Current liabilities

3. Acid-Test (Quick) ratio. This measures whether the entity could pay all its current liabilities if they fell due immediately.
   Acid-Test (Quick) ratio = (Current assets − Inventory)/ Current liabilities

4. Accounts Receivable Turnover. This measures a company's ability to collect cash from credit customers.

171

Accounts receivable turnover = Net credit sales / Average net accounts receivable

5. Inventory Turnover. This is a measure of the number of times a company sells its average level of inventory during a year.
Inventory turnover = Cost of goods sold / Average inventory

6. Rate of Return of Equity. This ratio shows the relationship between net income and stockholders' investment in the company.
Rate of return of equity = Total net profit / Equity

7. Rate of Return on Net Sales. This measures the ability of a company to earn taxes and profits from sales, and is different from the western concept which excludes taxes from the calculation.
Rate of return on net sales = (Total taxes + Total profits) / Net Assets

8. Rate of Return on Total Costs. This expresses the relationship between the profits and costs and achievements and effort.
Rate of return on costs = Total profits / Total costs

Effect-Chain Analysis

The Effect-Chain analysis method is the unique to China. Its purpose is to analyse the effect of each variable in relation to overall effects. For example, when analysing profit, we know that sales price, unit cost, and tax rate all have an effect on the profit, and we want to know to what extent these factors affect the overall profit figure. Effect-Chain analysis can be used as a tool to quantify the effects of each factor.

The procedures in Effect-Chain analysis are as follows:

1. identify each variable which affects the overall results;
2. identify the relationship between variables;
3. substitute each variable once;
4. calculate the result after substitution;
5. subtract the previous figure;
6. get the figures for the effect of each variable.

172

For example, the after tax profit is used to evaluate management performance. The after tax profit is equal to sale quantity × (sales price − unit cost), or the contribution margin, × tax rate, as in the following formula:

$$P_1 = \Sigma[Q_1 * (S_1 - C_1) * (1-t_1)] \quad (\text{The Profit in This Year})$$

$$P_0 = \Sigma[Q_0 * (S_0 - C_0) * (1-t_0)] \quad (\text{The Profit in Last Year})$$

P – Profit
Q – Sale's quantity
C – Unit cost
t – Tax rate

Suppose the after tax profit increases Δ_1 yuan this year:

$$\Delta_1 = P_1 - P_0$$

This may be because of an increase in sale price or a decrease in unit cost, or because of changes in the tax rate. The purpose of using Effect-Chain analysis is to identify the effect of each variable, such as sale price, quantity, unit cost and tax rate, on the overall increasing results. The calculations of the effect of each variable are as follows:

1. Sales quantity (Q) effect on Profit
   $$\Delta_Q = \Sigma [\mathbf{Q_1} * (S_0 - C_0) * (1-t_0)] - \Sigma [Q_0 * (S_0 - C_0) * (1-t_0)]$$

2. Sales price (S) effect on Profit
   $$\Delta_S = \Sigma [Q_1 * (\mathbf{S_1} - C_0) * (1-t_0)] - \Sigma [Q_1 * (S_0 - C_0) * (1-t_0)]$$

3. Unit cost (C) effect on Profit
   $$\Delta_C = \Sigma [Q_1 * (S_1 - \mathbf{C_1}) * (1-t_0)] - \Sigma [Q_1 * (S_1 - C_0) * (1-t_0)]$$

4. Tax rate (t) effect on profit
   $$\Delta_T = \Delta C = \Sigma [Q_1 * (S_1 - C_1) * (1-\mathbf{t_1})] - \Sigma [Q_1 * (S_1 - C_1) * (1-t_0)]$$

5. Total effects of variables on the results
   $$\Delta_1 = \Delta_Q + \Delta_S + \Delta_C + \Delta_T$$

The weakness of Effect-Chain analysis is that if the substituting order is changed, the effect for each variable will be different.

Economic Accounting System

The Economic Accounting System is also sometimes called the Internal Economic Accounting System. It was brought into China from the Soviet Union in the early 1950s (Kwang, 1966). An Economic Accounting System includes: (1) Planning, (2) Financial and management accounting, (3) Management of funds (4) Analysis of enterprise economic activity. Therefore an Economic Accounting System is a broad concept. The methods discussed previously are regarded as parts of this system. Although this system was introduced into China in the 1950s, the implementation has never achieved complete success. Only parts of this system, such as the workshop and work-team accounting and funds stratification management system have been implemented in some enterprises. In the 1970s, leading state-owned enterprises such as Daqin Oil Corporation succeeded in the implementation of this system. The reasons for incomplete success in the adoption of the Economic Accounting System are:

1. The political and economic situations were unstable in the 1950s to 1970s because of the Great Leap Forward and the Cultural Revolution;
2. The ideological sensitivity of implementation of such a system which was sometimes regarded as a capitalist or revisionist method rather than a proletarian method;
3. The inherent complexity of the system which includes not only accounting but also statistics and analysis of the activities of enterprises.

The Growth of Responsibility Accounting in the 1980s

The development of responsibility accounting in China has dominated management accounting. From the historical view, China has implemented various forms of internal economic accounting, such as the work-team and workshop accounting system of the 1950s, the stratification of fund and cost management system of the 1960s, the internal economic accounting system of the 1970s. These systems have formed the basis of the current responsibility accounting system. The western version of responsibility accounting has been introduced since China reopened the door to the outside. Western responsibility accounting concepts, such as controllable and uncontrollable cost, variable and fixed cost, standard costing systems and the budgeting system were quickly adopted by Chinese academics and practitioners and this stimulated them to establish China's own responsibility accounting system. The other factor to foster the establishment of a responsibility accounting system was the implementation of the Contract Management Responsibility System (CMRS) in enterprises in 1987. The main feature of CMRS was the use of contracts to define the economic interests of enterprises and the State. The submission of taxes and profits to the State was fixed by contract according to certain criteria. Any surplus or deficiency after submission belonged to the enterprises themselves. The managers of enterprises used the same method to subdivide targets, and an internal responsibility system was established subsequently in order to subdivide the overall targets among departments and workshops. The internal responsibility accounting system was installed in most state-owned enterprises to monitor, and evaluate the performance of sub-divisions.

There is debate about how to solve the relationship between the responsibility accounting system and the traditional financial accounting system. One approach is to establish a separate internal responsibility accounting system alongside the traditional financial accounting system. The other approach is to integrate the internal responsibility accounting system within the traditional financial accounting system. These two approaches have advantages and disadvantages. For example, the two system approach is more expensive than a single system approach because there are so many similar accounting tasks in the two systems, however, the two system approach clarifies the different objectives and functions of both systems. No matter which form is adopted, the procedure to establish an internal responsibility accounting system is similar. The procedure includes: (a) to establish internal responsibility centres or internal accounting units as in the Chinese concept; (b) to set up targets and responsibility plans; (c) to set up an internal bank to deal with internal transactions; (d) to control the operation of the internal responsibility accounting system; (e) to calculate and collect the responsibility accounting and costing data; and (f) to evaluate the performance of responsibility plans and achievements.

Establishment of the Internal Responsibility Centres

There are three principles in setting up an internal responsibility centre: (1) the internal responsibility centre structure must be compatible with the existing organisational structure of the enterprise; (2) the centre must be able to conduct its accounting affairs independently, and its economic responsibilities must be clarified; and (3) the responsibilities, authorities and benefits of the centre must be integrated. According to these principles a responsibility centre can be one of the following:

1. Cost responsibility centre
    A cost responsibility centre can be established at the level of: (a) the workshop or sub-factory, (b) the work-team or work section, (c) the worker or machine, or (d) the administration department. The manager of a cost responsibility centre is only accountable for cost and the use of funds.

2. Profit responsibility centre
    Because the market mechanism has not been totally implemented in China, enterprises are subject to the market and to state plans. Some enterprises have been granted decision-making powers over sales, but not all. Accordingly, profit responsibility centres are classified as either natural profit responsibility centres which have the power to sell their products to the market, or artificial profit responsibility centres which do not sell their products to the market directly.

3. Fund-cost responsibility centres
    Fund-cost responsibility centres are the storage departments for materials, semi-finished goods and finished goods. The main goal of these centres is to minimise the funds spent on materials, semi-finished goods and finished goods. Another goal is to control the expenses of these departments.

Setting up and Breaking down the Responsibility Targets or Plans

Whereas responsibility targets in western countries are mainly financial targets, those in China include not only financial targets but also non-financial targets. Usually responsibility targets include profit, cost, fund turnover, product quantity and quality, product variety, the labour productivity rate, the

176

working time utilisation rate, the raw material consumption rate, the production safety plans, and the product innovation plans.

After the overall targets are set, they must be broken down into segments and assigned to various internal units for fulfilment. The targets are usually broken down in two ways: vertically, from enterprise level to workshop, and then from workshop to work-team and workers; and horizontally, from enterprise level to each department, and then to the persons in charge of management functions.

Setting up the Internal Transfer Prices

The methods for determining internal transfer prices in China are similar to those in western countries. A transfer price is based on: (1) planned cost; (2) planned cost plus internal profit; (3) planned variable cost plus planned fixed cost; (4) planned variable cost; (5) market price; and (6) negotiated price.

Setting up an Internal Banking System in Charge of Internal Transactions

The unique feature of the Chinese responsibility accounting system is that it usually contains an internal banking system in charge of internal transactions. There are several reasons for using such a system. Firstly, the internal responsibility units are not legal entities, and so, according to Chinese commercial law, they are not allowed to open bank accounts. Secondly, they cannot apply for bank loans from commercial banks and the only source of funding is the headquarters of the enterprise. Thirdly, from the enterprise's point of view, the headquarters wants to use interest as a tool to monitor and direct the use of funds and to allocate resources among the internal units. Therefore, most large and medium size state-owned enterprises have established internal banking systems.

The Forms and Functions of an Internal Bank

The functions of an internal bank include: (a) deciding the limit of working capital, or current funds in the Chinese concept, of each responsibility unit; (b) issuing limited working capital loans; (c) printing and issuing internal transaction documents and internal currency; (d) being in charge of internal transactions among the internal units; and (e) monitoring and controlling the efficient use of working capital or current funds.

There are two ways to set up an internal banking system: one is to set up the system in the accounting department, and the other is to set up a separate internal bank department to manage the overall funding of an enterprise. These two forms do not differ much in their functions. In the following example, we assume that an internal banking system is set up in the accounting department.

In order to establish an internal banking system, the enterprise should (a) open an internal bank account for each internal unit; (b) set operation procedures for the internal banking system; (c) clarify the authorisation for signing internal cheques and withdrawing money for each internal unit; (d) set the settlement time; (e) decide the method of calculation of the interest on internal deposits and loans.

Accounting in the Accounting and Banking Department

There are two levels of accounting in an enterprise after the establishment of an internal banking system. At the top is the accounting and banking department, which is in charge of internal transactions, adjustments of actual costs of products and evaluation of the performance of each internal unit. At the bottom level are the accounting divisions in internal units, such as in the workshops and departments which carry out routine cost accounting and internal financial reporting.

In order to perform internal banking functions, the accounting department should establish additional internal accounts as follows: (a) "Internal Working Capital", which reflects the movement of working capital in each internal unit; (b) "Internal Out-of-limit Loan", which reflects the movement of out-of-limit loans for each internal unit; (c) "Internal money", which calculates the increase or decrease of internal money in treasury; (d) "Internal Deposit", which reflects the increase and decrease of the deposit of each internal unit in the enterprise; and (e) "Issue of Internal Money", which reflects the increase or decrease of the issuing of internal money. In the Case Study 5 of the Appendix, a detailed description of the operations of an internal banking system is given based on the Nanjing Chemical Machinery Corporation.

Accounting in the Internal Units

Each internal unit has to establish its own accounting division in charge of the internal transactions with headquarters, calculation of the responsibility cost of the unit and the planned cost of products, and transferring variances to the

178

accounting department. This will adjust the cost at the enterprise level. An internal unit has to operate the following accounts to perform its tasks: "Internal Money", "Internal Deposit", "Internal Working Capital", "Internal Out-off Limit Loan", "Internal Sale" and "Internal Profit". The operation of these accounts is similar to that in a normal business.

Consolidation of Reporting in the Accounting and Banking Departments

At the end of the accounting period, the accounting and banking department needs to prepare the consolidated accounting reports. Unlike the consolidation accounting in western countries which consolidates the parent company's account with subsidiaries' accounts, the consolidation of internal reporting is quite simple under the internal banking system used in China. The reasons are: firstly, the transactions are always recorded opposite the accounts in the accounting and banking department and in the internal units; secondly, the relationship between headquarters and internal units is simpler than that between a holding company and its subsidiaries, and the headquarters and its internal units are still an integral legal entity; thirdly, all internal profits are regarded as variances of production and are transferred to the accounting department, after which the accounting department applies variances to the products to get the actual cost of products. There are no issues like unrealised profit, tax effect and goodwill. Thus, the consolidation of internal accounting used in China and consolidation accounting in the western concept is quite different except for one point in common, which is that both are adjusted in a worksheet not in the accounts themselves. At the end of the accounting period, the accounts should be off-set between the accounting and banking departments and internal units.

Figure 7-3 The Elimination of Accounts for Consolidated Accounting

Accounts used in Headquarters	Accounts used in Internal Units
Internal working Capital to Units	Σ Internal working capital from headquarters
Internal loan to units	Σ Internal loan from headquarters
Issuing of internal money – Internal money	Σ Internal Money
Internal Deposit	Σ Internal Deposit of units
	Σ (Internal profit – Internal profit appropriation) = 0

179

After the elimination of these accounts, a balance sheet of the enterprise can be derived. A profit and loss statement for the enterprise can be prepared by the accounting department directly based on the internal profit report of the final step, which is usually the sales department. The variances, administrative expenses and other receipts and expenses are adjusted.

Calculation and Collection of Accounting Data

Different accounting systems need different accounting data. For example, financial accounting needs to calculate the actual and planned costs of products; responsibility accounting needs to calculate the controllable and uncontrollable costs of responsibility centres, and decision-making accounting needs the information of variable and fixed costs to make short-term and long-term production and investment decisions. In the current situation, it may be impossible for an enterprise to have a costing system to calculate and collect all these data for different needs. The relationship between these accounting systems is illustrated in Figure 7-4.

Traditionally, the costing system is for the needs of financial accounting. With the introduction of responsibility accounting, it is necessary to have another costing system for collecting responsibility costs. Some Chinese enterprises do have two separate costing systems; one for financial accounting and the other for responsibility accounting, especially when first implementing responsibility accounting. The advantage of keeping two systems is that the traditional accounting system can operate normally and is not interrupted by the new system. However, the cost of keeping two systems is greater than the benefit because of the repetition involved. Therefore most enterprises have tried to integrate the two systems. There are two ways to integrate costing systems for financial accounting and for responsibility accounting: one is based on product costs and adjusting the responsibility costs; the other is based on responsibility costs and calculating the product cost.

Adjusting the Responsibility Costs Based on the Product Costs

Many enterprises use a costing system in which normative costs are transferred sequentially and normative variances are transferred in parallel. Although the main purpose of this method is to calculate the actual cost of products, the responsibility cost can easily be derived under this method. The features of the method are: the cost of semi-finished goods, which is calculated under normative costs; and the variances of semi-finished goods, which are transferred firstly to the account of semi-finished goods cost variance and then applied to the cost of finished goods. The procedure is illustrated in Figure 7-5.

The actual cost of products and the responsibility cost for each centre can be calculated as follows:

- Actual cost of finished goods = normative cost of finished goods ± variances of semi-finished goods and finished goods assigned to finished goods.

- Actual cost of each responsibility centre = normative cost of semi-finished goods (or finished goods) ± total variances of semi-finished goods (or finished goods).*

  Note: It is assumed that all variances are controllable by the responsibility centre. If not, the formula will be:

  Actual cost of each responsibility centre = normative cost of semi-finished goods (or finished goods) ± variances of semi-finished goods (or finished goods) - uncontrollable cost.

Adjusting the Product Cost Based on the Responsibility Cost

The costing system used in this method is mainly focused on calculation and collection of responsibility data. The actual cost of products will be adjusted based on these data. This method is not in popular use. The procedure is as shown in Figure 7-6.

- Actual responsibility cost of each unit = planned cost of controllable cost in each step ± variances of controllable cost.

- Actual costs of products = planned costs of controllable costs assigned to finished goods ± variances of controllable costs and uncontrollable costs assigned to finished goods.

181

Figure 7-4 The Needs and Relationships Between Different Accounting Systems

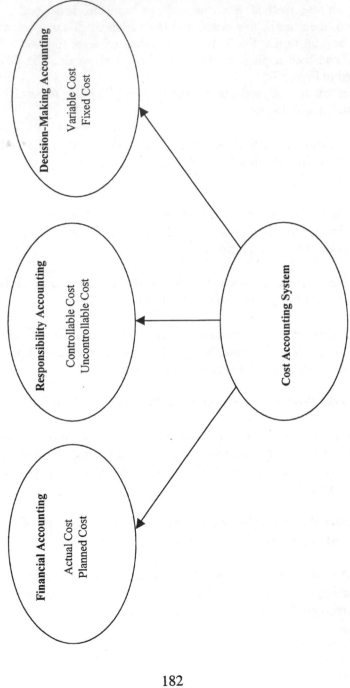

Figure 7-5 Adjusting the Responsibility Costs Based on the Product Costs

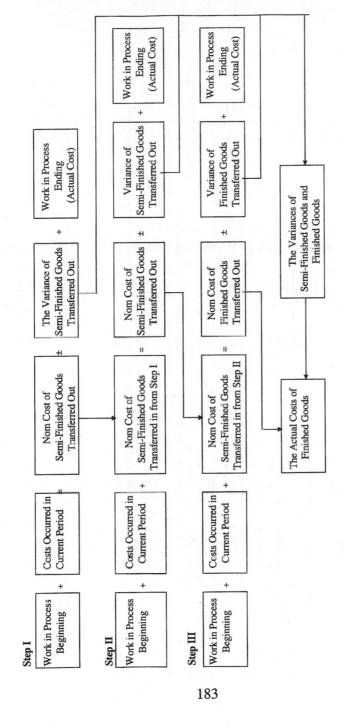

Figure 7-6 Adjusting Product Costs Based on Responsibility Costs

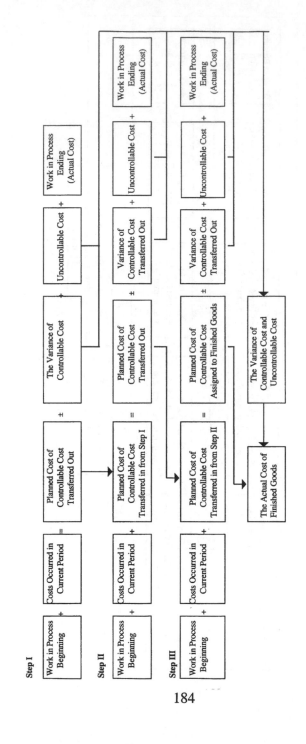

184

Some academics have suggested that using the direct cost method can provide the cost data not only for product cost, but also for responsibility cost accounting and decision-making accounting. In this system, the planned variable cost will be used in calculating the cost of semi-finished goods and work in process and the variances of variable cost and fixed cost will transfer directly to a joint account in the headquarters. Then, the joint cost will be applied to individual departments and products. However, this cost system has not yet been adopted regularly by enterprises because of its inherent complexity.

Evaluation of the Performance of Each Responsibility Centre

As targets for each responsibility centre include financial targets and also non-financial targets, the evaluation of the performance of each responsibility centre is based on a synthetic figure which integrates the measure of each target. Usually, a point evaluation system is used by an enterprise to evaluate the performance of each responsibility centre, as illustrated in Figure 7-7.

The incentive system consists of material incentives and moral incentives. Material incentives include bonuses, housing, and cars which are given to individuals who achieve their personal targets. Moral incentives are intended to encourage workers to work for the good of the enterprise as a whole, and include allowing workers to participate in decision-making. Also certificates and medals are given to excellent workers. Before economic reform, moral incentives were the main incentives used to motivate and promote workers, especially in the 1950s. The reactions from workers were quite positive, with most workers proud to get a medal for excellent work. Since 1979, enterprises have heavily used material incentives to motivate and promote workers because the appetites of most workers have changed and they have become more realistic and money-oriented. In some enterprises the bonus payments are two or three times normal wage payments. However the reactions from workers are indifferent and their working enthusiasm has not been lifted very much. The reason is that with the high inflation rate in China, workers regard the bonus payments as compensation for high inflation rather than as incentives (He and Lin, 1991).

185

Figure 7-7 Point Evaluation System

Targets	Basic point	Fluctuate point
Production Quantity	20	+(-) 0.1 points as quantity +(-) 10%
Production Cost	20	+(-) 2 points as cost - (+) 1%
Production Quality	20	No point if the quality does not meet the requirement
Production Variety	20	No point if the variety does not meet the requirement
Internal Profit	20	+(-) 2 points as internal profit +(-) 1%
Utilising of Funds	20	+ (-) 0.2 points as utilising of funds +(-) 1%
Total:	120	

Conclusion

The history of modern Chinese management accounting is relatively short. Management accounting was developed from early this century under the influence of the west. After the 1949 revolution, Chinese management accounting followed the Soviet model. Workshop and work-team accounting, target stratification management systems, economic activity analysis and economic accounting systems were all developed from the Soviet Union. The real improvement in management accounting came from the development of the Chinese version of responsibility accounting in the early 1980s. This system is inspired by the standard cost system used in the west and has developed into a form that is suitable for Chinese economic conditions. This can be regarded as the Chinese contribution towards management accounting, especially in decentralised organisations, for the measurements of a division's performance.

8 A Survey of the Application of Western Management Accounting in China

While management accounting theory had existed in the west for decades, it was not known in China until the late 1970s. Since China re-opened its doors in 1978, western management accounting theories and practices have been gradually introduced and accepted by Chinese accounting academics and practitioners (Yang, 1982). Table 8-1, derived from a survey conducted in China by the author in 1995/96, shows this adoption process.

Table 8-1 The Adopting Pattern of Western Management Accounting in China

Items	Numbers	Percentage (%)
Time of learning about western management accounting		
(1) Before 1979	1	2.2
(2) 1979-1984	35	77.8
(3) 1984-1994	7	15.6
(4) Still unknown	2	4.4

As can be seen in Table 8-1, most accountants learned about western management accounting in the late 70s and early 80s. Only one accountant said that he learned western management accounting before 1979. Nowadays, management accounting is regarded as a core course in tertiary accounting education. The contents in the management accounting course in China are almost identical to those in western countries. The young generation of accountants has mastered western management accounting theories and techniques. However, their successful application in practice is still doubtful. The aim of this chapter is to investigate the application of western management accounting theories and techniques in Chinese enterprises and to look at Chinese accountants' comments on their usefulness.

Research Design

The gap between management accounting theory and practice has been addressed by many western academics (Kaplan, 1984, Emmanuel and Edwards 1990, Drury et al, 1992). This thesis will provide further evidence of the practical value of management accounting in a different cultural environment, China. Considering the previous surveys conducted by western scholars, a special questionnaire was designed which integrated the traditional Chinese management accounting methods with western management accounting techniques. There were 22 questions in the survey that covered all of the aspects of management accounting methods, from short term to long term decision models and from budgeting methods to responsibility accounting. The questionaries were translated into Chinese and sent to 150 financial managers, financial controllers and chief accountants in different types of Chinese enterprises, including state-owned, private and foreign-funded enterprises. A total of 52 responses were returned – a 34.6 per cent response rate, and 45 responses were useable.

Besides mailing the questionaries to the Chinese enterprises, 21 interviews were conducted in Chinese enterprises in Nanjing, Beijing and Shanghai. On several occasions, financial managers, financial controllers and chief accountants attended the interviews.

Results and Analysis

Although it is alleged that there are fundamentally ideological differences between Chinese management accounting and western management accounting, western ideas have proved to be acceptable to the Chinese, at least from an academic point of view. Just as McDonalds, KFC and other western fast foods have been accepted in this oriental country, so have different methods of western management accounting received varying degrees of favour from Chinese practitioners according to the "practical value" they are perceived to have. The findings and comments on this survey are summarised as follows.

Accountants' Role in Management

Despite the overwhelming approval of western management accounting methods, the traditional management accounting methods still dominate in practice. Most accountants believe that these management accounting practices existed in China before people were aware of western ideas (see Table 8-2).

Most respondents recognised their enterprises as profit centres or investment centres. It is worthwhile to note that nearly 40 per cent of them classified their enterprises as investment centres. This is consistent with the recent trend of enterprise structure reforms, transforming most state-owned enterprises to shareholder corporations. However, in comparing the answers for question 4 with those for question 8, some contradictions can be found. In question 8, 68.9 per cent of respondents admitted that the long-term investment decision powers still belong to government authorities. This would seem to imply that it is possible, even after most enterprises transform successfully into shareholders' corporations in the future, they may not get substantial investment decision powers.

Compared with accountants in western countries, accountants in China play a less important role in management decision-making. Only 22.2 per cent of them said that they are heavily involved in decision-making. This is because in a traditional enterprise management, the planning department rather than the accounting department is in charge of long term and short term investment. The functions of the accounting department are to provide accurate and timely cost, profit and fund data to the related government authorities and internal departments. The role of the accounting department in such organisations is rather passive and the suggestions and opinions from the accounting department are often regarded by management as too conservative and lacking in foresight. This conflict between management and accountants should be investigated further. The Chinese management style is to exaggerate achievements and to minimise weaknesses. Sometimes the management ignores the accounting figures and even forces accountants to change the figures to fit with what they want to claim.

Table 8-2 Recognition of Traditional Management Accounting Methods

Items	Numbers	Percentage (%)
Do you believe management accounting practices existed before you became aware of western theories and practices?		
(1)Yes	40	88.9
(2) No	3	6.7
(3) Cannot decide	2	4.4
Which of the following can be classified as management accounting with Chinese characteristics		
(1) Workshop and work-team accounting	40	88.9
(2)Targets stratification management accounting		84.4
(3) Economic accounting	35	77.8
(4) Finance management	30	66.7
(5) Economic activity analysis	38	84.4

Table 8-3 Classification of Enterprises

Items	Numbers	Percentage (%)
Cost centre	7	15.6
Profit centre	20	44.4
Investment centre	18	40

Table 8-4 The Role of Accountants in Management

Items	Numbers	Percentage (%)
Do accountants in your enterprise play an important role in management decision-making?		
(1) Yes	10	22.2
(2) No	25	55.6
(3) Cannot decide	10	22.2

Technically, enterprises can design their own costing systems. However, they should follow certain governmental regulations. This is particularly true for the state-owned enterprises. As shown in this survey, there are similarities among the costing systems in different enterprises. In most of the enterprises, costs are sub-classified as direct materials, direct labour, and overhead. The methods for allocation of overheads are similar to the two-stage overhead allocation method in the west, in which costs are allocated from functional departments to production departments, and then from production departments to products, although the detailed procedures are more complicated than in the west. The overheads absorbed are mostly based on direct labour costs or direct labour hours and machine hours.

The use of normative costing has declined since the introduction of standard costing. Normative costing was designed mainly for the purpose of cost determination rather than cost control. Under the standard costing method, variances are categorised in accordance with responsibility centres, whereas under normative costing, variances are categorised in accordance with products. Chinese academics and practitioners argued against the normative costing system because of the variability of its norms and its neglect of cost behaviour, so that this system is greatly restricted in its use for cost control (Dai, 1984).

Table 8-5 Application of Costing Methods

Items	Numbers	Percentage (%)
Usage of costing systems:		
(1) Full-absorption costing system	0	0
(2) Manufacturing costing system	45	100
(3) Direct costing system	0	0
(4) Activity-based costing system	0	0
Associated with:		
(1) Standard costing	15	33.3
(2) Normative costing	8	17.9
(3) Actual costing	22	48.8
Total	45	100

If an enterprise has more than one workshop, the multi-overhead pools are used and normally each workshop has its own overhead pool. As the submission of production cost statements was mandatory before the issue of the first Chinese accounting standard in 1993, the contents of the overheads prior to 1993 were standardised among enterprises. Although the production cost information is no longer required by the government authorities and cost management has been deregulated, in the short-term practices in cost accounting have not changed significantly. The contents of overheads in a typical enterprise are shown in Table 8-7.

Internal Transfer Price

As shown in Table 8-8, popular methods for setting up internal transfer prices are: full cost of product, full cost plus internal profit and negotiated price.

Table 8-6 Absorption of Overheads

Items	Numbers	Percentage (%)
How do you apply overhead to the products? The Bases are:		
(1) Direct labour costs	13	28.9
(2) Direct labour hours	15	33.4
(3) Machine hours	10	22.2
(4) Units produced	3	6.7
(5) Material costs	2	4.4
(6) Material quantities	2	4.4
(7) Other cost drivers	0	0

**Table 8-7 The Overhead Costs in Workshop II in Orient Printing
Corporation**

Items	Costs
(1) Wages of non-production personnel (including workshop managers and supporting staff)	3,050
(2) Welfare of non-production personnel	1,100
(3) Depreciation costs	5,450
(4) Maintenance costs	2,000
(5) Office costs	150
(6) Water and electricity costs	4,300
(7) Heating costs	250
(8) Rent costs	4,780
(9) Sundry materials costs	2,430
(10) Insurance premiums	120
(11) Work-protection costs	180
(12) Loss on work-in-process	1,030
(13) Design costs	690
(14) Testing and investigating costs	970
(15) Travelling costs	200
(16) Transportation costs	150
(17) Other costs	70
Total:	26,920

Table 8-8 Internal Transfer Price Bases

How do you decide an internal transfer price, is it according to:	Numbers	Percentage (%)
(1) Market price	5	11.1
(2) Full cost of product	11	24.4
(3) Direct cost	1	2.3
(4) Full cost plus internal profit	15	33.3
(5) Direct cost plus internal profit	3	6.7
(6) Negotiated price	10	22.2

Slack Reaction in Practice to Western Management Accounting Methods

Response to the Cost-Profit-Volume (CVP) Model

The Cost-Profit-Volume model is the most successful method used by practitioners in western countries. This model was introduced into China at the end of the 1970s. It seems that the CVP has been accepted by most Chinese enterprises: 68.9 per cent use this method in different ways as shown in Table 8-9. However, nearly one-fourth of businesses have not used the CVP in making short-term decisions and some enterprises do not know of the CVP at all.

There are reasons for the acceptance of the CVP technique in China: (a) The model is technically rather than ideologically oriented; (b) The Chinese economy is open to outside markets and enterprises are becoming more market oriented; and (c) the CVP technique is easy to understand and practice.

Table 8-9 Application of CVP Analysis in Chinese Enterprises

Items:	Numbers	Percentage (%)
Usage of CVP analysis	31	68.9
(1) In the analysis of past costs, production and profit	30	66.7
(2) In forecasting of costs, production and profit	25	55.6
(3) In deciding of product pricing	11	24.4
(4) In the decision whether to make or buy products	8	17.8
(5) In the decision about whether to continue or drop current products	4	8.9
Non-usage of CVP analysis	12	26.7
Unknown CVP analysis	2	4.4
Total:	45	100

Response to Responsibility Accounting and Standard Costing

In the early 1980s when western management accounting was introduced into China, western responsibility accounting systems and standard costing attracted considerable interest from Chinese academics and practitioners.

Most of them argued that western methods were superior and should replace the existing methods.

There did exist a Chinese version of responsibility accounting, known as Internal Economic Accounting (IAE) (Kwang, 1966), prior to the introduction of western responsibility accounting (RA). There are two differences between IEA and RA: (1) the general goal of the system, which in IEA is to maximise quantitative output, and in RA it is to maximise profit; and (2) performance measures and incentive devices, which in IEA have a collective orientation and in RA have an individual orientation. The IEA system puts more emphasis on moral incentives than material incentives.

The western responsibility accounting and standard costing systems have been familiar to the Chinese for over 15 years. The application of these methods is shown in Table 8-10:

Table 8-10 Application of Responsibility Accounting

Items	Numbers	Percentage (%)
(1) The Responsibility Accounting System been established	34	75.6
Based on: Workshops as cost centres	11	32.3
Workshops as profit centres	15	44.1
Functional departments as costs centres	5	14.7
Functional departments as profit centres	3	8.9
(1-1) The Responsibility Accounting System is efficient	18	52.9
(1-2) The Responsibility Accounting System is not efficient	16	47.1
(2) The Responsibility Accounting System has not been established	11	22.4
Total	45	100

It is worthwhile noting that, although 75.6 per cent enterprises have established responsibility accounting systems they themselves do not seem to be efficient. Nearly half of the respondents indicted that their responsibility accounting systems are ineffective because they found these systems were too complicated to implement. The efforts of managers and accountants to enhance and improve the systems are declining. The reasons can be summarised as: (a) The responsibility accounting system was linked with the

195

Contract Responsibility System implemented in most state-owned enterprises during the middle of the 1980s. Since the Contract Responsibility System has been substituted by various types of shareholder systems, the responsibility accounting system has lost its popularity; (b) China has advocated a socialist market economy and so most enterprises have been driven into competitive markets. With high inflation and intensive competition, managers have recognised that it is easy to increase the profit by increasing product price rather than reducing cost. Therefore their attention has shifted from emphasising internal management and cost reduction to increasing prices and/or expanding their market. As the main goals of the responsibility accounting system are to enhance the internal management and reduce costs, there is no doubt that the system has lost favour with managers and accountants; (c) The Chinese market is still developing and prices of commodities have not been rationalised. Also, there is a high inflation rate in China now. Therefore, it is difficult for accountants to design standard costs. These might change every year, or even every month.

Response to Budgeting Methods

Some Chinese scholars have asserted that western budgeting methods are very similar to the production and financial planning systems already used in Chinese enterprises. The only real difference between the two systems at a technical level is that the budgeting process in the west begins with the sales budget, whereas the traditional Chinese planning process begins with production plans (Bromwich and Wang, 1991). However the differences between Chinese and western budgeting are, in fact, quite wide. A typical budgeting system in China is illustrated in Figure 8-1:

Figure 8-1 The Budgeting and Planning System Used in China

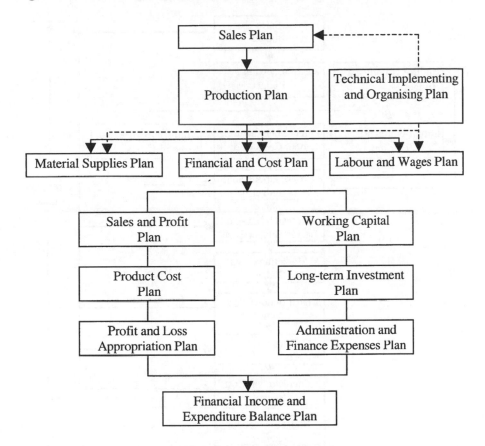

A typical western budgeting system is illustrated as in Figure 8-2 by Charles T. Horngren and Foster (1991) in his well-known text, *Cost Accounting: A Managerial Emphasis* (p. 177).

Figure 8-2 Master Budget for Halifax Engineering

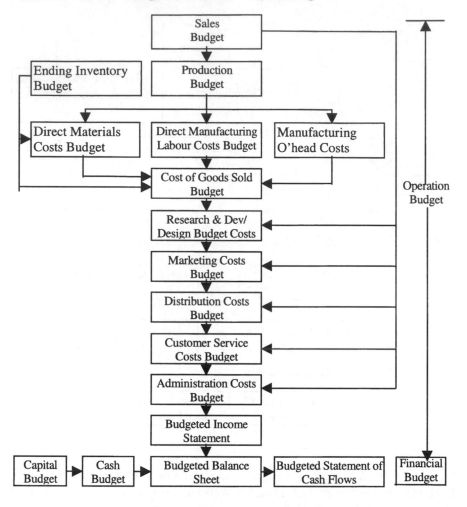

When these two budget systems are compared, it is easy to recognise that the western budget system is more systematic than the Chinese. In China, the budgeted income statement, the budgeted balance sheet and the budgeted statement of cash flow are not required. Therefore, in fact, there are two different budgeting approaches: the Chinese traditional budgeting approach, which ends up with the financial income and the expenditure balance plan; and the western master budget, which contains a set of budgeted income statements, a balance sheet and a statement of cash flows. The use of budgeting approaches and methods in Chinese enterprises is shown in Table 8-11:

Table 8-11 Application of Budgeting Approaches and Methods

Items	Numbers	Percentage (%)
Usage of budgeting approach		
(1) Chinese traditional budgeting approach	41	91.1
(2) Western budgeting approach	4	8.9
Usage of budgeting methods		
(1) Rolling budget (based on historical data)	25	55.6
(2) Zero base budget	1	2.2
(3) Flexible budget	4	8.9
(4) Planning budget (based on planned targets)	15	33.3

As shown in Table 8-11, 91.1 per cent of Chinese enterprises still use the traditional budget approach. The rolling budget (55.6 per cent) and planning budget (33.3 per cent) methods are most popular. Zero base and flexible budgeting have not yet been adopted by most enterprises. The biggest problem in adopting western budget methods, that the author has observed, is not ideological or cultural barriers: most managers and accountants are willing to use them. It is rather a technical problem because most accounting systems in China are still manual systems and the application of computer systems is in the early stages.

The second difference between the Chinese and western budgeting is the procedure of designing and implementing the budget. In China this procedure is a dual process in which both managers and workers participate in the budget-setting. The budget is designed by senior managers and accountants and is then sent to factories, workshops and individual workers for comment; a process which operates from top to bottom. Based on the budget draft and their own situation, each factory, workshop and worker adjusts the contents of the budget and then sends the revised budget back to the headquarters of the enterprise, by this process of bottom to top. This dual process reflects the unique features of Chinese management philosophy: democratic management, mass-line management and mass participation in decision-making. It is widely utilised in management accounting on the basis that, by participating in the budget setting process, workers and managers can recognise the value of self-motivation and self-development. They understand that their behaviour directly influences the attainment of enterprise targets.

Response to Long-term Investment Methods

As shown in Table 8-12, the authority for investment decision-making is mostly monopolised by higher governmental agencies. The capital budgeting techniques used at the enterprise level seem to be rather irrational. Most interviewees claimed that long term investment is decided by whoever has the power, no matter whether the project is profitable or not. The survey also shows only simple methods such as the pay-back period method and accounting return on investment are used in Chinese enterprises.

There are many factors restricting the use of western capital budgeting techniques. Firstly, in the traditional planned economy, people lacked awareness of the value of time, and this is still a serious problem in the current situation. For example, the interest on loans and deposits is still calculated as simple interest rather than compound interest. Therefore, Discount Cash Flow (DCF) methods are not appropriate in China. Secondly market mechanisms do not fully operate in China: there is limited availability of physical assets and electricity, investment is restricted and there is always a shortage of main production resources for enterprises. Thirdly, enterprises in China were only cost centres before reform, and are only profit centres since reform. They have never been granted the full title of investment centres. Therefore it is not necessary for enterprises themselves to use sophisticated capital budgeting methods to evaluate investment decisions, because the responsibility for evaluation belongs to government authorities. This situation may change in the future because most state-owned enterprises have now been reorganised into shareholder corporations, and this means that most enterprises will have more responsibility for their own investment.

Table 8-12 Application of Long-term Investment Methods

Items	Numbers	Percentage (%)
The decision maker of long-term investment		
(1) Government authorities	31	68.9
(2) Board of directors	5	11.1
(3) Managers of the enterprises	8	17.8
(4) Accounting department of enterprises		0
(5) Planning department of enterprises	1	2.2
Usage of method in long-term investment		
(1) Decided by person who has the power	26	57.8
(2) Pay-back period	11	24.4
(3) Accounting return on investment	4	8.9
(4) Return on investment	3	6.7
(5) Discounted pay-back period		
(6) Net present value	1	2.2
(7) Present value index		
(8) Internal rate of return		

Response to Advanced Costing Method: Activity-Based Costing

There are three cost approaches used in western countries: traditional costing, modern costing and activity-based costing. The features of each can be summarised as follows:

- In the traditional costing approach, the costs of a product can be calculated by: (a) charging each product for standard raw materials; (b) charging each product for standard labour costs; (c) assigning overhead costs to the product based on a two-stage allocation formula.
- In the modern costing approach some changes have been made in the calculation of product costs: (a) set-up labour is broken out from the overhead pool and charged to each product based on set-up time per production run divided by the number of units in a production run; (b) the overhead that is more related to material cost is broken out and charged to products based on material cost rather than labour cost; and (c) machine hours are substituted for labour dollars (or labour hours) in the measure of production value.

201

However, in activity-based costing (ABC), the fundamental concept of costing has been altered. Activity-based costing traces costs to products based on the production and marketing activities which give rise to the cost. This costing procedure is based on the premise that one should look at the actual transactions that drives overhead costs, rather than allocating costs solely on some measure of physical volume.

Activity-based costing is a new concept for Chinese accountants. Several articles on it have been published in Chinese accounting journals, but, as shown in Table 8-5, so far no enterprise is using this method and the response to it would seem to be indifferent. The reasons why the ABC method is not popular in China can be explained as follows:

1. Currently, cost information in China is generated largely by the direct costs of materials and labour. Cost is equal to direct materials plus direct labour and overhead (Cost = Direct Material + Direct Labour + Overhead), therefore overhead is equal to cost minus direct material and labour (Overhead = Cost - (Direct Material + Direct Labour)). This formula means that overhead is a residual item in the traditional costing approach. As long as the total cost of a product can represent the direct costs significantly, there is no need to adopt a new cost approach.

    Most industries in China are labour intensive. Direct materials and direct labour make up the major proportion of the cost of products. In some industries, direct materials and labour make up 80 per cent of total costs and even more. The overhead is still a residual item in the calculation of product costs. In contrast, in some western industries, if the cost of a product is based on the traditional cost approach in which overhead is applied to the product based on labour hours or value, this is misleading for management decision-makers because the overhead is no longer a residual item and may be three to five times the direct costs. Hence, the ABC method has been adopted in some western industries.

2. There is a lack of technology in China, e.g. computers, to measure transactions. Activity-based costing, which is in effect transaction costing, requires new technology, especially the use of computers in manufacturing, such as computer aided manufacturing (CAM), and flexible manufacturing systems (FMS). With these systems, the data

related to the costs of each activity can be collected easily and it is possible to use activity-based costing in such a high technical environment. However, the level of automation and computerised manufacturing in China is relatively low in most industries and it is impossible for enterprises to measure the costs of each activity. There is no doubt, however, that activity based costing will be adopted in high technology industries in the future.

3.   Chinese costing methods are regulated by governmental authorities and enterprises lack incentive to invent new costing methods. In China, accountants' ability and motivation to innovate and create are restricted by the rigid regulations imposed on enterprises, such as the uniform accounting system, cost regulation and depreciation scheme. Most Chinese accountants are rule followers and play a passive role in the development of accounting techniques. This situation has to be changed if China wants to catch up and compete with the rest of the world.

Response to Inventory Control and the Just-in-time (JIT) Method

The most widely accepted definition of Just-in-time (JIT) is the constant and relentless pursuit of the elimination of waste, with waste being defined as:

> anything that does not add value to a product such as inspection, queue time and stock. The common denominator for this concept is the pursuit of zero inventories, zero defects, flexibility, and zero schedule interruptions (McLhattan, 1987, p.21).

The Just-in-time philosophy has significant impact on cost accounting, for example, in the identification of cost drivers, the number of product cost elements, the application of product costs and the nature of performance measures. However, the implementation of JIT requires an extremely stable external environment, including constant stable supply and distribution markets. As the market is so fluctuating in China and there is almost always a shortage of the main raw materials, electricity, water, and funds, there is no doubt that the adoption of JIT in Chinese management accounting has a long way to go. The methods used in inventory control are shown in Table 8-13.

As indicated in Table 8-13, not only has the JIT not been applied in Chinese enterprises, but also the Economic-order-quantity method has not been widely adopted in China.

Table 8-13 Application of Inventory Control Methods

Items	Numbers	Percentage (%)
(1) Fund stratification management system	39	86.7
(2) Economic-order-quantity	4	8.9
(3) Just-in-time method	0	
(4) Classification management method	41	91.1

Response to Mathematical Modelling

All of the respondents indicated that no mathematical model (Table 8-14), such as linear programming, simple regression, multiple regression, non-linear programming is currently used in their enterprises. One can not draw the conclusion absolutely from this survey that mathematical modelling has not been used in China because only 45 enterprises were observed. However, the survey indicates that mathematical models are unpopular among enterprises.

Table 8-14 Application of Mathematical Models

Which of the following mathematical models are used in your enterprise's management planning and analysis?	Numbers	Percentage (%)
(1) Linear programming	0	0
(2) Simple regression	0	0
(3) Multiple regression	0	0
(4) Non-linear programming	0	0
(5) None of the above	45	100

The General Attitude of Chinese Accountants Towards Western Management Accounting

As shown in the above two sections, traditional Chinese cost methods have been predominant in the practice. The adoption of western management has been slow, except for the short-term decision methods, such as CVP analysis and variable and fixed cost concepts. The general attitude of Chinese accountants towards western management accounting is very important because this attitude indicates the future trend and the possibility of western methods being adopted.

Three questions were designed to test the attitude of Chinese accountants towards western management accounting. The first question was: "Do you think western accounting theories and practices are suitable for China?". As shown in Table 8-15, most Chinese accountants (68.9 per cent) replied that western accounting theories and practices are suitable for China but need to be modified. However, 15.6 per cent indicated that western management accounting is not suitable for China because the level of management development in China is low, and there are also other environmental factors, such as lack of market mechanisms. It is interesting to note that the ideological differences between capitalism and socialism no longer hampers the adoption of western management skills. Only three people replied that western accounting is not suitable for China because it is based upon capitalist economic theory. This is in contrast to the situation when western management accounting was first introduced into China at the end of the 1970s, when there was a great debate over the suitability of western management methods to China (Bromwich and Wang, 1991).

Table 8-15 General Attitude towards Western Accounting

Do you think western accounting theories and practices are suitable for China?	Numbers	Percentage (%)
(1) Yes, absolutely suitable	4	8.8
(2) Yes, but need to be modified	31	68.9
(3) No, because western management accounting is based upon capitalist economic theory	3	6.7
(4) No, because the level of management development in China is lower and there are also other environmental factors	7	15.6

When the respondents were asked which western accounting concepts and methods are most useful for Chinese enterprises, their answers were: cost-volume-profit analysis (93.3 per cent); variable and fixed cost concepts (88.9 per cent); responsibility accounting systems (84.4 per cent); budgeted methods (77.8 per cent); standard costing (per cent); and quality accounting and Total Quality Control (TQC) (66.7 per cent) are the most popular. The most impractical methods are long-term investment appraisal techniques (44.4 per cent), mathematical models for cost estimating and forecasting (22.2 per cent), agency theory (6.7 per cent) and behavioural theories (2.2 per cent).

Table 8-16   The Perception of the Usefulness of Western Management Accounting Methods

Which of the following western accounting concepts and methods are most useful for Chinese enterprises?	Numbers	Percentage (%)
(1) Variable and fixed cost concepts	40	88.9
(2) Cost-volume-profit analysis	42	93.9
(3) Long-term investment appraisal techniques	20	44.4
(4) Budgeted methods	35	77.8
(5) Responsibility accounting systems	38	84.4
(6) Standard costing	32	71.1
(7) Agency theory	3	6.7
(8) Mathematical models for cost estimating and forecasting	10	22.2
(9) Quality accounting and total quality control (TQC)	30	66.7
(10) Behavioural theory	1	2.2

It is not surprising that quality accounting and total quality control (TQC) are recognised by Chinese as the most useful western methods. Recently, a series of Total Quality Control campaigns have been promoted by the governmental authorities among enterprises in order to solve one of the two serious management problems in China: low efficiency and poor product quality. Under the inspiration of TQC from western countries, especially Japan, Chinese practitioners have devised a number of quality cost accounting systems in several enterprises. The objective of quality cost accounting is to enhance quality control. The elements of quality accounting include: (a) prevention costs, such as costs of designing quality control systems, employee

206

training, and quality improvement; (b) scrutiny costs, such as materials inspection costs, product inspection costs and inspection equipment costs; (c) defect costs, which include internal defect costs such as the costs of spoilage, reworking and production procedure break-down, and (d) external defect costs, such as warrant expenses, the cost of returned products, the discounting of defective products, and liability claims.

Agency theory has not received much attention among accounting academics and practitioners in China, although it has been suggested that the responsibility contract system used in China can be explained as an agency relationship (Scapens and Meng, 1993). However, this principal-agent relationship is quite different from the western concept. It is our belief that more and more Chinese scholars will pay attention to agency theory because it is potentially useful to explain the failure of the experiments of responsibility contract systems and to define the precise relationship between the State as an owner and enterprises as agents.

Compared to the agency theory, behavioural theories have suffered more criticism in China. Although they have been studied for a long time, the attitudes of most researchers are biased and these theories are regarded as non-scientific and sometimes as anti-Marxist and anti-Maoist. The fundamental issue is that the nature of the human being has never been recognised by the authorities: people are treated as physical beings without feelings who are supposed to act like robots and follow strictly the commands of the authorities (Ji, 1990).

The third question was "Do you think you need to establish your own management accounting procedures with Chinese characteristics? If the answer is 'yes', what are the Chinese characteristics?". Fifty-three point three per cent of the respondents said "yes" and 46.7 per cent said "no". The controversy remains as only a few people identified the Chinese features essential in developing its own management accounting. The three major features suggested are mass participation, emphasis on the moral incentive and understandability.

Table 8-17 The Needs of Management Accounting with Chinese Features

Do you need to establish your own management accounting procedures with Chinese characteristics? If the answer is yes, please identify three features you think are needed to establish a Chinese management accounting system.	Numbers	Percentage (%)
(1)Yes	24	53.3
(a) mass participation	6	13.3
(b) emphasis on moral incentive	3	6.7
(c) understandability	4	8.9
(2) No	21	46.7

Conclusion Remarks on the Survey

This survey has examined the application of western management accounting methods in China. The major findings are: (1) the traditional Chinese cost methods have been predominant in practice; (2) the adoption of western management is slow, except in the short-term decision methods, such as CVP analysis and variable and fixed cost concepts; (3) the Chinese accountants' attitude towards western management accounting is enthusiastic and encouraging. It is interesting to see from this survey that most accountants in China have overcome the ideological barriers between capitalism and socialism. This indicates western management accounting methods will eventually be accepted by the Chinese. The major obstacles in absorbing western ideas are environmental factors rather than political factors: the market mechanism in China is not mature, the enterprise structure is still under reform, and entrepreneurial spirits have not been fully encouraged to date.

9 Empirical Research Factors Influencing the Development of Chinese Accounting

Introduction

Accounting researchers have tried to identify the reasons why different accounting patterns exist in the world (Mueller, 1967, Choi and Mueller, 1992, Gray, 1988). They argue that the accounting system in a particular country is a consequence of political, economic and social interaction and then analyse the influence of environmental factors on the development of accounting. Choi and Mueller (1992) listed a wider set of influences which they believed had a direct effect upon accounting development. These included (1) legal system; (2) political system; (3) nature of business ownership; (4) differences in size and complexity of business firms; (5) social climate; (6) level of sophistication of business management and the financial community; (7) degree of legislative business interference; (8) presence of specific accounting legislation; (9) speed of business innovations; (10) stage of economic development; (11) growth pattern of an economy and (12) status of professional education and organisation.

Farmer and Richman (1966) classified environmental characteristics into four major groups: educational, sociocultural, legal and political, and economic. There are a number of elements within each group: for example, the educational characteristics encompass (1) the degree of literacy, including the ability to use simple mathematics, (2) the percentage of people who have received formal schooling at various levels, (3) the basic orientation of the educational system (religious, vocational, liberal arts, scientific, professional), and (4) the educational match – the appropriateness of the educational system's output for the country's economic and social needs.

Belkaoui also presented an international accounting contingency framework to explain national differences in international accounting (Belkaoui, 1985). The main elements of the framework include cultural relativism, linguistic relativism, political and civil relativism, economic and demographic relativism, and legal and tax relativism.

Alhashim and Arpan (1988) classified environmental influences on accounting into sociocultural conditions, legal and political conditions and economic conditions. They claim that economic conditions have the greatest influences on accounting:

> Fundamentally, the complexity of the economy is directly related to accounting complexity. As an economy becomes more complex, so too do types of economic transactions, such as credit sales, leases, mergers, and acquisitions – complexities that also require more complex accounting procedures (p.8).

In the sociocultural conditions, they argue that a people's attitude towards secrecy, time, fate and business can influence accounting. The attitude toward secrecy is related to the degree of trust that people have in each other and in their institutions. Where people are generally secretive, they are not likely to provide much information to others, whether in accounting or in any other field.

The attitude towards time is related to whether people take a long-term or short-term view of business. Alhashim and Arpan argue that, where people have a longer view of time and a diminished sense of urgency, the balance sheet is likely to be given more importance than the income statement, and financial reports are likely to be published less frequently.

Alhashim and Arpan believe that a people's attitude towards fate also affects accounting, particularly certain aspects of managerial accounting. If the dominant belief is that there is no control over events or life in general, then there is little perceived need for planning, budgeting, performance evaluation, or other means of control.

Finally, they argue that a people's attitude towards business in general affects the degree of public disclosure and the amount of social responsibility of accounting. A negative or distrustful attitude towards business will be more likely to result in legislation that requires greater disclosure in, and greater reliability or verifiability of, financial statements.

Lawrence (1996) believes that environmental factors that influence the development of the national accounting framework that exists in the world are cultural, political, legal and economic factors. Cultural factors include people's assumptions and attitudes towards reporting. Personal beliefs, aspirations and motivations affect information requirements; interpersonal relationships affect the level of acceptance of governmental control; and social structure determines the status of the accountant. Political factors are more concerned about governmental interventions into accounting regulations and professions. Legal factors include the national legal framework, details of accounting legislation and legal enforcement of accounting decisions. Economic factors include forms of organizations, sources of finance, role of the accounting profession and sophistication of users of accounting information.

Cultural Influences on Accounting

Hofstede's Cultural Dimensions

The impact of culture on accounting has attracted more and more researchers. Among them, Gray (1988) is one of the first papers to introduce Hofstede's cultural dimensions into accounting. Since then, the number of papers on culture and accounting have grown quickly (Perera, 1989; Doupnik and Salter, 1995; Salter and Niswander, 1995; Cray and Vint, 1995; and Zarsekei, 1996). Culture has been defined by Kroeber and Kluckhohn (1952) as follows:

> Culture consists of patterns, explicit and implicit, of and for behaviour acquired and transmitted by symbols, constituting the distinctive achievements of human groups, including their embodiments in artefacts; the essential core of culture consists of traditional (i.e. historically derived and selected) ideas and especially their attached values; Cultural systems may on one hand be considered as products of actions, on the other as conditioning elements of further action.

Hofstede (1980, 1984, 1987 and 1991) is the pioneer of culture researchers and his model is widely accepted as the analytical tool to diagnosis the cultural influences on not just accounting, but other disciplines. Hofstede (1980) defined culture as:

> The collective programming of the mind which distinguishes the members of one group from another.

He argued that culture is "the software of mind" which includes a set of societal values that underpin people's thinking, feeling and potential acting. Based on extensive surveys carried out on employees in a multinational corporation, IBM, located in more than 50 countries, Hofstede identified four universal dimensions of national culture that are significantly different among countries. They are individualism versus collectivism; large versus small power distance; strong versus weak uncertainty avoidance; and masculinity versus femininity. He described them in details as follows (Hofstede, 1984):

Individualism versus Collectivism

Individualism stands for a preference for a loosely knit social framework in society wherein individuals are supposed to take care of themselves and their immediate families only. Its opposite, collectivism, stands for a preference for a tightly knit social framework in which individuals can expect their relatives, clan, or other in-group to look after them in exchange for unquestioning loyalty. The fundamental issue addressed by this dimension is the degree of interdependence a society maintains among individuals.

Large versus Small Power Distance

Power Distance is the extent to which the members of a society accept that power in institutions and organisations is distributed unequally. This affects the behaviour of the less powerful as well as of the more powerful members of society. People in Large Power Distance societies accept a hierarchical order in which everybody has a place which needs no further justification. People in Small Power Distance societies strive for power equalisation and demand justification for power inequalities. The fundamental issue addressed by this dimension is how a society handles inequalities among people when they occur.

Strong versus Weak Uncertainty Avoidance

Uncertainty Avoidance is the degree to which the members of a society feel uncomfortable with uncertainty and ambiguity. This feeling leads them to beliefs promising certainty and to maintaining institutions protecting conformity. Strong Uncertainty Avoidance societies maintain rigid codes of belief and behaviour and are intolerant towards deviant persons and ideas. Weak Uncertainty Avoidance societies maintain a more relaxed atmosphere in which practice counts more than principles and deviance is more easily tolerated. The fundamental issue addressed by this dimension is how a society reacts on that fact that time only runs one way and that the future is unknown: whether it tries to control the future or to let it happen. Like Power Distance, Uncertainty Avoidance has consequences for the way people build their institutions and organisations.

Masculinity versus Femininity

Masculinity stands for a preference in society for achievement, heroism, assertiveness, and material success. Its opposite, Femininity, stands for a preference for relationships, modesty, caring for the weak, and the quality of life. The fundamental issue addressed by this dimension is the way in which a society allocates social (as opposed to biological) roles to the sexes.

Hofstede and Michael Bond (1988) found later that the dimension of uncertainty avoidance was not appropriate to eastern cultures, which are influenced mainly by Confucianism. Confucianism is derived from Confucius' teaching two thousand years ago and has profound influence not only on China but also on Japan, Korea and South East Asia.

Confucius

Confucius was born in 551 B.C, and died in 479 B.C. When he was young his great goal was to be a governmental official because this was the path to upgrade his social status. He taught himself many skills, e.g. practising rituals, playing music, archery, driving, learning literature and calculating. When he was 26 years old, he was appointed as an accountant in a rich family business. Later, he became a professional teacher, taking tuition-paying disciples and teaching them his view on life and government. He and his disciples travelled around from state to state to persuade feudal lords to accept his principles on life and government which were based on the practices of the previous Zhou Dynasty. Confucius admired the prosperity and the way of life in the Zhou Dynasty and regarded it as a perfect model of government. He spent his whole life trying to restore the rules of Zhou Dynasty in the Waring States. Although his political ambitions were unsuccessful because none of the lords of states took his advice, his philosophy on life, family and government lay down the foundation stone of Chinese culture. Confucius' teachings are about the ethics of practices and not about religion. Hofstede and Bond (1988) summarised the key principles of Confucian teachings as follows:

1. The stability of society is based on unequal relationships between people. This "wu lun", or five basic relationships, are ruler/subject, father/son, husband/wife, older brother/younger brother and friend/friend. These relationships are based on mutual, complementary obligations: the junior partner owes the

senior respect and obedience: the senior owes the junior partner protection and consideration.

2.   The family is the prototype of all social organisations. A person is not primarily an individual; rather, he or she is a member of a family. Children should learn to restrain themselves, to overcome their individuality so as to maintain the harmony in the family (if only on the surface); one's thoughts, however, remain free. Harmony is found in the maintenance of an individual's "face", meaning one's dignity, self-respect, and prestige. The use of our own word "face" in this sense was actually derived from the Chinese. Losing one's dignity, in the Chinese tradition, is equivalent to losing one's eyes, nose, and mouth. Social relations should be conducted in such a way that everybody's face is maintained. Paying respect to someone else is called "giving face".

3.   Virtuous behaviour toward others consists of treating others as one would like to be treated oneself: a basic human benevolence – which, however, does not extend as far as the Christian injunction to love the enemies. As Confucius said, if one should love one's enemies, what would remain for one's friend?

4.   Virtue with regard to one's tasks in life consists of trying to acquire skills and education, working hard, not spending more than necessary, being patient, and persevering. Conspicuous consumption is taboo, as is losing one's temper. Moderation is enjoined in all things (p.6).

Based on the Chinese Value Survey conducted by Michael Bond in 22 countries, Hofstede and Michael Bond found another cultural dimension, "Confucian Dynamism", which indicates whether a society has a long-term orientated or short-term orientated value.

Long-Term orientation versus Short-Term Orientation

A society with a long-term orientation will value persistence, ordering of relationships by status and observing this order, thrift, and having a sense of shame, whereas a society with a short-term orientation values personal steadiness and stability, protecting your face, respect for tradition and reciprocating of greetings, favours and gifts (Hofstede and Bond, 1988).

As shown in the Chinese Value Survey (Hofstede and Bond, 1988), Japan and South Korea have the higher scores on the dimension of Confucian Dynamism while the United States has a lower score on this dimension. This reveals that eastern countries and regions (e.g. Japan, Taiwan, Singapore, South Korea, and Hong Kong) are more long-term orientated and western countries are more short-term orientated. Hosftede and Bond (1988) argued that there is a strongly associated relationship between the scores of Confucian Dynamism and economic growth. Persistence or perseverance in the pursuit of goals is an important attribute of the success of eastern entrepreneurship, and thrift leads to high savings in the eastern societies which facilitates the accumulation of capital and investment.

There are some controversies about the Confucian Dynamism. Firstly, Hofstede and Bond argued that the reasons for the success of Five Dragons (two Dragons are now in serious financial crisis) are, at least, because of the Confucian values which are deeply rooted in people's lives, such as persistence and thrift.

In ancient China, people were classified based on Confucian social status into four classes: nobles, farmers, artisans and merchants. Merchants were at the bottom of the society and commercial activities were always constrained and even suppressed. Fu (1968) said "In Chinese, the characters for 'merchant' are pronounced exactly the same as the characters for 'harmful people'". Berry (1988) argued that the negative attitude towards merchants "prevented men of intellect and sensitivity from going into business, thus, this tended to restrict the expansion of business. This in turn delayed the development of accounting". It is hard to contribute the Asian success in the development of economy to an ideology which was strongly against merchants and business.

Secondly, based on the scores each country has from the Chinese Value Survey, it seems that people from western countries, such as the United States, are more concerned about their face than their eastern counterparts. People in western countries play more respect to tradition than people in eastern countries, and western businessmen favour more the reciprocation of greetings, favours, and gifts. It is arguable that the opposite is true. Kirkbirde and Tang (1990) discussed strategies and principles of negotiations with the Chinese, and emphasised the importance of the "face":

> The face mechanism operates to influence a person to behave in a certain way that reinforces his social position as well as that of others. The influence of face in social interactions is universal but is particularly important to the Chinese. [Chinese subdivided face into two dimensions. "Lian" and "Mianzi"]. The former one is normally ascribed while the latter is more achieved than ascribed. A person is socially condemned if he has no "Lian" and is seen to be unsuccessful and low in status of he has no "Mianzi". They are externally mediated and people interact with a purpose to add, give, take, complete, exchange or borrow "face". In negotiating situations, aggressive behaviour from either party can easily injure the

"face" of other party. As not giving face to a person is perceived as denying the person's pride and dignity, Chinese will hesitate to engage in such aggressive actions under normal circumstances. In addition, the adoption of face-giving or face-saving behaviour in conflict situations is valued as a means of maintaining group harmony.

The respect of tradition is another virtue of Chinese culture. Confucius himself was an active advocator of going back to the tradition of the ancient society. As mentioned his ideal model of society was the "Zhou Dynasty" which had been replaced by the Waring States at that time. He told people to "restrain yourself to restore the rites of Zhou". The ancient Chinese left volumes of books on history but a few books on science and technology. When the society was in crisis, rulers always tried to find the solutions from their ancestors. More than five thousand years of history and traditions might be a heavy burden to the Chinese and this might be the reason why China fell behind western countries from the middle of the eighteenth century.

If one has experience of dealing with the Chinese in business, one may find that reciprocation of greetings, favours and gifts is a common strategy used by the Chinese. The purpose of having many banquets, gifts and even bribes is to establish a good relationship, which is so called "Gunxi". Without the strong personal trust and contact with each other, it is hard to be successful in business.

In summary, protecting one's face, respecting the tradition and the reciprocation of greetings, favours and gifts are representing the strong characteristics of Chinese culture. They have been preserved and are practised currently. These factors may not be used to distinguish the *long-term* and *short- term* perspectives between the westerners and easterners.

The reason why the Chinese and Japanese scored higher on Confucian Dynamism while western respondents had relatively lower marks may be because changes are occurring in our world. The Chinese Survey (Hofstede and Bond, 1988) might convey an important message that the culture in a particular country can be changed over time. As Hofstede and Bond (1988) observed:

> The Chinese and Japanese peoples were known to value thrift and perseverance before the present boom started; their belief in tradition and "face" (negative on the "Confucian Dynamism" scale) was heavily shaken by the events of the 1940s and 1950s; therefore, we assume the values to be at least part of the cause, and economic growth to be the effect (p.18).

216

In other words, it can be argued that the growth of the economy was caused partly by the changes in people's beliefs about values such as tradition, "face" and personal relationship. These changes made the easterners more westernised, and more likely to adopt western thought. And then this in turn accelerated the growth of the Asian economy.

Trompenaars' Cultural Dimensions

Although Hofstede's cultural dimension analysis has been widely accepted and applied in many fields, his model is not the only study on cultural dimensions. Trompenaars' study (1994) provides an excellent contribution to cross-cultural research. His study covered over 15 years and involved 15,000 participants. 900 cross-cultural training programmes were conducted in 18 countries. Thirty companies, with departments spanning 50 different countries, participated in the study. In order to gather a comparable sample, a minimum of 100 people with similar backgrounds and occupations were surveyed in each of the countries in which the companies operated. Approximately 75 per cent of the participants belong to management, with the remaining 25 per cent being general administrative staff.

Trompenaars states that "cultural is the way in which a group of people solves problems". Every culture distinguishes itself from others by the specific solutions it chooses to solve particular problems. These problems may be sub-classified as (1) those which arise from our relationships with other people; (2) those which come from the passage of time; and (3) those which relate to the environment.

Trompenaars identified seven cultural dimensions and five of these come from the first category: universalism versus particularism; individualism versus collectivism; neutral versus emotional; specific versus diffuse; achievement versus ascription. The sixth dimension is related to attitudes towards time: synchronic versus sequential. The seventh dimension is about the relationship between the human being and environment: inner-directed versus outer-directed.

When Hofstede's five cultural dimensions are compared with Trompenaars's seven cultural dimensions, some similarities can be found in both studies. Both of them identified the cultural dimensions of individualism versus collectivism. Hofestede's cultural dimensions of masculinity versus femininity may be related to Trompenaars's cultural dimensions on emotional versus neutral, specific versus diffuse, achievement versus ascription and inner-directed versus outer-directed.

People in general from a masculine society tend to prefer controlling their emotions; separating personal relationships from working relationship; admiring achievements rather than ascription; and believing they can control nature by imposing their will on it.

Trompenaars' cultural dimensions on universalism versus particularism can be related to Hofstede's large versus small power distance and strong versus weak uncertainty avoidance. People in a large power distance and strong uncertainty avoidance society prefer to resolve problems according to relationships rather than to rules. They want to solve the problem personally and not involve any challenge towards regulations and rules.

Gray's Accounting Values and the Connections to Hofstede and Trompenaar's Cultural Values

Gray (1988) tried to link societal values to accounting values. Each different country has an identical accounting system which reflects a country's accounting values and accounting values are derived from the cultural values of that country. Gray identified four accounting values as follows:

Professionalism versus Statutory Control
A preference for the exercise of individual professional judgement and the maintenance of professional self-regulation as opposed to compliance with prescriptive legal requirements and statutory control.

Uniformity versus Flexibility
A preference from the enforcement of uniform accounting practices between companies and for the consistent use of such practices over time as opposed to flexibility in accordance with the perceived circumstances of individual companies.

Conservatism versus Optimism
A preference for a cautious approach to measurement so as to cope with the uncertainty of future events as opposed to a more optimistic, laissez-faire, risk-taking approach.

Secrecy versus Transparency
A preference for confidentiality and the restriction of disclosure of information about the business only to those who are closely involved with its management and financing as opposed to a more transparent, open and publicly accountable approach.

218

Then, Gray (1988) analysed the relationship between accounting values and Hofstede's societal values, and made the following hypotheses:

H1: The higher a country ranks in terms of individualism and the lower it ranks in terms of uncertainty avoidance and power distance then the more likely it is to rank highly in terms of professionalism.

H2: The higher a country ranks in terms of uncertainty avoidance and power distance and the lower it ranks in terms of individualism then the more likely it is to rank highly in terms of uniformity.

H3: The higher a country ranks in terms of uncertainty avoidance and the lower it ranks in terms of individualism and masculinity then the more likely it is to rank highly in terms of conservatism.

H4: The higher a country ranks in terms of uncertainty avoidance and power distance and the lower it ranks in terms of individualism and masculinity then the more likely it is to rank in terms of secrecy.

Roxas et al (1997) tried to establish the linkage between Trompenaars' cultural values and Gray's accounting values. They proposed the following hypotheses:

HT1: The higher a country ranks on particularism and individualism, the higher it will rank on professionalism

HT2: The higher a country ranks on universalism, the higher it will rank on uniformity.

HT3: The higher a country ranks on synchronism and out directedness, the higher it will rank on conservatism.

HT4: The higher a country ranks on individualism and specificity, the higher it will rank on secrecy.

How can Hofstede's fifth cultural value be linked with Gray's accounting values. Chow et al (1995) suggested that a country with a long-term orientation is more likely to be conservative and secretive in accounting. It is argued that there should be the fifth accounting value which is better related to Hofstede's long-term versus short-term cultural dimensions. The fifth accounting value suggested is profitability versus liquidity.

Profitability versus Liquidity
A preference for the ability of making profit as opposed to the ability of converting assets into cash.

These two values are most important for every success in business. They are the fundamental aspects which concern the accountant. They are not mutually exclusive but are emphasised by people from different cultural backgrounds. This difference is represented by the preference for the statement of profit and loss or the balance sheet. The information about a company's profitability is disclosed in the profit and loss statement while the information on the company's liquidity is revealed in the balance sheet. People with a long-term view about business are concerned with the profitability of the company, while people with a short-term view of business are focused on the balance sheet. Jones and Aiken (1995) reviewed the developments of accounting both in the United Kingdom and the United States and concluded that the emphasis on income statements by Britain is because of its collective culture and statutory requirements of protecting the interests of shareholders. American's early emphasis on the balance sheet is because of its individual culture which advocated the laissez-faire economy. The fifth hypothesis can be envisaged as:

H5: A country which has a short-term orientation and scores the higher in terms of individualism is more likely to emphasise liquidity over profitability.

The Hofstede-Gray model has been tested empirically by some scholars (Doupnik and Salter, 1995; Salter and Niswander, 1995; Gray and Vint, 1995; and Zarsekei, 1996). Doupnik and Salter (1995) viewed accounting in any country as a complex interaction between the external environment, institutional structure and culture and tested whether relationships existed between the accounting system and the above elements for a wide range of countries using a hierarchical cluster analysis and a canonical correlation analysis. They concluded that all three elements were important to the accounting diversity around the world, and the institutional structure appeared to be the most significant factor.

Salter and Niswander (1995) tested the Gray theory directly by using data from 29 countries. They treated Gray's accounting values as the dependent variables and Hofstede's cultural values as independent variables and used the linear regression techniques to test the link between Hosftede's cultural values and Gray's accounting values. They found that the model was best at explaining actual financial reporting practice but was relatively weak at explaining extant professional and regulatory structures from a cultural base.

Cultural Influences and Harmonisation of Accounting Practices

Although extensive research has been carried out by many scholars to try linking accounting with the cultural influences, culture is only one of the environmental factors which affect the development of accounting. Other

220

factors are neglected such as economic and political influences. Culture has the influence on the development of accounting, however, to what degree it does has not yet been addressed by academia. It seems that the development of economy has more dominant influence on accounting than culture does, and politics has a more direct influence on accounting than culture does. Without taking economic and political influences into account, the development of accounting can hardly be explained based on the single variable of culture.

The second question is about the role of culture on the development of accounting. Does culture have positive or negative influences on accounting? What is the impact of cultural differences on the harmonisation of the process of accounting? It seems that the cultural differences among countries are the major obstacles of harmonisation.

The final question is whether the culture in a particular country can be changed. Hofstede and Gray both implicitly took a static persistence of view about culture. With the globalisation of the economy and mobilisation of human resources around the world, we can see a trend of dilution of culture. If culture is changing, what is the impact of changes of culture on accounting?

Environmental Influences on the Development of Chinese Accounting

Based on the research described above and by analysing the historical development and current practices of Chinese accounting, it is possible to identify some environmental factors that have direct effects upon Chinese accounting developments.

Political Influences

Within the last 150 years countries in the West have not generally experienced such dramatic social and political changes as those which have occurred in China. China has moved from a feudal to a semi-colonial and semi-feudal society and then finally to a socialist society. These political and structural changes have had a great influence on the development of accounting. Even within one social and political pattern, government policy changes can still have some influence on accounting development. For example, during the Great Leap Forward which began in 1958, a campaign based on "leftist" ideas brought about many absurd accounting concepts and practices; notably, as previously mentioned the practice of "accounting without books", a reference not to the use of computers but to the elimination of all accounting journals and ledgers. This was based on the socialist principle that property belongs to the people and that it is unnecessary to distinguish individual ownership. Later, during the Cultural Revolution, many accounting teachers and practitioners were forced to give up their positions and to accept re-education from peasants and workers. Zhao (1983) described "... the record-keeping and statistical services which were vital for central planning purposes were virtually abandoned. Any accounting measures designed to aid management, such as the regular comparison of major ratios among enterprises in the same industry and of similar size, were denounced as running counter to the 'revolutionary line' and were dropped".

Economic Influences

The Chinese national economy from 1949 to 1979 was a planned economy. The structure of enterprises was mainly based on public ownership (including ownership by the State and ownership by "collectives"). The government directly provided most capital funds and administered all economic enterprises, including factories, farms, and commerce. The State also controlled transactions between enterprises through a system of material allocations and price-setting. It eliminated the labour market by assigning life-time employment to school leavers. Under such a situation uniform accounting systems were implemented through all economic sectors because the main and dominant users of accounting information were government administrative agencies. As enterprises were all owned by the State there was lack of incentive to pursue the interests of enterprises themselves and economic efficiency and management accounting could not be emphasised. Although, as discussed earlier, some forms of management accounting, such as work-team accounting, fund management and economic accounting were attempted in order to improve the efficiency of the state-controlled enterprises, the results were poor and the economy deteriorated.

Since 1979 China has implemented a reformist and open policy and the economic structure has changed dramatically. Now China is in a transitional period from a centrally planned economy to a socialist market economy. The changes in economic structure and operation have had strong influences on the development of accounting. For example, the improvement of Chinese responsibility accounting and the introduction of the internal banking system are closely linked to the implementation of the responsibility contract system in state-owned enterprises. Currently most state-owned enterprises have been transformed into shareholder corporations, and corporate accounting issues such as the consolidation and disclosure requirements have become a reality.

Cultural Influences

Cultures are complex and are capable of being viewed from many different perspectives. One view of culture is furnished by Edward Sapir. He writes "The genuine culture is the expression of a richly varied and yet somehow unified and consistent attitude toward life...." (Spair, 1960).

Some scholars suggest that although cultures are complex configurations which need to be characteristic of whole societies, they can be analysed in terms of their components. Hofstede did his cross-cultural research which was aimed at detecting the structural elements of culture (Hofstede, 1980). Gray (1988) establishes a framework for analysing the impact of culture on the development of accounting systems internationally. He gives value dimensions at the accounting subculture level: professionalism versus statutory control, uniformity versus flexibility, conservatism versus optimism and secrecy versus transparency. These are linked to the cultural value dimension as identified by Hofstede, *viz.* individualism, power distance, uncertainty avoidance, and masculinity. Grey's matrix of the relationship of accounting values with societal values is shown in Table 9-1.

Using the framework provided by Gray, we can identify some culture value effects on the development of Chinese accounting. China is a typical eastern society, with the societal values of collectivism, large power distance, strong uncertainty avoidance and femininity. Therefore its accounting values appear to be statutory control, uniformity and secrecy. However, this framework cannot explain why Chinese accounting appears to be more optimistic than conservative. Conservatism was not recognised until 1992 when the first accounting standard was promulgated. For example, short-term investment was presented at historical cost; the cost or market, whichever is lower basis, was not allowed and no provision was made for doubtful debts. Even since the new accounting standard was issued, conservatism has not been fully adopted by the Chinese. For example, the lowering of cost and market rule is still not allowed in determination of the costs of inventories. This is in contradiction to Gray's hypothesis, which asserts that Chinese accounting should be more conservative, based on the societal values which China has.

As Baladouni points out, viewed in the broad perspective, technology connotes the bodies of skills, knowledge, and procedures for accomplishing or attaining a recognised useful purpose. Technologies are an ensemble of techniques or means employed by man for the purpose of adapting to his continually changing environment – physical, biological, and social (Baladouni, 1987).

It would be neither possible nor desirable to try to isolate the history of technology from related disciplines. Accounting itself is a technology in its own right and a product of the technological environment. As a technology, accounting involves the application of reliable empirical knowledge and rational techniques to achieve specific objectives.

We can see the influence of the technological change on accounting development by looking at specific events in the world history of technology. The most significant episode, it is agreed by technological historians, was the Industrial Revolution which had a definite impact on the development of accounting thought. The direct effects were the development of the concept of depreciation and the development of cost accounting (Chatfield, 1977). Prior to the 19th century, depreciation was not an important concept, largely because fixed assets were not a significant aspect of commerce and industry. With the advent of the factory system and mass production, fixed assets became a sizeable cost in the production and distribution process. There also arose a need for management information regarding the costs of production and the costs to be assigned to inventory valuations. The rapid development and growth of railroads in Europe and the United States during the 19th century also had a definite influence on accounting development. Railroads required a much larger investment and considerably longer-lasting equipment than most of the industrial activities of the mid-19th century. Both of these factors increased the importance of making a distinction between capital and income. The wide use of computers in recent decades has also had a great influence on accounting development.

Table 9-1 Matrix of Relationships of Accounting Values with Societal Values

Values	Professionalism	Statutory Control	Uniformity	Flexibility	Conservatism	Optimism	Secrecy	Transparenc
Individualism	Positive	Negative	Negative	Positive	Negative	Positive	Negative	Positive
Collectivism	Negative	Positive	Positive	Negative	Positive	Negative	Positive	Negative
Lager Power Distance	Negative	Positive	Positive	Negative	n/a	n/a	Positive	Negative
Small Power Distance	Positive	Negative	Negative	Positive	n/a	n/a	Negative	Positive
Strong Uncertainty Avoidance	Negative	Positive	Positive	Negative	Positive	Negative	Positive	Negative
Weak Uncertainty Avoidance	Positive	Negative	Negative	Positive	Negative	Positive	Negative	Positive
Masculinity	n/a	n/a	n/a	n/a	Positive	Negative	Positive	Negative
Femininity	n/a	n/a	n/a	n/a	Negative	Positive	Negative	Positive

Source: Redebaugh. L.H., and Gray. S., *International Accounting and Multinational Enterprises* 3rd edition, p.73.

Table 9-2:   Relationship of Accounting Values with Societal Values in China

Societal Values in China	Accounting Values in Gray's Framework	Accounting Values in Chinese Reality
Collectivism	Statutory Control	Statutory Control
Larger Power Distance	Uniformity	Uniformity
Strong Uncertainty Avoidance	Conservatism	Optimism
Femininity	Secrecy	Secrecy

The development of technology has also had a significant influence on accounting in China. For example, the invention of paper and the abacus in the Eastern Han Dynasty and the invention of paper money and the block printing technique in the Song Dynasty had a strong influence on Chinese accounting history and also on world accounting developments. It is expected that computer and communication technology will play an increasingly important role in future accounting developments in China.

Outside Influences

In ancient times, Chinese accounting had some influences on other countries, such as Japan, Korea and South-east Asian countries. However, modern Chinese accounting is under strong outside influence. There have been three periods in the development of modern Chinese accounting: the first period (1840-1949) was under the influence of Japan and the United States; the second period (1949-1979) was under the Soviet Union influence; and the third period (1979-present) is under the influence of international accounting.

Empirical Evidence on Environmental Influences on the Development of Chinese Accounting

As analysed above, the development of the Chinese accounting systems has been influenced by China's political and economic systems, culture, technical progress, and outside influences. In this section, a set of models will be established to verify this assertion. The influences from the economy, politics and culture have been tested in the following model. However, the technical and other influences have not been included in the model for two reasons.

226

Firstly, the proper surrogates for these variables have not been found. Secondly, technical and other influences are indirect with respect to the development of accounting.

Development of Research Hypotheses

Dependent variables. The development of accounting in China is represented by the percentage of CPAs in the total population of China (CPAs/Population).

Independent variables. Three independent variables have been chosen which represent the economic, political, cultural influences on accounting. Rates of real gross domestic production (RGDP) per person represent the economic influences.

The percentages of trade value between the United States and China in the total Chinese trade value represent the political influence. The United States has been concerned with political stability in China for a long time and has raised some sensitive issues, such as human rights, nuclear proliferation and Taiwanese and Tibetan issues. These all have had an impact on bilateral trade. The percentages of trade value between the United States and China in the total Chinese trade value is thus a proper surrogate and matches the pattern of the changes of the political situation in China.

Between 1983 and 1987, the political situation became more uncertain in China. A campaign against "spiritual pollution" was carried out in October 1983, student demonstrations occurred in many cities in 1986, and the General Secretary Hu Yaobang was removed from his position in January 1987. During the same period the percentages of trade value between the United States and China in total Chinese trade value declined. In 1989, the Tiananmen Incident occurred and Zhao Ziyang was removed from office. A year late, the percentage of trade value between the United States and China in the total Chinese value of trade dropped from 11.46 per cent to 10.85 per cent.

The percentage of the employment of non-state sectors in total employment shows the cultural influences on accounting. Hofstede (1980) described culture as a static variable which could not be changed in the long run. However, we argue that culture is a dynamic variable and that it changes with changes in economic, political, and legal systems. It was observed that there has been a dramatic change in people's attitudes in China since the reforms. There is a significant move towards commercialism. The growth of non-state sectors reflects this trend of cultural changes. The following hypotheses will be tested:

- Hypothesis 1: *There is a positive association between the growth of CPAs, and the growth of real GDP. The increase of real GDP will result in an increase in demand for CPAs.*

- Hypothesis 2: *There is a positive relationship between the relaxation of political controls and the growth of an accounting profession. The more the relaxed political situation, the higher the growth rate of accounting development.*

- Hypothesis 3: *There has been a positive association between the cultural changes towards commercialism and the growth of the accounting profession. The quicker the growth of non state sectors, the higher the growth of CPAs.*

Data collection The yearly data from 1980 to 1993 for: the CPAs; population in China; real GDP; real GDP per person; trade value; percentage of US-China bilateral trade value in total trade value; total employment; and percentage of the employment in non state sector of total employment is shown in Table 9-3.

Data about numbers of Certified Public Accountants come initially from Xu (1995), "The Development of the Certified Public Accountant System in the People's Republic of China". Data about Real GDP and population in China come from the *International Financial Statistics Yearbook* published by the International Monetary Fund. Data for the total trade value of China are in the *International Financial Statistics Yearbook* and the bilateral trade value between China and the United States is from *Direction of Trade Statistics*, which is published by The International Monetary Fund (IMF). Also, data about total employment and employment in non-state sectors are from the *China Statistical Yearbook*, 1995, 1994, 1993, compiled by the State Statistical Bureau, People's Republic of China. Non-state sectors include all sectors except the state-owned units and collective-owned units.

Model design The following multiple regression models will be estimated. It is assumed there is a linear relationship between the dependent variables and the independent variables. To make it clear the second formulation of each

228

model is not a different model but spells out in detail how our variables CPA, ECO, POL and CUL were obtained from preliminary data.

Model A:

$$CPA = \beta_0 + \beta_1 ECO + \beta_2 POL + \beta_3 CUL + e \qquad (1)$$

$$\frac{CPAS}{POP} = \beta_0 + \beta_1 \frac{RGDP}{POP} + \beta_2 \frac{UCTRADE}{TRADE} + \beta_3 \frac{NSEMPLOYMENT}{EMPLOYMENT} + e$$
$$(2)$$

Model B:

$$CPA = \beta_{01} + \beta_{11} ECO + e_1 \qquad (3)$$

$$\frac{CPAS}{POP} = \beta_{01} + \beta_{11} \frac{RGDP}{POP} + e_1 \qquad (4)$$

Model C:

$$CPA = \beta_{02} + \beta_{12} ECO + \beta_{22} POL + e_2 \qquad (5)$$

$$\frac{CPAS}{POP} = \beta_{02} + \beta_{12} \frac{RGDP}{POP} + \beta_{22} \frac{UCTRADE}{TRADE} + e_2 \qquad (6)$$

Model D:

$$CPA = \beta_{03} + \beta_{13} ECO + \beta_{33} CUL + e_3 \qquad (7)$$

$$\frac{CPAS}{POP} = \beta_{03} + \beta_{13} \frac{RGDP}{POP} + \beta_{33} \frac{NSEMPLOYMENT}{EMPLOYMENT} + e_3 \qquad (8)$$

Model E:

$$LogCPA = \beta_{04} + \beta_{14}LogECO + \beta_{24}LogPOL + \beta_{34}LogCUL + e_4 \qquad (9)$$

$$Log\frac{CPAS}{POP} = \beta_{04} + \beta_{14}Log\frac{RGDP}{POP} + \beta_{24}Log\frac{UCTRADE}{TRADE} +$$
$$\beta_{34}Log\frac{NSEMPLOYMENT}{EMPLOYMENT} + e_4 \qquad (10)$$

CPA = the growth of Certified Pubic Accountants (CPAs) in China as presented by the percentage of CPAs in the total population of China;
ECO = the economic variable as presented by the rates of Real Domestic Production per person in China;
POL = the political variable as presented by the percentage of trade value between the United States and China in total Chinese trade value;
CUL = the cultural variable as represented by the percentage of the employment of non-state sectors in total employment;
CPAS = numbers of CPAs;
POP = the population in China;
RGDP = real gross domestic products in billions of RMB Yuan;
UCTRDE = bilateral trade value between the United States and China;
TRADE = the total trade value in China;
NSEMPLOYMENT = the employment in non state sectors;
EMPLOYMENT = total employment in China.

Table 9-3 Basic Data for the Surrogates of Accounting, Economic, Political, and Cultural Variables

Year	CPAs	Population (Millions)	Real GDP (Billions RMB)	Total trade value (Millions $US)	US-China bilateral trade value (Millions $US)	Total Employment (Thousands)	Employment In Non State Sectors (Thousands)
1980	71	996	753	36,394	4,811	4,236,100	3,191,700
1981	143	1,008	787	42,204	6,187	4,382,000	3,302,375
1982	214	1,021	852	40,014	6,070	4,533,325	3,415,756
1983	286	1,040	941	41,850	4,465	4,682,044	3,525,017
1984	357	1,055	1,077	51,286	6,149	4,819,700	3,634,400
1985	429	1,070	1,216	66,113	7,537	4,987,300	3,755,900
1986	500	1,087	1,320	70,303	7,354	5,128,200	3,852,800
1987	1,750	1,104	1,466	79,085	7,869	5,278,300	3,964,100
1988	3,000	1,122	1,631	98,221	10,028	5,433,400	4,082,300
1989	4,233	1,139	1,702	106,795	12,239	5,532,900	4,171,900
1990	5,467	1,155	1,768	111,031	11,747	5,674,000	4,284,500
1991	6,700	1,170	1,910	130,434	14,152	5,836,000	4,406,800
1992	10,000	1,184	2,161	158,871	17,508	5,943,200	4,492,200
1993	15,000	1,196	2,460	185,546	27,665	6,022,000	4,590,700

Source: Xu. Z. D. "The Development of Certified Public Accountant System in People's Republic of China" in Tsuji and Carner (ed) *Studies in Accounting History*, Greenwood Pres 1995 Yang, S.Z., "The Evolution of Certified Public Accountant System in China", *Accounting Communication*, (Chinese), vol 3, 1995. *China Statistical Yearbook*, 1995, 1994, 1993, State Statistical Bureau, People's Republic of China. *International Financial Statistics Yearbook, Direction of Trade Statistics*, International Monetary Fund.

The correlation matrix of dependent variable CPA and three independent variables, ECO, POL and CUL is shown in Table 9-4. Three independent variables are not correlated and the model does not suffer the problem of mutlicollinearity.

Table 9-4 Correlation Matrix of Dependent and Independent Variables

	CPA	ECO	POL	CUL
CPA	1.0000	0.9196	0.0996	0.8441
ECO	0.9196	1.0000	-0.2340	0.6113
POL	0.0996	-0.2340	1.0000	0.5031
CUL	0.8441	0.6113	0.5031	1.0000

The results of the estimation are shown in Table 9-5. It was found that there is a significant relationship between the dependent variables and the independent variables.

Model A:
CPA =   -337.43 + 6.73ECO + 17.76POL + 490.20CUL
        (-3.23)   (6.89)   (0.90)   (3.08)

In model A, it is shown that there are positive and statistically significant relationships between accounting development and the growth of real GDP, and changes in the political situation in China and in Chinese culture (the statistic scores are shown in brackets). This model indicates that if real GDP increases 1 per cent, the demand for the members of CPAs will increase 6.7 per cent. However, the changes in the political situation and culture have more significant impacts on the development of accounting in China. This finding is consistent with the reality in China that the development of the accounting profession is a consequence of political adjustment and the growth of non public sectors which fundamentally change the Chinese society. A rapid growth in the accounting profession did not occur during planned economy and only eventuated when China carried out the economic reforms and initiated its "open door" policy. The changes in Chinese society which have been orientated towards more commercialism has created the demand for the accounting services and, therefore an accounting profession.

Model B:

CPA =   -8.1   + 8.61ECO
       (-5.69)   (8.11)

Model B attempts to quantify the relationship between the development of CPAs and economic growth alone. The results indicate that there is a positive and significant relationship between the dependent variable and independent variable. However, the Durbin-Watson test is much lower.

Model C:

CPA =   -17.24 + 9.34ECO   + 68.92POL
       (-8.31)   (14.45)   (4.82)

The results from Model C show there are positive and statistically significant relationships between the development of the accounting profession in China, growth in the Chinese economy and changes in the political situation in China. R^2, and Durbin-Watson results are better than these in Model A.

Model D:

CPA =   -464.95 + 6.03ECO+ 610.25CUL
       (-7.26)   (10.21)   (7.13)

Model D attempts to quantify the impact of growth in the Chinese economy and changes in Chinese culture on the accounting profession. It shows that changes in culture have had the most significant impact on the growth of CPAs (610 times).

Model E:

Log CPA = -0.45 + 5.19LogECO +0.414LogPOL -1.14LogCUL
          (-0.03)   (7.38)   (0.27)   (-0.02)

Model E is log form regression model. It was shown that only variable ECO is significant. If economy (GDP) grows by 1 per cent, the demand on CPAs will grow by 5 per cent.

Table 9-5 Estimation Results

Dependent Variable: CPA	Sample: 1980 1993				
Included observations: 14					
	A	B	C	D	E
Variable	Coefficient	Coefficient	Coefficient	Coefficient	Coefficient
C	-377.479 *	-8.100 *	-17.2360*	-464.9582*	-0.451
ECO	6.728 *	8.611 *	9.3407*	6.0340*	5.189 *
POL	17.755		68.9175*		-0.414
CUL	490.265 **			610.2604*	-1.144
R-squared	0.974	0.845	0.9504	0.9725	0.958
Adjusted R-squared	0.967	0.832	0.9414	0.9675	0.945
Durbin-Watson test	1.576	0.317	1.6836	1.2588	0.959
F-statistic	127.853 *	65.730 *	105.4905*	194.7919*	76.191 *

Note: *: significant at 1; **: significant at 5; ***: significant at 10 per cent level, respectively.

234

In this section an empirical model is established to test the assertion that the development of accounting in China has been strongly influenced by the political, economic, and cultural environments of China. Although we have found there is a statistically significant relationship between growth in the accounting profession and growth in the economy, changes in the political situation and changes in Chinese culture, we do not conclude that there are no influences from other aspects, such as the development of technologies including calculation techniques, constitutional arrangements, and educational and outside influences. If we can find proper and independent surrogates to represent and measure these variables, the current model could be refined. Nevertheless, this is an early attempt to apply empirical research methodology to Chinese accounting issues. The results confirm our hypotheses that the recent development of accounting in China has been strongly influenced by its economic, political and cultural dimensions.

In particular we note from our model C and D, a significant additional (contributory) power (after allowing for the effect of ECO) is afforded by our conclusion of CUL or POL being a multiple regression study. The analysis has provided a modelling over a unique period of only 14 years. This has experienced the liberalisation of trade, particularly with US, and changes in the nature of the enterprises which have contributed most to Chinese economic growth in the period. The selection of a small sample size in terms of years is inescapable. Results in Table 9-4 are nevertheless significant in explaining the unique era of transition as applied to the development of accounting in China.

Conclusion

In this chapter, Hofstede's and Trompenaars' cultural values have been examined. It is argued that the fifth cultural dimension suggested by Hofstede and Bond (1988) misplaced Confucian values on long-term versus short-term orientation. Secondly, the link between Gray's accounting values and Hofstede's cultural dimensions are evaluated. It is suggested that there is a fifth accounting value: profitability versus liquidity which is more consistent with Hofstede's long-term and short-term orientation. Thirdly, it is argued that although cultural influences on accounting are emphasised, it is not the only factor which influences the evolution of accounting. The development of accounting is strongly influenced by other factors, especially political and economic factors. Finally, a model is established to test the influences of environmental factors on the development of Chinese accounting. It concludes that the evolution of Chinese accounting is the consequence of complex interactions between political, economic and cultural influences.

10   Conclusion

Although Chinese accounting has a longer history than most other civilisations, the most significant improvements occurred during the post-revolutionary period (after 1949). This book examines the developments of Chinese accounting in this modern era. Special attention is given to those areas which are represented the typically Chinese characteristics and neglected by previous researches, such as the developments in cost and management accounting. The development of accounting during the modern era (after 1949) may be broadly divided into two phases: the first phase was called the centrally planned economy period which was from the establishment of the People's Republic of China to the beginning of economic reforms in 1978; the second phase is called the transition economy period that started from 1979 and continues to the present. The development of Chinese accounting during the first period was influenced by the Soviet Union's accounting model and traditional Chinese accounting thought. Some unique features of Chinese accounting system were developed, e.g. the diversity of bookkeeping methods and a centralised administration system for management of accounting affairs. The accounting system in this period was significantly different from these systems in western countries. During the second phase, China opened its door to the outside and carried out a series of reforms. The economic and social structures underwent substantial changes. The economic outputs and living standards have been improved. In response to these changes, Chinese accounting has moved away from serving a central economy to serving a market economy. Many aspects of accounting have been changed under the banner of "matching up with international practices". The positive results of this movement are Chinese accounting systems have become more open and comparable. The accounting information has become more transparent and reliable. However, the negative side of this rush is that some unique characterises of Chinese accounting have been abandoned without careful examination.

One of the examples is the disallowance for diversity in the bookkeeping methods. The Chinese invented several double-entry bookkeeping methods, for example the increase-decrease double entry method and the receipt-disbursement double entry method. These methods are disallowed extrinsically in governmental regulations issued in recent years. This argument was that the diversity of bookkeeping methods was harmful for the internationalising and modernising of Chinese accounting and that only the debit-credit double entry method should be used. However, this assertion is incorrect because a bookkeeping system is only a processing device, just like the computer system or a manual system. It may have no impact on the passage of accounting information through the system. Therefore it is not necessary to unify the bookkeeping methods as long as accountants are accustomed to systems and can use them to provide correct and timely information. The diversity of bookkeeping methods as a symbolic characteristic of Chinese accounting can be maintained (Aiken and Lu, 1993a). Even some ancient bookkeeping methods, such as single-entry, three feet entry, and Longmen accounts may be allowed in individual and small businesses because they represent the cultural heritage of accounting.

The findings and comments from previous chapters are summarised as followings.

Comments and Findings of the Research

Accounting History

Chinese accounting history is an important part of world accounting history. Ancient Chinese accounting made great contributions to the world, and modern Chinese accounting development offers an excellent example of the transferring of accounting patterns from one society to another. There are many areas in Chinese accounting history which deserve further research, for example:

- Chinese civilisation, the emergence of Chinese writing and its impact on the earlier development of accounting;
- the government accounting system in the Western Zhou Dynasty (1100-722 B.C.);
- the government accounting system in the Tang and Song Dynasties (618-1279 A.D.);
- the innovation of technology and its impact on the development of accounting in ancient times;
- Chinese culture, Confucism, Taoism and Legalism and their impact on the development of accounting;
- the development of non-governmental accounting, especially in the Ming and Qing Dynasties;

- the emergence of Chinese double-entry bookkeeping and whether there is a historical link between the Italian double-entry system and the Chinese system[26];
- the introduction of western accounting theory and practice and the Chinese accounting reform movement in the early twentieth century;
- accounting in the centrally controlled economy and under the influence of Maoism.

Financial Accounting and Accounting Standards

Before the promulgation of the first accounting standard, the financial accounting system was fund management oriented and was very hard to comprehend. The issue of the new accounting standard paved the way to link Chinese financial accounting and reporting to the outside world. There is little doubt that the future development of financial accounting will be more internationally comparable. Currently, most academics' attention is on how to deal with the old uniform accounting systems and the new accounting standards. The uniform accounting systems have been used in China for more than 40 years and have not yet been abolished, even after the issuing of the new accounting standard. A question has arisen about the destiny of the uniform accounting systems. Some scholars say that these systems should be abolished, while others suggest that they may exist concurrently with the accounting standards.

The second option is more realistic for these reasons: (1) The uniform accounting systems do exist concurrently with the accounting standard. The 13 uniform accounting systems for different industries were issued by the Ministry of Finance at the same time as the first accounting standard was promulgated. (2) The impression that industrial countries like the United States, the United Kingdom, and Australia only have accounting standards and do not have uniform accounting systems is mistaken. Most corporations in western countries have their own uniform accounting systems including uniform accounts, procedures, and policies in order to keep the accounting system operating correctly and efficiently. The question here is that in China,

---

[26] Marco Polo, a missioner, went to China in the fifteenth century to learn Chinese technology and culture. After spending 15 years in China he eventually returned to Italy and brought back a lot of techniques. It was said that pizza, the most popular food in Italy and the world, was brought from China by Polo. Therefore some scholars suspect that he also brought the Chinese double-entry system to Italy. It is an extraordinary and very interesting historical hypothesis and I leave it here for debate and criticism.

a government agency, the Ministry of Finance, performs tasks which could otherwise be done by the corporations themselves. There may also be some advantages in using uniform accounting systems; accounting procedure could be more open to the public and the accounting data is more comparable across industries. (3) The level of eduction of most accountants in China is lower than that in western countries and their attitude is passive and rule-following. Therefore, they do need detailed instructions to perform their tasks. It is strongly suggested that China needs to consider carefully the relationship between uniform accounting systems and accounting standards.

Cost Accounting

The Chinese cost accounting system originated in the Soviet Union and since then few changes have been made. The only change made in recent years is to treat financial and administrative expenses as period expenses rather than previous inventoriable expenses. However, the classification and accounting for cost elements and the procedures of accumulating and allocating costs have not yet been changed. Compared with the cost system used in western countries, the following findings have been observed: (1) The main purpose of the cost system in China is for product cost determination rather than cost control, and the actual cost of product is required to be used in financial reports. (2) The classification and accounting for cost elements are complicated and too detailed. For example, inventory is classified as materials, low-value and perishable articles, containers, semi-finished goods, finished goods and so on, and the accounting treatment for them is also different. (3) The procedure of accumulating and allocating production cost is more complicated. The question here is the accuracy of the product cost derived from this procedure, because too many arbitrary allocation methods are used, and (4) the cost-restored procedure in which the costs of finished goods should be represented retrospectively in cost elements, direct materials, direct labour and overhead, produces data of doubtful accuracy and usefulness for decision-making purpose.

Management Accounting

Some management accounting techniques have been used in China since the 1950s although the word "management accounting" did not appear until 1979. However, these methods used in the centrally planned economy were restricted to the responsibility accounting area. They include work-team accounting, target stratification management, economic accounting, and financial analysis. There is no evidence that management accounting methods for decision-making were created and used in that period.

Since China re-opened the door in 1978, western management accounting theories and practices have been gradually introduced. However, the absorption of western ideas and methods has made slow progress. Some methods have been easily accepted by the Chinese, such as short-term decision models, standard costing and western responsibility accounting, while some methods have been resisted or even rejected by the Chinese. These include the Just-in-time philosophy and behavioural theories. The reason is that the development of management accounting is strongly linked to the political system, economic growth and cultural patterns. It is not surprising that some western methods have not been accepted by China because its political, ideological, economic and societal environments have not been ready for these western ideas and techniques. With the reform of the political and economic structure; the growth of the economy and the opening up of the market, western management accounting will be adopted by the Chinese.

The most successfully developed area in management accounting in China is responsibility accounting. Chinese responsibility accounting was initiated and developed based on the Soviet model in the 1950s to 1970s. After the absorption of western responsibility accounting, standard costing and budgeting methods, and also given the strong influence of enterprise structure reform, with the implementation of the Contract Responsibility System, Chinese responsibility accounting reached its peak. It carried its own distinct features: the internal banking system, mass participation and management doctrines, integration of costing systems with financial accounting and responsibility accounting. Also, decision-making accounting, and material and moral incentive systems are included. Chinese responsibility accounting deserves the attention of western scholars.

The Accounting Profession

China's first certified professional accountant appeared in Beijing in 1918. After the establishment of the People's Republic of China the activities of CPAs actually stopped and the system was abandoned in 1956. The system of CPAs was resumed in 1980 and the first *Certified Public Accountants Act* was promulgated in 1992. The accounting profession in China is quite young and the quality of CPAs is lower than in western countries. The CPAs and their organisation, CICPA, have not been truly granted an independent statute, and governmental interference is the biggest problem in the development of the profession in China.

So far, foreign CPAs are not allowed to conduct their own business in China although the big six international accounting firms have all established joint venture accounting firms in China. It is possible that China will open its CPA market to the outside world soon and that competition will enhance the quality of Chinese CPAs and CPA firms.

Accounting Education

Compared with other aspects of accounting, accounting education has suffered much criticism. Although some reforms have been carried out in accounting education, such as revising the curriculum, the system is still based on the Soviet Union model and fails to provide capable graduates for the needs of economic reform and the internationalising of commercial activities. There are several reasons why accounting education reform has lagged behind the development of the economy. Firstly, most accounting instructors and lecturers were trained under the older Soviet accounting education system and most of them lack knowledge about western economic theory, communications and computer technology, research methodology and modern accounting theory and practice. They need to re-train in order to understand contemporary accounting theory and practice. Secondly, western accounting textbooks are not easily accessible for most teachers and students because they are too expensive and most have not yet been translated into Chinese. Thirdly, although China has sent accounting scholars overseas to learn advanced accounting theory and practice, it seems the numbers are too small and the scope of the international cooperation in accounting education is too narrow.

Accounting research undertaken by the Chinese is quite different from that in western countries. The descriptive method is mainly used by Chinese academics and practitioners and empirical and behavioural research methods are quite new to them. There is a long way to go for the Chinese to catch up with accounting research in developed countries.

Taxation Reform

The Chinese taxation system was restructured in 1994. Unlike western countries in which income tax is the main financial source of government revenue, in China turnover taxes are the main sources. After the reform, the main taxes in China are Value-added Tax, Consumption Tax, Business Tax, Domestic Enterprise Income Tax, Foreign Investment Enterprise Income Tax, and Individual Income Tax. The Chinese taxation system is now more rational and internationally comparable. However, there are still some problems in the implementation of the new tax system, such as in the administration and sharing of tax income between the central government and local governments.

Enterprise Reform

Accounting reforms are strongly associated with the enterprise reforms. Enterprise reforms are pre-requisites for accounting reforms. Since 1979, several enterprise reform packages have been adopted by the Chinese government in order to revive the state-owned enterprises. However, more and more state-owned enterprises continued to slip into deficit and their share in the national economy has constantly declined. By contrast non state-owned enterprises, such as private enterprises and foreign investment enterprises have grown dramatically. The following reforms of state-owned enterprises have been suggested: separation of the living and political support function from the business operations function; establishment of job security, social medical insurance, and a pension insurance system; recognition of the professional status of entrepreneurs; establishment of a free labour market and of a modern enterprise system, e.g. the shareholder corporation. However, the reform of state-owned enterprises in fact is much more complicated than this. It requires the reorganisation of the political and social pattern in China. Therefore the progress of enterprise reform will be slow. The Chinese government is, to some extent, willing to smooth this procedure in order to keep the society stable.

Future Direction and Characteristics of Chinese Accounting

There is a debate about the future direction of Chinese accounting. One group of accounting scholars and practitioners asserts that Chinese accounting should be internationalised and that China should follow the Singapore model, using international accounting standards as its own accounting standards. Other scholars insist that Chinese accounting should be nationalised. They have tried to establish China's own accounting framework, standards and theory. As the first Chinese accounting standard is more internationally

243

oriented, it seems that the international group's thinking is prevailing. However, China is a big country with a long and proud history and a huge population and nationalism is deeply rooted in the society. Therefore, Chinese accounting will no doubt have its own characteristics. These appear to be as follows:

Government Domination in Accounting Affairs

Historically and culturally, the government has dominated the country for more than two thousand years, and the current government still controls the society tightly. Accounting is no exception and is under the control of the government. The Accounting Affairs Administration Department (AAAD) in the Ministry of Finance (MOF) is the real power centre in the management of all aspects of accounting, from accounting standards, uniform accounting systems to accounting education and even the promotion of accountants. This situation will apparently remain, whatever may be the future directions of accounting development. The accounting professional body, CICPA, is a quasi-government agent which will play an important role in the future. However, it cannot be as powerful an organisation as the American Institute of Certified Public Accountants (AICPA), The Institute of Chartered Accountants in Australia (ICAA) and Australian Society of Certified Practising Accountants (ASCPA) because of governmental control.

Concurrence of Uniform Accounting Systems and Accounting Standards

As accounting standards have come into the reality of China, the future of the uniform accounting systems is doubtful. However, from both the historical and the practical point of view, the uniform accounting systems will continue to exist alongside the accounting standards. There are several forms in which the uniform accounting systems can survive. Firstly, the many different uniform accounting systems for different industries may be combined and reduced to one or a few uniform accounting systems, which will make accounting data comparable across industries. Some scholars have undertaken this project. Secondly, a uniform accounts plan may be integrated into the accounting standards as a separate accounting standard. This is more like the French model. Thirdly, the current situation may be retained. In some Chinese scholars' views, the accounting standards should not only include guidelines to identify, measure, calculate and disclose accounting elements; they should also include the guidelines on how to record accounting transactions. This

244

would mean incorporating the uniform accounting systems and bookkeeping methods into the accounting standards.

The Internationalism and Nationalism of Chinese Accounting

Should Chinese accounting be internationalised or nationalised? Both total internationalising and total nationalising seem wrong. Before adopting other countries' accounting models, China should take stock and consider carefully which areas of accounting should be internationalised and which should keep their own features. Financial accounting will be more internationalised in the future; the recognising and measuring criteria, and the disclosure requirements of financial information will be in line with international accounting standards. On the other hand, management accounting and accounting administration may keep their own unique features. Obviously, the Chinese must adopt some advanced management accounting theory and practice but they should not forget their own management accounting experience. Pro-western attitudes may affect some academics and practitioners in accounting. They can assert that Chinese accounting should be totally westernised. It is suggested here that the Chinese should absorb all the advanced accounting theory and practice of the world as well as valuing its own experience. China should establish a system which is internationally comparable with, but not identical to models such as those of the United States, the United Kingdom, Japan, and Germany, however, they would maintain some unique Chinese characteristics.

Conclusion

Chinese accounting is in a transition period. Its reforms are an interesting experiment in accounting transformation from one social pattern to another. Chinese accounting is becoming more internationalised with the opening-up of its society. It is willing to accept all advanced accounting systems in the world. Its development has been influenced, and will be continually affected by its political, economic and cultural systems. Chinese accounting made a great contribution to the development of accounting in the world in the past, including the ancient past, and will play an important role in international accounting in the future.

245

Appendix:

Case Study 1: Sequential Process Costing System in the New Star Electronic Company

The New Star Electronic Company manufactures one product, Z, which has to go through three processing steps. Raw material is input at the beginning of the production in Step 1, where it is transformed into semi-finished goods X. The semi-finished goods X are transferred into storage I. In Step 2, semi-finished goods X are transformed into semi-finished goods Y, which are stored temporarily at storage II. In Step 3, semi-finished goods Y are transferred into product Z. Finished goods are installed in Storage III. The company uses the sequential process costing method, and the relevant cost data of the New Star Electronic Company is as follows:

(a)   The quantities of product A

Steps	Work-in-process, beginning	Started at current period	Finished at current period	Work-in-process ending
Step 1	80	250	260	70
Step 2	50	300	320	30
Step 3	70	230	240	60

Note: raw material is input at the start of Step 1. The other expenses are incurred constantly and the finishing degree of work in process is 50%.

(b)   Costs of work in process, beginning

Steps	Direct material	Semi-finished goods	Direct labour	Overhead	Total
Step 1	3,200		750	1,200	5,150
Step 2		8,200	820	1,420	10,440
Step 3		10,500	3,250	2,800	16,550
Total:	3,500	18,750	4,820	5,420	32,140

(c) The beginning balance of semi-finished goods and finished goods in Storages

	Quantity	Unit cost	Total
Storage I	50	95	4,750
Storage II	60	140	8,400
Storage III	75	240	18,000

(d) Cost incurred in the current month

Steps	Direct material	Direct labour	Overhead	Total
Step 1	12,000	2,400	3,250	17,650
Step 2		5,250	9,420	14,670
Step 3		10,520	8,750	19,270
Total:	12,000	18,170	21,420	51,590

Solution:

The costs of product Z can be calculated as follows:

(a)   Costs of semi-finished goods X in Step 1

Item	Direct materials	Direct Labour	Overhead	Total
Work-in-process, beginning	3,200	750	1,200	5,150
Costs in current month	12,000	2,400	3,250	17,650
Total:	15,200	3,150	4,450	22,800
@ cost of elements	46	11	15	
Costs of semi-finished goods	11,946	2,776	3,922	18,674
Work-in-process, ending	3,224	374	528	4,126

Note: The per-unit cost of the cost elements of semi-finished goods in step 1 is calculated as follows:
@ Direct Materials = 15,200/(260+70) = 46
@ Direct Labour =3,150/(260+70*50%) = 11
@ Overhead = 4,450/(260+70*50%) = 15

The sub-ledger of semi-finished goods X in Step 1:

Item	Quantity	Unit cost	Total costs
Beginning balance	50	95	4,750
Hand-in from step 1	260	72	18,674
Sub-total	310	76	23,424
Hand-out to step 2	300	76	22,668
Ending balance	10		756

Note: The unit cost of semi-finished goods hand-out is computed as (4,750+18,674)/ (50+260) = 76.

(b) Costs of semi-finished goods in Step 2

Item	Semi-finished goods from step 1	Direct Labour	Overhead	Total
Work-in-process, beginning	8,200	820	1,420	10,440
Costs in current month	22,668	5,250	9,420	37,338
Total:	30,868	6,070	10,840	47,778
@ cost of elements	88	18	32	138
Costs of semi-finished goods	28,223	5,798	10,355	44,375
Work-in-process, ending	2,646	272	485	3,403

Note: The per-unit cost of the cost elements of semi-finished goods in Step 2 is calculated as follows:
@ Semi-finished goods of X = 30,868/(320+30) = 88
@ Direct Labour = 6,070/(320 +30*50%) = 18
@ Overhead =10,355/(320+30*50%) = 32

The sub-ledger of semi-finished goods Y in Step 2:

Item	Quantity	Unit cost	Total costs
Beginning balance	60	140	8,400
Hand-in from step 2	320	139	44,375
Sub-total	380	139	52,755
Hand-out to step 3	230	139	31,943
Ending balance	150		20,832

Note: The unit cost of semi-finished goods Y hand-out is computed as (8,400+44,375)/ (60+320) = 139

(c) Costs of finished goods in Step 3

Item	Semi-finished goods Y from step 2	Direct Labour	Overhead	Total
Work-in-process, beginning	10,500	3,250	2,800	16,550
Costs in current month	31,943	10,520	8,750	51,213
Total:	42,443	13,770	11,550	67,763
@ cost of elements	141	51	43	235
Costs of finished goods	33,954	12,240	10,267	56,461
Work-in-process, ending	8,489	1,530	1,283	11,302

Note: The per-unit cost of the cost elements of finished goods in Step 3 is calculated as follows:
@ Semi-finished goods of $Y = 42,443/(240+60) = 141$
@ Direct Labour $= 13,770/(240+60*50\%) = 51$
@ Overhead $= 11,550/(240+60*50\%) = 43$

Ledger of finished goods in Step 3:

Item	Quantity	Unit cost	Total costs
Beginning balance	75	240	18,000
Hand-in from step 3	240	235	56,461
Sub-total	315	236	74,461
Sold	300	236	70,915
Ending balance	15		3,546

Note: The unit cost of goods sold of Z is computed as $(18,400+56,461)/(75+240) = 236$

(d) Cost- restored

As shown in the calculation of costs of finished goods in Step 3, the cost of finished goods 56,461 yuan, or approximately, 235 yuan per unit. However, we only know that the 235 yuan cost consists of the cost of the semi-finished goods Y 141 yuan, the direct labour 51 yuan and the overhead 43 yuan in Step 3. It is necessary for government agencies and the management of enterprises to figure out how much the cost of direct materials, direct labour and overhead is in a finished product. Therefore the costs of semi-finished goods should be divided into the cost elements. This procedure is called cost-restored in China. The proportion of cost elements in semi-finished goods is as follows:

249

Proportion of each cost element in semi-finished goods

Item		Direct materials or semi-finished goods	Direct labour	Overhead	Total
@ cost of semi-	Amount	46	11	15	72
finished goods (X)	%	64%	15%	21%	100%
@ cost of semi-	Amount	88	18	32	138
finished goods (Y)	%	64%	13%	23%	100%

The costs of finished goods can be restored, based on the proportion of each cost element in the semi-finished goods. The calculation is illustrated in next page.

After calculating cost-restored, the amount of each cost element can be derived. The unit cost of product Z is 235 yuan, and the direct materials are 58 yuan, direct labour is 83 yuan, and overhead is 94 yuan.

Calculation of Cost-restored

Item	Semi-finished goods Y	Semi-finished goods X	Direct Material	Direct Labour	Overheads	Total
Total costs before restoration	33,95			12,24	10,26	56,46
Unit cost of semi-finished goods Y		8		1	3	13
Percentage of cost elements bear unit						
Cost of semi-finished goods Y		64		13	23	
(1) Decompose the costs of Semi-finished goods Y	-33,95	21,65		4,42	7,87	
Unit cost of semi-finished goods X			4	1	1	7
Percentage of cost elements bear unit						
Cost of semi-finished goods X			64	15	21	
(2) Decompose the cost of Semi-finished goods X		-21,65	13,83	3,30	4,51	
Total decomposed costs			13,83	19,97	22,65	56,46
Unit Cost			5	8	9	23

Case Study 2: The Parallel Costing System in the Pacific Clothing Company

The Pacific Clothing Company mainly produces men's shirts. There are three procedures: cutting, sewing, and ironing and packing. The cloth is input in the cutting workshop (Step 1), and cut to semi-finished goods A. A is transferred to the sewing workshop (Step 2), and produced to semi-finished goods B. B is transferred to the ironing and packing workshop (Step 3), and completed as men's shirts C. The finished degree of work in process is 50 per cent. The company uses the parallel costing system and the data of quantities and costs in each step are illustrated below.

(a) The data of quantities in each step:

Item	Step 1	Step 2	Step 3
Work-in-process, beginning	100	80	40
Amount incurred in current period	460	500	480
Amount of transferred out	500	480	360
Work-in-process, ending	60	100	160

(b) The data of costs in each step

Items	Work-in-Process, Beginning				Costs Occurred in Current Period			
	Direct material	Direct labour	Over-head	Total	Direct material	Direct labour	Over-head	Total
Step 1:	1,500	780	1,000	3,280	17,500	6,000	1,850	25,350
Step 2:		560	650	1,210		6,200	5,950	12,150
Step 3:		1,750	960	2,710		18,250	10,250	28,500

Solution:

(1) Production Cost Statement in Step I

Item	Direct material	Direct labour	Over-head	Total
Work-in-process, beginning	1,500	780	1,000	3,280
Costs occurred in current period	17,500	6,000	1,850	25,350
Total costs	19,000	6,780	2,850	28,630
Equivalent units*	680	650	650	
Application rate	48	10	4	
Costs transferred to finished goods	10,059	3,755	1,578	15,392
Work-in-process, ending	8,941	3,025	1,272	13,238

* Note:
- The equivalent units for direct material = (Semi-finished goods, beginning in this step) + (Semi-finished goods transferred in this month) + (Work-in-process, ending in this step; narrow concept) = (final finished goods) + (Work-in-process, ending, broad concept) = $(80+40) + 500 + 60 = 680$ or $= 360 + (60+100+160) = 680$
- The equivalent units for direct labour = $(80+40+500+60*50\%) = 650$ or $= (360+160+100+60*50\%) = 650$
- The equivalent units for overhead = $(80+40+500+60*50\%) = 650$ or $= (360+160+100+60*50\% = 650$

(2) Production Cost Statement in Step 2

Item	Direct Labour	Overhead	Total
Work-in-process, beginning	560	650	
Costs occurred in current period	6,200	5,950	12,150
Total costs	6,760	6,600	13,360
Equivalent units*	570	570	
Application rate	12	12	
Costs transferred to finished goods	4,269	4,168	8,438
Work-in-process, ending	2,491	2,432	4,922

253

*Note:
- The equivalent units for direct labour = (40+480+100*50%) = 570 or (360+160+100*50%) = 570
- The equivalent units for overhead = (40+480+100*50%) = 570 or (360+160+100*50%) = 570

(3) Production Cost Statement in Step 3

Item	Direct Labour	Overhead	Total
Work-in-process, beginning	1,750	960	2,710
Costs occurred in current period	18,250	10,250	28,500
Total costs	20,000	11,210	31,210
Equivalent units*	440	440	
Application rate	45	25	
Costs transferred to finished goods	16,364	9,172	25,535
Work-in-process, ending	3,636	2,038	5,675

* Note:
- The equivalent units for direct labour = (360+160*50%) = 440
- The equivalent units for overhead = (360+160*50%) = 440

(4) The cost of finished goods of C

Item	Direct Material	Direct Labour	Overhead	Total
Step 1	10,059	3,755	1,578	15,392
Step 2		4,269	4,168	8,438
Step 3		16,364	9,172	25,535
Total Costs	10,059	24,388	14,919	49,366
Unit Cost	28	68	41	137

254

Case Study 3: Normative Costing System in the Victory Plastics Factory

Victory Plastics uses normative costing to calculate actual product costs. There is only one product produced by the factory; plastic chairs. If one hundred plastic chairs are produced in one month, the related data can be illustrated as follows:

Table A3-1 Normative Cost and Actual Cost in the Work-in-process and Current Period

Item	Quantity	Normative Cost	Actual Cost
Work in process, beginning:	20		
Direct materials		100	110
Direct labour		60	65
Overhead		40	50
Started during current period	110		
Direct materials		550	630
Direct labour		330	400
Overhead		220	180
Work in process, ending:	30		

If standard costing was to be used in the valuation of the finished goods, the total cost of finished goods would be 1000 yuan (quantity 100, @ direct materials 5 yuan, @ direct labour 3 yuan and @ overhead 2 yuan). However, under normative costing used by Victory Plastics, only actual costs can be utilised in financial statements and therefore, the normative costs of products must be conversed to actual costs. The actual costs of 100 plastic chairs under normative costing can be calculated as follows:

Table A3-2 Calculation of the Actual Costs of Plastic Chair in Normative Costing System

	Work in process, beginning		Started in current period		To account for	
	Norm cost	Variance	Norm cost	Variance	Norm cost	Variance
	(1)	(2)	(3)	(4)	(5)=(1)+(3)	(6)=(2)+(4)
Materials costs	100	10	550	80	650	90
Labour costs	60	5	330	70	390	75
Overhead	40	10	220	-20	260	-10
Total	200	25	1,100	130	1,300	155

Proportion rate	Finished goods				Work in process, ending	
	Norm cost	Variance	Actual cost	Unit cost	Norm cost	Variance
(7)=(4)/(5)	(8)	(9)=(8)*(7)	(10)=(8)+(9)	(11)=(10)/100	(12)	(13)=(6)-(9)
13.85%	500	69.23	569.23	5.69	150	20.77
19.23%	300	57.69	357.69	3.58	90	17.31
-3.85%	200	-7.69	192.31	1.92	60	-2.31
11.92%	1000	119.23	1,119.23	11.19	300	35.77

Case Study 4: Effect-chain Analysis in the Eastern Meat Company

The Eastern Meat Company has one product of ham. The profits of the company increased by 180,000 Yuan in this year. The related data are as follows.

	Sale Volume	Sale Price	Unit cost	Tax rate	Profit
This year	1,200	20	12	20%	7,680
Last year	1,000	18	8	25%	7,500
Increase or Decrease	200	2	4	-5%	180

(1) Volume effect of sales on profit

	Sale Volume	Sale Price	Unit cost	Tax rate	Profit
Substitute 1	1,200	18	8	25%	9,000
Last year	1,000	18	8	25%	7,500
Increase or Decrease	200	0	0	0%	1,500

(2) Price effect of sales on profit

	Sale Volume	Sale Price	Unit cost	Tax rate	Profit
Substitute 2	1,200	20	8	25%	10,800
Substitute 1	1,200	18	8	25%	9,000
Increase or Decrease	0	2	0	0%	1,800

257

Unit cost effect on profit

	Sale Volume	Sale Price	Unit cost	Tax rate	Profit
Substitute 3	1,200	20	12	25%	7,200
Substitute 2	1,200	20	8	25%	10,800
Increase or Decrease	0	0	4	0%	(3,600)

(3) Tax rate effect on profit

	Sale Volume	Sale Price	Unit cost	Tax rate	Profit
Substitute 4	1,200	20	12	20%	7,680
Substitute 3	1,200	20	12	25%	7,200
Increase or Decrease	0	0	0	-5%	480

(5) Total effects on profits

$\Delta 1 = \Delta q + \Delta s + \Delta c + \Delta t = 1,500 + 1,800 - 3,600 + 480 = 180$

Case Study 5: Internal Banking System in the Chinese Chemical Machinery Corporation

The Chinese Chemical Machinery Corporation has two workshops: Workshop I, which produces semi-finished goods; and Workshop II, which produces finished goods. In addition, the Corporation has a supply department, sales department, semi-finished-goods storage, and administrative department. Before implementing an internal banking system, the trial balance of relevant accounts of the Corporation was as follows:

Table A5-1 Trial Balance before Implementation (Renmibi $,000 Yuan)

Accounts	Debit	Credit
Material	12,000	
Variances of material	100	
Work-in-process	3,100	
Semi-finished goods	1,500	
Finished goods	7,500	
Variances of finished goods		150
Cash	4,400	
Deposit in bank	35,000	
Working capital		63,450
Total:	63,600	63,600

Two years ago, the corporation decided to set up an internal banking system. It therefore calculated the limit of working capital for each unit, it assigned to the units a total internal working capital of 45,000 yuan and also issued 2,000 internal money. The details of the total working capital 1 and its utilisation in each unit are illustrated in Table A5-2.

259

Table A5-2 Utilisation of Internal Working Capital ($,000)

Internal Units	Limit of working capital	Utilising of the working capital
Workshop I	3,500	1,000
Workshop II	4,500	2,000
Supply department	16,500	12,000
Sales department	12,000	7,500
Semi-finished Goods Storage	5,000	1,500
Administrate department	3,500	
Total:	45,000	24,000

The bookkeeping entries in the Accounting and Banking Department for setting up an internal banking system were as follows:

(a) Calculating and assigning the internal working capital to each unit

Dr.	Working capital to internal units	45,000,000
Cr.	Internal deposit – workshop I	3,500,000
	– Workshop II	4,500,000
	– Supply department	16,500,000
	– Sales department	12,000,000
	– Semi-finished goods storage	5,000,000
	– Administrate department	3,500,000

(b) Utilising the working capital in each unit

Dr.	Internal deposit – Workshop I	1,000,000
	– Workshop II	2,000,000
	– Supply department	12,000,000
	– Sales department	7,500,000
	– Semi-finished goods storage	1,500,000
Cr.	Work-in-process – Workshop I	1,000,000
	Work-in-process – Workshop II	2,000,000
	Material	12,000,000
	Finished goods	7,500,000
	Semi-finished goods	1,500,000

(c) Transferring the production variances

Dr.   Variances of production cost   100,000
   Cr.   Work-in-process   100,000

(d) Issuing of internal money

Dr.   Internal money   2,000,000
   Cr.   Issuing of internal money   2,000,000

Journal entries in each internal unit for setting up the internal banking system were shown as follows:

(a)   Supply Department

(i) Receiving internal working capital from the accounting and banking department

Dr.   Internal deposit   16,500,000
   Cr.   Internal working capital   16,500,000

(ii) Using internal deposit to purchase the materials from the accounting and banking department

Dr.   Materials   12,000,000
   Cr.   Internal deposit   12,000,000

(b)   Workshop I
(i) Receiving internal working capital from the accounting and banking department

Dr.   Internal deposit   3,500,000
   Cr.   Internal working capital   3,500,000

(ii) Using internal deposit to purchase the work-in-process from the accounting and banking department

Dr.   Work-in process –Workshop I   1,000,000
   Cr.   Internal deposit   1,000,000

(c)   Workshop II
(i) Receiving internal working capital from the accounting and banking department

Dr. Internal deposit	4,500,000
Cr. Internal working capital	4,500,000

(ii) Using internal deposit to purchase the work-in-process from the accounting and banking department

Dr. Work-in process –Workshop I	2,000,000
Cr. Internal deposit	2,000,000

(d)   Semi-finished goods storage
(i) Receiving internal working capital from the accounting and banking department

Dr. Internal deposit	5,000,000
Cr. Internal working capital	5,000,000

(ii) Using internal deposit to purchase semi-finished goods from the accounting and banking department

Dr. Semi-finished goods	1,500,000
Cr. Internal deposit	1,500,000

(e)   Sales department
(i) Receiving internal working capital from the accounting and banking department

Dr. Internal deposit	12,000,000
Cr. Internal working capital	12,000,000

(ii) Using internal deposit to purchase finished goods from the accounting and banking department

Dr. Finished goods	7,500,000
Cr. Internal deposit	7,500,000

(f)   Administration department
(i) Receiving internal working capital from the accounting and banking department

Dr.   Internal deposit   3,500,000
   Cr.   Internal working capital   3,500,000

The trial balances of the enterprise after the adjustment for implementing the internal banking system were as follows:

Table A5-3 Trial Balance of the Accounts after Adjustment in the Accounting and Banking Department ($,000)

Accounts	Debit	Credit
Working capital in internal units	45,000	
Variances of material	100	
Variances of production cost	100	
Variances of finished goods		150
Cash on hand	4,400	
Deposit at bank	35,000	
Internal money	2,000	
Internal deposit		21,000
Working capital		63,450
Issuing of internal money		2,000
Total	86,600	86,600

**Table A5-4 Trial Balance of the Accounts after Adjustment in Each
Internal Unit ($,000)**

	Debit	Credit
Supply Department		
Materials	12,000	
Internal deposit	4,500	
Working capital		16,500
Workshop I		
Work-in-process	1,000	
Internal deposit	2,500	
Working capital		3,500
Workshop II		
Work-in-process	2,000	
Internal deposit	2,500	
Working capital		4,500
Semi-finished goods storage		
Semi-finished goods	1,500	
Internal deposit	3,500	
Working capital		5,000
Sales department		
Finished goods	7,500	
Internal deposit	4,500	
Working capital		12,000
Administration department		
Internal deposit	3,500	
Working capital		3,500
Total	45,000	45,000

In the following month, these transactions occurred and the journal entries in the Accounting and Banking Department are shown as follows:

A. Accounting in the Accounting and Banking Department

(a) The supply department purchased the material 3,500,000 at actual price.

Dr.   Internal deposit – Supply department   3,500,000
   Cr.   Deposit at bank   3,500,000

(b) The planned price of the material was 3,250,000 and the supply department submitted the losses to the accounting department.

Dr.   Variances of material   250,000
   Cr.   Internal deposit – Supply department   250,000

(c) Workshop I brought materials from Supply department for 1,750,000.

Dr.   Internal deposit – Workshop I   1,750,000
   Cr.   Internal deposit – Supply department   1,750,000

(d) The accounting department withdrew cash from bank for the employee's wages.

Dr.   Cash at hand   1,200,000
   Cr.   Deposit at bank   1,200,000

(e) Each internal unit received cash from the accounting department and paid employees wages.

Dr.   Internal deposit – Workshop I   450,000
                  – Workshop II   400,000
                  – Administration department   350,000
   Cr.   Cash at hand   1,200,000

(f) The accounting department paid the outside expenses on the behalf of each internal unit.

Dr.   Internal deposit – Workshop I   150,000
                  – Workshop II   180,000
                  – Administration department   240,000
   Cr.   Cash at hand   570,000

(g) Workshop I transferred the semi-finished goods to storage at the planned cost of 2,000,000 Yuan.

Dr. Internal deposit – Storage   2,000,000
   Cr. Internal deposit – Workshop I   2,000,000

(h) The actual cost of semi-finished goods was 1,750,000 yuan. Workshop I calculated the internal profit and charged it to the accounting department

Dr. Internal deposit – Workshop I   250,000
   Cr. Variances of production cost   250,000

(i) Workshop II borrowed internal loans from Internal bank

Dr. Internal out-of-limit loan   1,500,000
   Cr. Internal deposit – workshop II   1,500,000

(j) Workshop II bought semi-finished goods from semi-finished foods storage

Dr. Internal deposit – Workshop II   3,000,000
   Cr. Internal deposit – Storage   3,000,000

(k) Workshop II transferred the finished goods at planned cost of 2,500,000 yuan.

Dr. Internal deposit – Sales department   2,500,000
   Cr. Internal deposit – Workshop II   2,500,000

(l) Workshop II returned the out-off-limit loan of 1,000,000 yuan

Dr. Internal deposit – Workshop II   1,000,000
   Cr. Internal out-off-limit loan   1,000,000

(m) The Accounting department charged the interest on loans of Workshop II

Dr. Internal deposit – Workshop II   75,000
   Cr. Variances of finished goods   75,000
(the interest on internal deposit is treated adversely)

(n) The actual cost of finished goods was 2,640,000 yuan, Workshop II transferred the internal loss to the accounting department (2,500,000 – 2,640,000 – 75,000)

Dr.   Variances of finished goods   215,000
   Cr.   Internal deposit – Workshop II   215,000

(o) The Administration department cashed out the internal money by using an internal cheque of 800,000.

Dr.   Internal deposit – administration department   800,000
   Cr.   Internal money   800,000

(p) The Administration department paid outside the expenses using internal money

Dr.   Internal money   550,000
   Cr.   Deposit at bank   550,000

(q) The Sales department sold the products for 6,5000,000 yuan.

Dr.   Deposit at bank   6,500,000
   Cr.   Internal deposit – sales department   6,500,000

(r) The Sales department calculated the sales tax payable

Dr.   Internal deposit – sales department   350,000
   Cr.   Sales tax payable   350,000

(s) The Sales department submitted the sales profit to the accounting department

Dr.   Internal deposit – sales department   3,200,000
   Cr.   Profit – Sales profit   3,200,000

(t) The Administration department reimbursed the expenses to the accounting department

Dr.   Administration expenses   1,290,000
    Cr.   Internal deposit – Administration department   1,290,000

(u) Charging administrative expenses as period expenses

Dr.   Profit   1,290,000
    Cr.   Administration expenses   1,290,000

(v) The Accounting department adjusted the product costs

(i) Charging the variances of materials to materials delivered to workshops

Dr.   Variances of production costs   100,000
    Cr.   Variances of materials   100,000

(ii) Charging the variances of production costs to the finished goods

Dr.   Variances of finished goods   150,000
    Cr.   Variances of production costs   150,000

(iii) Charging the variances of finished goods to the goods sold

Dr.   Profit   140,000
    Cr.   Variances of finished goods   140,000

Trial Balance in Accounting and Banking Department at End of Month ($,000)

Accounts	Beginning Balance		Month's Incurrence		Ending Balance	
	Debit	Credit	Debit	Credit	Debit	Credit
Working capital in internal units	45,000				45,000	
Internal loan			1,500	1,000	500	
Variances of materials	100		250	100	250	
Variances of production costs	100		100	400		200
Variances of finished goods		150	365	215		
Administrative expenses			1,290	1,290		
Cash on hand	4,400		1,200	1,770	3,830	
Deposit at bank	35,000		6,500	5,250	36,250	
Internal money	2,000		550	800	1,750	
Internal deposit		21,000	20,195	19,005		19,810
Working capital		63,450				63,450
Sales tax payable				350		350
Profit			1,430	3,200		1,770
Issuing of internal money		2,000				2,000
Total	86,600	86,600	32,350	32,350	87,580	87,580

B. Accounting in Internal Units

Accounting in internal units includes calculating the production costs, transferring the variances to the Accounting and Banking department, and calculating the internal profit. In order to perform the internal accounting tasks, several accounts were set up, including; Internal money, Internal deposit, Internal working capital, Internal loan, Internal sales, and Internal profit.

(a) Accounting in the Supply department

(i) Purchasing materials from the outside

Dr.	Materials purchasing	3,500,000	
	Cr. Internal deposit		3,500,000

(ii) Receiving the materials purchased and the planned cost was 3,250,000.

Dr.	Materials	3,250,000	
	Cr. Materials purchasing		3,250,000

(iii) Calculating the variances of materials

Dr. Materials purchasing   250,000
   Cr.   Variances of materials   250,000

(iv) Submitting the variances to the Accounting and Banking department

Dr. Variances of materials   250,000
   Cr.   Internal deposit   250,000

(v) Delivering the materials to workshops at planned cost

Dr. Internal deposit   1,750,000
   Cr.   Materials   1,750,000

Table A5-6 Trial Balance of Supply Department at the End of Month ($,000)

Accounts	Beginning Balance		Month's Incurrence		Ending Balance	
	Debit	Credit	Debit	Credit	Debit	Credit
Internal deposit	4,500		2,000	3,500	3,000	
Materials	12,000		3,250	1,750	13,500	
Materials purchasing			3,500	3,500		
Variances of materials			250	250		
Internal working capital		16,500				16,500
Total:	16,500	16,500	9,900	9,900	16,500	16,500

(b) Accounting in Workshop I

(i) Purchasing materials from Supply department at the planned cost 1,750,000

Dr. Work-in-process I   1,750,000
   Cr.   Internal deposit   1,750,000

(ii) Paying workers' wages

Dr. Cash on hand   450,000
   Cr.   Internal deposit   450,000

270

Dr.	Wages payable	450,000	
	Cr.	Cash on hand	450,000

Dr.	Work-in-process	400,000	
	Overhead	50,000	
	Cr.	Wages payable	450,000

(iii) Calculating monthly depreciation cost

Dr.	Overhead	150,000	
	Cr.	Accumulated depreciation	150,000

(iv) Expenses incurred in current month

Dr.	Overhead	150,000	
	Cr.	Internal deposit	150,000

(v) Applying overhead cost to production costs

Dr.	Work-in-process	350,000	
	Cr.	Overhead	350,000

(vi) Selling semi-finished goods to semi-finished goods storage

Dr.	Internal deposit	2,000,000	
	Cr.	Internal sales	2,000,000

(vii) Calculating the costs of semi-finished goods sold

Dr.	Internal sales	1,750,000	
	Cr.	Work-in-process	1,750,000

(viii) Calculating the internal profit

Dr.	Internal sale	250,000	
	Cr.	Internal profit	250,000

271

(ix) Submitting the internal profit, variances of production costs, to the Accounting and Banking department

Dr. Internal profit – variances of production cost   250,000
   Cr. Internal deposit   250,000

Table A5-7 Trial Balance of Workshop I at the End of Month ($,000)

Accounts	Beginning Balance		Month's Incurrence		Ending Balance	
	Debit	Credit	Debit	Credit	Debit	Credit
Internal deposit	2,500		2,000	2,600	1,900	
Work-in-process I	1,000		2,500	1,750	1,750	
Overhead			350	350		
Cash on hand			450	450		
Internal working capital		3,500				3,500
Wages payable			450	450		
Accumulated depreciation				150		150
Internal sales			2,000	2,000		
Internal profit			250	250		
Total	3,500	3,500	6,950	6,950	3,650	3,650

(c) Accounting in Workshop II

(i) Borrowing money from internal bank

Dr. Internal deposit   1,5000,000
   Cr. Internal loan   1,500,000

(ii) Purchasing semi-finished goods from semi-finished storage at the planned cost of 3,000,000

Dr. Work-in-process II   3,000,000
   Cr. Internal deposit   3,000,000

(iii) Paying workers' wages

Dr. Cash on hand   400,000
   Cr. Internal deposit   400,000

Dr. Wages payable   400,000
   Cr. Cash on hand   400,000

Dr.	Work-in-process	320,000	
	Overhead	80,000	
Cr.	Wages payable		400,000

(iv) Calculating monthly depreciation cost

| Dr. | Overhead | 120,000 | |
| Cr. | Accumulated depreciation | | 120,000 |

(v) Expenses incurred in the month

| Dr. | Overhead | 180,000 | |
| Cr. | Internal deposit | | 180,000 |

(vi) Applying overhead cost to production costs

| Dr. | Work-in-process | 380,000 | |
| Cr. | Overhead | | 380,000 |

(vii) Selling finished goods to Sales department

| Dr. | Internal deposit | 2,500,000 | |
| Cr. | Internal sales | | 2,500,000 |

(viii) Calculating the costs of finished goods sold

| Dr. | Internal sales | 2,640,000 | |
| Cr. | Work-in-process | | 2,640,000 |

(ix) Calculating the internal loss

| Dr. | Internal profit | 140,000 | |
| Cr. | Internal sale | | 140,000 |

(x) Returning internal loan 1,000,000.

| Dr. | Internal loan | 1,000,000 | |
| Cr. | Internal deposit | | 1,000,000 |

(xi) Charging the interest on internal loan

Dr.   Internal profit   75,0000
    Cr.   Internal deposit   75,000

(xii) Reimbursing the internal loss, as variances of finished goods, to the Accounting and Banking department

Dr.   Internal deposit   215,000
    Cr.   Internal profit – variances of finished goods   215,000

(d) Accounting in semi-finished goods storage

(i) Purchasing semi-finished goods from Workshop I at planned cost

Dr.   Semi-finished goods   2,000,000
    Cr.   Internal deposit   2,000,000

(ii) Selling semi-finished goods to Workshop II at planned cost

Dr.   Internal deposit   3,000,000
    Cr.   Semi-finished goods   3,000,000

Table A5-8 Trial Balance of Workshop II at End of the Month ($,000)

Accounts	Beginning Balance		Month's Incurrence		Ending Balance	
	Debit	Credit	Debit	Credit	Debit	Credit
Internal deposit	2,500		4,215	4,655	2,060	
Work-in-process II	2,000		3,700	2,640	3,060	
Overhead			380	380		
Cash on hand			400	400		
Internal working capital		4,500				4,500
Internal loans			1,000	1,500		500
Wages payable			400	400		
Accumulated depreciation				120		120
Internal sales			2,640	2,640		
Internal profit			215	215		
Total	4,500	4,500	12,950	12,950	5,120	5,120

274

Table 5A-9 Trial Balance of Semi-finished Goods Storage at the End of Month ($,000)

Accounts	Beginning Balance		Month's Incurrence		Ending Balance	
	Debit	Credit	Debit	Credit	Debit	Credit
Internal deposit	3,500		3,000	2,000	4,500	
Semi-finished goods	1,500		2,000	3,000	500	
Working capital		5,000				5,000
Total	5,000	5,000	3,500	3,500	5,000	5,000

(e) Accounting in Administrative departments

(i) Paying administrative staff salaries

Dr.	Cash at hand		350,000	
	Cr.	Internal deposit		350,000
Dr.	Administrative expenses		350,000	
	Cr.	Salary payable		350,000
Dr.	Salary payable		350,000	
	Cr.	Cash at hand		350,000

(ii) Calculating the depreciation expenses

Dr.	Administrative expenses		150,000	
	Cr.	Accumulated depreciation		150,000

(iii) Paying administrative expenses

Dr.	Administrative expenses		240,000	
	Cr.	Internal deposit		240,000

(iv) Cashing internal money

Dr.	Internal money		800,000	
	Cr.	Internal deposit		800,000

(v) Using internal money to pay administrative expenses

Dr.	Administrative expenses	550,000
Cr.	Internal money	550,000

(vi) Reimbursing administrative expenses from the Accounting and Banking department

Dr.	Internal deposit	1,290,000
Cr.	Administrative expenses	1,290,000

Table A5-10   Trial Balance of Administrative Departments at the End of Month ($,000)

Accounts	Beginning Balance		Month's Incurrence		Ending Balance	
	Debit	Credit	Debit	Credit	Debit	Credit
Internal deposit	3,500		1,290	1,390	3,400	
Internal money			800	550	250	
Cash on hand			350	350		
Administrative expenses			1,290	1,290		
Internal working capital		3,500				3,500
Accumulated depreciation				150		150
Salary payable			350	350		
Total:	3,500	3,500	2,700	2,700	3,650	3,650

(f) Accounting in the Sales department

(i) Purchasing finished goods from Workshop II at planned cost

Dr.	Finished goods	2,500,000
Cr.	Internal deposit	2,500,000

(ii) Selling products to the outside

Dr.	Internal deposit	6,500,000
Cr.	Sales	6,500,000

276

(iii) Calculating the costs of finished goods sold

| Dr. | Sales | 2,950,000 | |
| | Cr. | Finished goods | 2,950,000 |

(iv) Calculating the sales tax

| Dr. | Sales | 350,000 | |
| | Cr. | Sales tax payable | 350,000 |

(v) Transferring the sales tax payable to the Accounting and Banking department

| Dr. | Sales tax payable | 350,000 | |
| | Cr. | Internal deposit | 350,000 |

(vi) Calculating the sales profit

| Dr. | Sales | 3,200,000 | |
| | Cr. | Profit | 3,200,000 |

(vii) Transferring the sales profit to the Accounting and Banking department

| Dr. | Profit | 3,200,000 | |
| | Cr. | Internal deposit | 3,200,000 |

Table A5-11   Trial Balance in Sales Department at the End of Month ($,000)

Accounts	Beginning Balance		Month's Incurrence		Ending Balance	
	Debit	Credit	Debit	Credit	Debit	Credit
Internal deposit	4,500		6,500	6,050	4,950	
Finished goods	7,500		2,500	2,950	7,050	
Internal working capital		12,000				12,000
Sales tax payable			350	350		
Sales			6,500	6,500		
Profits			3,200	3,200		
Total	12,000	12,000	19,050	19,050	12,000	12,000

(3) Consolidating accounting in the Accounting and Banking department

At the end of each accounting period, the Accounting and Banking department has to prepare the consolidated financial statements based on the trial balances in the internal units and in the Accounting and Banking department itself. The elimination entries are as follows:

(a) Dr.   *Working capital in internal units*   45,000,000
     Cr.   Internal working capital   45,000,000

(b) Dr.   *Internal loan in internal units*   500,000
     Cr.   Internal loan   500,000

(c) Dr. *Internal deposit in internal units*   19,810,000
     Cr.   Internal Deposit   19,810,000

(d) Dr.   *Issuing of internal money*   2,000,000
     Cr.   *Internal money in internal units*   2,000,000

(e) Dr.   *Internal money in internal units*   250,000
     Cr.   Internal money   250,000

Note: The accounts in the Accounting and Banking department are italicised.

After the elimination of these accounts, a Balance Sheet for the enterprise was derived as showed in Table A5-15. Based on the internal profit and loss statement of the Sales department, a profit and loss statement for the enterprise was prepared by the Accounting and Banking department as in Table A5-16.

Table A5-12 Consolidation Worksheet of Internal Units ($,000)

Items	Supply Department Debit	Supply Department Credit	Workshop I Debit	Workshop I Credit	Workshop II Debit	Workshop II Credit	Semi-finished Goods Storage Debit	Semi-finished Goods Storage Credit	Administration Department Debit	Administration Department Credit	Sales Department Debit	Sales Department Credit	Total Debit	Total Credit
Internal deposit	3,000		1,900		2,060		4,500		3,400		4,950		19,810	
Internal money									250					250
Materials	13,500												13,500	
Work-in-process														
Work-in-process I			1,750										1,750	
Work-in-process II					3,060								3,060	
Semi-finished goods							500						500	
Finished goods											7,050		7,050	
Internal working capital		16,500		3,500		4,500		5,000		3,500		12,000		45,000
Internal loan						500								500
Accumulated depreciation				150		120				150				420
Total	16,500	16,500	3,650	3,650	5,120	5,120	5,000	5,000	3,650	3,650	12,000	12,000	45,920	45,920

Table A5-13 Consolidation Worksheet of the Accounts between the Accounting and Banking Department and the Internal Units ($,000)

Items	Internal Units		Accounting and Banking Department		Elimination		Consolidated Accounts	
	Debit	Credit	Debit	Credit	Debit	Credit	Debit	Credit
Accounts in Internal Units:								
Internal deposit	19,810					19,810		
Internal money	250					250		
Materials	13,500						13,500	
Work-in-process								
Work-in-process I	1,750						1,750	
Work-in-process II	3,060						3,060	
Semi-finished goods	500						500	
Finished goods	7,050						7,050	
Internal working capital		45,000			45,000			
Internal loan		500			500			
Accumulated depreciation		420						420

Accounts in Accounting and Banking Department:					
Working Capital in internal units			45,000	45,000	
Internal loan in internal units			500	500	
Cash on hand			3,830		3,830
Deposit at bank			36,250		36,250
Internal money			1,750	2,000	250
Variances of materials			250	250	
Variances of production costs					200
Variances of finished goods	200				
Internal deposit			19,810	19,810	
Working capital			63,450		63,450
Sales tax payable			350		350
Profit			1,770		1,770
Issuing of internal money			2,000	2,000	
Total:	45,920	45,920	87,580	67,560	66,190

Table A5-14   Balance Sheet of the Chinese Chemical Machinery Corporation at the End of Month ($,000)

Items	Debit	Credit
Materials	13,500	
Work-in-process and Semi-finished goods	5,360	
Finished goods	7,050	
Cash on hand	3,830	
Deposit at bank	36,250	
Accumulated depreciation	(420)	
Sales tax payable		350
Working capital		63,450
Income tax payable		584
Retained profit		1,186
Total:	65,570	65,570

Table A5-15   Profit and Loss Statement for Chinese Chemical Machinery Corporation for the Month ($,000)

Items	Sales Department	Accounting and Banking Department	Total
Sales income:	6,500		6,500
Less: Cost of goods sold	2,950		2,950
Sales tax	350		350
Operation profit	3,200		3,200
Less: Variances of finished goods		140	140
Administrative expenses		1,290	1,290
Financial expenses			
Add: other income			
Less: other expenses			
Profit before income tax		1,770	1,770
Less: income tax (33%)			584
Profit after income tax			1,186

Bibliography

Abdel-khalik, A.R. and Ajinkya, B.B. (1979), *Empirical Research in Accounting: A Methodological Viewpoint*, American Accounting Association.

Aiken, M. and Lu, W. (1993a), "Historical Instances of Innovative Accounting Practices in Chinese Dynasties and Beyond", *The Accounting Historians Journal*, Vol.20, No.2, December, pp.163-186.

_____ (1993b), "Perception, Culture and Research Method in Accounting History: Its Evolution in Modern China", *Accounting History*, Vol.5, No.1, pp. 11-20.

_____ (1993c), "Chinese Government Accounting: Historical Perspective and Current Initiatives", *British Accounting Review*, Vol.25, No.2, pp 109-129.

Aiken, M., Lu, W. and Ji, X.D. (1995), "The New Accounting Standard in China: A Critical Analysis", *Perspectives on Accounting and Finance in China*, Routledge, pp. 159-177.

_____ (1997), "The Certified Public Accounting Profession in China: Its Development and Impact on Financial Control of Business Operations", *Australian Accounting Review*, Australian Society of Certified Practicing Accountants, Vol.7, No.2, pp.45-53.

Alchian, A. A. and Demsetz, H. (1972), "Production, Information Costs and Economic Organization", *American Economic Review*, Vol. 62, pp.777-795.

Alhashim, D.D. and Arpan, J.S. (1988), *International Dimensions of Accounting*, PWS-KENT Publishing Company.

Australian Accounting Research Foundation (1994), *Accounting Handbook 1994*, Sydney, Prentice Hall.

Baladouni, V. (1987), "The Study of Accounting History", *The Academy of Accounting Historians Working Paper Series*, Vol. 1, Virginia Commonwealth University, pp.318- 327.

Ball, R. and Brown, P. (1968), "An Empirical Evaluation of Accounting Income Numbers", *Journal of Accounting Research*, Vol. 6, pp.159-178.

Barnett, B. (1980), "Observations of CPA in China", *The Journal of Accountancy*, January, pp. 80-83.

Barrow, N. and Liu, K.C. (1994), "A Cross-Cultural Investigation of Ethical Attitudes of Prospective Accountants in China, Hong Kong and the UK", Paper presented at International Symposium on Chinese Accounting and Financial Management Lancashire Business School, Preston, UK, 21 March.

Barzun, J. and Graff, H.F. (1985), *The Modern Researcher*, San Diego: Harcourt Brace, Jovanovich.

Beaver, W.H. (1968), "The Information Content of Annual Earnings Announcements", *Journal of Accounting Research*, Vol. 6 (Supplement), pp.67-92.

Beijing Review (1978), No.52, p.11.

Belkaoui, A. (1985), *International Accounting*, Quorum Books Press.

Bennett, S. (1993), "Chinese and Western Accounting Practices Compared", *Management Accounting*, February, pp. 26-27.

Berry, M. (1988), "The Cultural Development of Accounting in the People's Republic of China", *Recent Accounting and Economic Developments in the Far East*, Centre for International Education and Research in Accounting, Urbana-Champaign, Ill, The University of Illinois, pp.1-26.

Birkett, B. (1987), "Perspectives on Accounting Education", *The Chartered Accountant in Australia*, February, pp. 31-32.

Blake, J. and Gao, S. (1995), *Perspectives on Chinese Accounting and Finance in China*, Routledge.

Bowen, R., Noreen, E. and Lacey, J. (1981), "Determinants of Corporate Decision to Capitalize Interest", *Journal of Accounting and Economics*, Vol 3, pp.151-179.

Bromwich, M. and Bhimani, A. (1989), *Management Accounting: Evolution not Revolution*, Chartered Institute of Management Accountants.

Bromwich, M. and Wang, G.Q. (1991), "Management Accounting in China: A Current Evaluation", *The International Journal of Accounting*, Vol.26, No.1, pp. 51-66.

Bryd, W. (1983), "Enterprise-level Reforms in Chinese State-Owned Industry", *American Economic Review*, May, pp.8-11.

Cai, X.Y. (1993), *Lian Huan Zhan Bu (Chain Accounting System)* (Chinese), WuHan People's Press, Reprint.

Centre for International Education and Research in Accounting (1988), *Recent Accounting and Economic Developments in the Far East*, The University of Illinois.

Certified Public Accountants Act 1993, Chinese Economy and Finance Publishing.

Chambers, R. (1966), *Accounting, Evaluation and Economic Bahavior*, Englewood Clidds, NJ: Prentice-Hall.

Chatfield, M. (1977), *A History of Accounting Thought*, New York: Robert E.K. Publishing.

Chen, H. P. and Tran. A. (1995), "Recent Accounting Reform in China", *Asian Review of Accounting*, Vol.3, No.1, pp.3-24.

Chen, M. (1995), *Asian Management System*, Routledge.

Cheng, P.C.(1980), "Political Accounting in China: What the West Should Know", *The Journal of Accountancy*, January, pp.76-80.

Chen, Y., Jubb, P. and Tran, A., (1997), "Problems of Accounting Reform in the People's Republic of China", *The International Journal of Accounting*, Vol.32, No.2, pp.139-154.

Chen, Y.Q., Zheng, P.J. and Chen, J.Z. (1993), *New Industrial Enterprise Accounting* (Chinese), Lixing Accounting Publishing.

Chen, Y.Z., Dong, F. and Li, Y.Z. (1993), *Industrial Enterprise Accounting and Reporting Under New Accounting System* (Chinese), Astronavigation Publishing.

Cheung, S.N.S. (1983), "The Contractual Nature of the Firm", *Journal of Law and Economics*, Vol.26, pp.1-21.

Choi, F.D.S. and Mueller, G.G. (1992), *International Accounting*, Second Edition, Prentice-Hall.

Chow, L.M., Chau, G. K. and Gray S. J. (1995), "Accounting Reforms in China: Cultural Constraints on Implementation and Development", *Accounting and Business Research*, Vol.26, No.1, pp. 24-49.

Christie, A.A. (1990), "Aggregation of Test Statistics: An Evaluation of the Evidence on Contracting and Size Hypotheses", *Journal of Accounting and Economics*, Vol.12, pp.12-36.

Coase, R. (1937), "The Nature of the Firm", *Economica*, New Series 4, pp. 386-405.

Coffman, E.N. (1979), *Academy of Accounting Historians: Working Paper Series*, The Academy of Accounting Historians.

Collingwood, R. G. (1946), *The Idea of History*, Oxford University Press.

Creswell, J.W. (1994), *Research Design: Qualitative and Quantitative Approaches*, Thousand Oaks: Sage.

Dai, X.M. (1984), "Differences Between Standard Costing System and Normative costing System", *Accounting Research* (Chinese), No.3, June, pp. 22-25.

Davidson, R., Gelardi, A.M.G. and Li, F. (1996), "Analysis of the Conceptual Framework of China's New Accounting System", *Accounting Horizons*, Vol.10, No.1, March, pp. 58-74.

Devine, C.T. (1963), "The Rule of Conservatism Re-examined", *Journal of Accounting Research*, Vol. 1, pp. 127-138.

Dickinson, J.P. (1990), *Statistical Analysis in Accounting and Finance*, Philip Allan.

Ding, P.Z. (1993), "Answers to Questions Regarding to Foreign CPA Firms and CPAs", *Journal of Certified Public Accountants*, No.12, p. 8.

Doupnik, T.S. and Salter, S.B. (1995), "External Environment, Culture and Accounting Practice: A Preliminary Test of A General Model of International Accounting Development", *International Journal of Accounting Education and Research*, Vol. 30, pp.189-207.

Drury, C.(1992), *Management and Cost Accounting*, 3rd Edition, Chapman and Hall Press.

Drury, C., Braund, S., Osborne, P. and Tayles, M. (1992), "A Survey of Management Accounting Practices in UK Manufacturing Companies", ACCA Research Occasional Paper, Chartered Association of Certified Accountants.

Duke, J.C. and Hunt Jr, H.G. (1990), "An Empirical Examination of Debt Covenant restrictions and Accounting-related Debt Proxies", *Journal of Accounting and Economics*, Vol 12, pp. 45-63.

285

Eisenhardt, K.M. (1989), "Building Theories from Case Study Research", *Academy of Management Review*, Vol.14, No.4, pp.532-550.

Emmanual, C.R. and Edwards, K. (1990), "Exploring The Relevance Gap", *Management Accounting*, November, pp. 44-46.

Enthoven, A.J.H. (1991), "Accounting, Auditing and Education in the People's Republic of China", in *Comparative International Accounting*, eds. C. Nobes and R. Parker, Prentice-Hall, pp.277-278.

Everitt, B. (1974), *Cluster Analysis*, Heinemann Educational Books.

Fang, Q.M. (1994), "State-owned Enterprise Reform in China: Incentives and Environment", *China's Economic Reforms*, edited by Fang, Q. M. and Nolan, P., St.Martin's Press.

Fang, Z. L. (1989), "Re-examining the Accounting Equation: How to Report Assets, Liabilities and Equity", *Accounting Research* (Chinese), No.3, pp.21-9.

Fang, Z. L. and Tang, Y. W. (1991), "Recent Accounting Developments in China: An Increasing Internationalisation", *International Journal of Accounting*, Vol.26, No.2, pp. 85-103.

Fang, Z. L. and Zhang, W. G., (1988), "New Issues Caused by Economics Structure Reform in Financial Accounting and Reporting", *Sichuan Finance and Accounting* (Chinese), No.2, pp.10-11.

Far Eastern Economic Review (1993), "Business briefing", 9 July, p.63.

Farag, S.M. (1988), "Accounting Developments in the People's Republic of China: A Commentary", *International Journal of Accounting*, Vol.23, No.2, pp.145-149.

Farmer, R. and Richman, B. (1966), *International Business: An Operational Theory*, Homewood, Irwin.

Ferris, K.R. (1988), *Behavioural Accounting Research: A Critical Analysis*, Century VII Publishing Company.

Finance and Accounting (1992a) (Chinese) No.2 p.56.

Finance and Accounting (1992b) (Chinese) No.4 p.29.

Financial Accounting Standards Board (1978), *Objectives of Financial Reporting by Business Enterprises*, Statement of Financial Accounting Concept, No.1, Stanford, FASB.

Firth, M. (1996), "The Diffusion of Managerial Accounting Procedures in the People's Republic of China and the Influence of Foreign Partnered Joint Ventures", *Accounting, Organisation and Society*, Vol.21, No.7/8, pp.629-654.

Fisher, L. (1994), "Go East, Brave Firms", *Accountancy*, June, pp.45-46.

Fleischman, R., Mills, P. and Tyson, T. (1996), "A Theoretical Primer for Evaluation and Conducting Historical Research in Accounting", *Accounting History*, Vol.1, No.1, pp. 55 –76.

Fowler, F.J. (1993), *Survey Research Methods*, Second Edition, Sage Publication Inc.

Fu, P.Y. (1968), *A Study of Governmental Accounting in China: with Special Reference to the Song Dynasty, Ph.D Dissertation*, University of Illinois at Urnana-Champaign.

_____ (1971), "Government Accounting in China During the Chou Dynasty", *Journal of Accounting Research*, Vol.9, No.1, pp. 40-51.

Gang, J. (1992), "Initial Practice in the Development of the Chinese Accounting Standards", *Accounting Research* (Chinese), No.2, pp. 26-30.

Gao, S. (1996), *China's Economic Reform*, St. Martin's Press.

Gay, L.R. and Diebl, P.L. (1992), *Research Methods for Business and Management*, Macmillan Publishing Company.

Ge, J.S. (1992), "Learning from International Experience to Establish Chinese Accounting Standards", *Accounting Research* (Chinese), No.2, pp.16-19.

Geng, Y.X.(1994), "Reform of State Enterprises to Enter New Stage", *Beijing Review*, November, pp. 21-27.

Godfrey, J., Hodgson, A., Holmes, S. and Kam, V. (1994), *Accounting Theory*, John Wiley and Sons.

Godsell, D. (1993), *Auditors' Legal Duties and Liabilities in Australia*, Longman Professional.

Graham, L.E. (1996), "Setting a Research Agenda for Auditing Issues in the People's Republic of China", *International Journal of Accounting*, Vol.31, No.1, pp.19-37.

Gray, S. J. (1988), "Towards a Theory of Cultural Influence on the Development of Accounting Systems Internationally", *Abacus*, Vol. 24, No.1, pp.1-15.

Gray, S.J. and Vint, H.M. (1995), "The Impact of Culture on Accounting Disclosures: Some International Evidence", *Asia-Pacific Journal of Accounting*, December, pp.34-43.

Graziano, A.M. and Raulin, M.L. (1989), *Research Methods: A Process of Inquiry*, New York: Happer and Row Publishers.

Gujarati, D.N. (1995), *Basic Econometrics*, Third Edition, McGrqw-Hill, Inc.

Guo, D.Y. (1982,1988), *The History of Chinese Accounting* (Chinese) (Vol.1 and 2), Beijing, Chinese Financial and Economics Press.

_____ (1984), "The Historical Contributions of Chinese Accounting", *Collected Papers of the Fifth World Congress of Accounting Historians*, The University of Sydney.

_____ (1986), *The History of Accounting Development* (Chinese), Beijing: Chinese Broadcasting and Television University Press.

_____ (1988), "Confucius and Accounting", *The Accounting Historians Notebook*, Spring, 1988, pp. 8-10.

Hagerman, R.L. and Zmijewshi, M. (1979), "Some Economic Determinants of Accounting Policy Choice", *Journal of Accounting & Economics*, Vol 1, pp. 141-161.

Hampden-turner, C. and Trompenarrs, F. (1994), *The Seven Cultures of Capitalism: Values Systems for Creating Wealth in the United States, Britain, Japan, Germany, France, Sweden, and the Netherlands*, Judy Piatkus Ltd.

He, L. X. and Lin, G. (1991), *Responsibility Accounting* (Chinese), Liaoling Science and Technology Publishing.

287

Henderson, S. and Peirson, G. (1993), *Issues in Financial Accounting*, Melbourne: Longman Cheshire.

Hendrikson, E. (1970), *Accounting Theory*, Homewood, Ill: Irwin.

Hofstede, G. (1980), *Culture's Consequences*, Sage Publications, 1980.

_____(1983), "Dimensions of National Cultures in Fifty Countries and Three Regions", *Explications in Cross-Cultural Psychology*, Swets and Zeitlinger.

_____ (1984), *Cultural Consequences: International Differences in Work Related Values*, abridged edition, Beverley Hills, CA, Sage Publications.

_____ (1987), "The Cultural Context of Accounting" in B.E. Cushing (ed) *Accounting and Culture*, American Accounting Association, pp.1-11.

_____ (1991), *Cultures and Organizations: Software of the Mind*, McGraw-Hill Book Company.

Hofstede, G. and Bond, M. H. (1988), "The Confucius Connection: From Cultural Roots to Economic Growth", *Organisational Dynamics*, Vol.17, pp.4-21. Reprinted in Blunt, P. and Richards, D. (1993), *Readings in Management, Organisation and Culture in East and South East Asia*, NTU Press, Northern Territory University, Darwin, NT Australia, pp.105-121.

Hoggett, J. and Edwards, L.(1992), *Accounting in Australia*, Second Edition, John Wiley & Sons Press.

Horngren, C.T. (1986), "Cost and Management Accounting: Yesterday and Today", in Bromwich, M. and Hopwood, A.G. (1986) (eds), *Research and Current Issues in Management Accounting*, Pitman Press, pp. 31-46.

Horngren, C. T. and Foster, G. (1991), *Cost Accounting*, Prentice-Hall, Inc.

Hsu, T.T. (1981), "Recent Business and Accounting Developments in China", *International Journal of Accounting*, Vol.17, No.1, pp. 157-60.

Huang, H.Q. (1987), "Auditing", in *Accounting and Auditing in the People's Republic of China: a review of its practices, systems, education and development*, Joint Research Study by Shanghai University of Finance and Economics and Center for International Accounting development, The University of Texas at Dallas, pp. 53-74.

Hussey, J. and Hussey, R. (1997), *Business Research*, Macmillan Press Ltd.

Hy, Y. and Marts, J.A. (1991), "How China's Central Government Administers Accounting in Industry" in Doupnik, T.S. (eds), *Advances in International Accounting*, Vol.4, London: JAI Press, pp. 47-53.

Ijiri, Y. (1972), "The Nature of Accounting Research", in Sterling, R. R. (1992) (ed), *Research Methodology in Accounting*, Scholars Book Company, pp. 59-70.

Jensen, M. and Meckling, W. (1976), "Theory of the Firm: Managerial Behaviour, Agency Costs and Ownership Structure", *Journal of Financial Economics*, Vol. 3, October, pp.305-360.

___ (1989a), "The Policies and Methods of Financial Inspection", *Jiangsu Accountancy* (Chinese), November, p. 1.

___ (1989b), "The Inadequacies of the System of Job Responsibility in Business Contract and Tentative Ideas of its Perfection", *Jiangsu Accountancy* (Chinese) August, pp.15-16.

___ (1989c) "The Significant Measure - on Inspection of Taxes, Finance Affairs and Prices in 1989", *Annual Economic Report of Jiangsu Province, 1990* (Chinese) Economics and Finance Press.

___ (1989d), *Evading Taxes and Anti-evading Taxes* (Chinese), Chinese International Broadcasting Press.

Ji, X.D. (1990), "The Analysis of Economic Benefit of Locally-administered State Enterprise in Jiangsu Province", *The Research on the Enterprises Economic Efficiency* (Chinese), Department of Finance, Jiangsu Province, May.

Ji, X.D. and Lu, W. (1992), "Chinese Accounting Reform: Looking Back and Forward", *Chinese Economy in Transition, 1992 Annual Conference of the Chinese Economic Association*, University of Adelaide, Adelaide, Australia, November 12-13.

___ (1995), "Current Failure and Future Direction of Management Reform of State Enterprises in China", *Asia Pacific International Business: Regional Integration and Global Competitiveness*, Academy of International Business, Southeast Asia regional Conference, Perth, Australia, June 20-23.

___ (1996), "A Survey of the Application of Western Management Accounting in China", *Eighth Asian-Pacific Conference on International Accounting Issues*, Vancouver, British Columbia, Canada, October 13-16.

___(1997), "Evaluation of Research on Chinese Accounting Issues", *Eighth World Congress of International Association for Accounting Education and Research*, Paris, 23-25 October.

Johnson, T. and Kaplan, R. S. (1987), *Relevance Lost: The Rise and Fall of management Accounting*, Harvard University Press.

Johnson, T. and Kaplan, R .S. (1991), *Advanced Management Accounting*, second edition, Prentice Hall.

Jones, S. and Aiken, M. (1995), "Introduction of the Emergence of Practice Descriptive Research in Accounting" in Jones, S., Romano, C. and Ratnatunga, J. (ed) *Accounting Theory: A Contemporary Review*, Harcourt Brace and Company, Australia, pp. 3-28.

Jong, H.H. (1979), "The Traditional Accounting Systems in the Oriental Countries – Korea, China, Japan" in Coffman, E.N. (eds), *Academy of Accounting Historians: Working Paper Series*, The Academy of Accounting Historians, Vol.2 pp.7-32.

Kaplan, R.S. (1984), "Yesterday's Accounting Undermines Production", *Harvard Business Review*, July/August, pp. 16-24.

Kirkbride, P. S. and Tang, S.F.Y. (1990), *Negotiation: Lessons from Behind the Bamboo Curtain*, in Blunt, P. and Richards, D. (1993), *Readings in Management, Organisation and Culture in East and South East Asia*, NTU Press, Northern Territory University, Darwin, NT Australia, pp.272-284.

Kroeber, A.L. and Kluckhohn, C. (1952), *Culture: A Critical Review of Concepts and Definitions*, Cambridge, Mass: Peabody Museum.

Kwang, C.W. (1966), "The Economic Accounting System of State Enterprise in Mainland China", *The International Journal of Accounting*, Spring, Vol.2, No.1, pp.61-99.

La Trobe University Handbook, 1997.

Lai, J. (1985), "Management Accounting in China", *Management Accounting*, September, pp.26-28.

Lau, A.H.L. and Yang, J.L.(1990), "Auditing in China: Historical Perspective and Current Developments", *The International Journal of Accounting*, Vol. 25, No.1, pp.53-62.

Lawrence, S. (1996), *International Accounting*, International Thomson Business Press.

Lefebvre, C. and Lin, L.Q. (1990), "Internationalisation of Financial Accounting Standards in the Peoples' Republic of China", *The International Journal of Accounting*, Vol.25, No.3, pp.170-183.

Li, J.Y. (1991), *Taxation in the people's republic of China*, Praeger Publishers.

Li, W.Z. (1988), "System of Cost and Management Accounting" in *Accounting and Auditing in the People's Republic of China: a review of its practices, systems, education and development*, Joint Research Study by Shanghai University of Finance and Economics and Center for International Accounting development, The University of Texas at Dallas. pp 31-52.

Lichtenstein, P.M. (1991), *China At The Brink*, Praeger Publishers, New York.

Lin, Z. (1989), "A Survey of Current Developments in Chinese Accounting" in T.S.Doupnik,(eds) *Advances in International Accounting*, London, JAI Press Inc, Vol.2, pp. 99-110.

___ (1992), "Chinese Double-entry Bookkeeping before the Nineteenth Century", *The Accounting Historians Journal*, Vol.19, No.2, pp. 103-122.

Lin, Z. and Deng, S.L. (1992), "Educating Accounting in China: Current Experiences and Future Prospects", *The International Journal of Accounting*, pp.164-177.

Lippit, V.D., (1987), *The Economic Development of China*, New York: E. Sharp, Inc.

Liu, J.C. and Xu, L.L. (1992), "Industrial Reforms and Enterprise Management in Shanghai", *Research in Asian Economic Studies*, Vol. 4B, JAI Press, pp.443-458.

Liu, W. and Eddie, I.A. (1995), "Developments in Accounting Regulation", *Perspectives on Accounting and Finance*, Routledge, pp. 139-158.

Loft, A. (1991), "The History of Management Accounting: Relevance Found" in *Issues in Management Accounting*, ed. Ashton, D., Hopper, T. and Scapens, R. W., Prentice Hall, pp.17-38.

Lou, E. X. (1984), *Socialist Accounting Theory* (Chinese), Shanghai University of Finance and Economics, Shanghai.

Lou, E.X. and Zhang, W.G. (1992), "A Comparative Study on Sino-foreign Accounting Standards", *Accounting Research* (Chinese), No.2, pp. 5-15.

290

Lu, W. (1992), *Accounting Development in China During the Modern Era*, Masters Thesis, La Trobe University, Bundoora, Vic. Australia.

Lu, W. and Ji. X.D. (1994), "The Reform of Accounting Education in China – The Need for a Third Blood Transfusion", *Sixth Annual Conference of Accounting Academics*, Hong Kong, 28-29 April 1994, pp. 533-544.

_____ (1995a), "The Evolution of Bookkeeping in China", *Proceedings of the Second Bi-annual Swedish Accounting & Auditing Research Colloquium*, Umes University, pp. 231-236.

_____ (1995b), "The Development of Certified Public Accounting in China: a Prerequisite for International Trade and Economic Growth", *Seventh Asian-Pacific Conference on International Accounting Issues*, Seoul, South Korea, November 8-11.

Lung, J. (1989), "Socialism Burdens Chinese Car Venture", *The Wall Street Journal*, 13 April.

Ma, X.M. (1994), "The legal Liabilities of CPAs and CPA firms in China", *Accounting Research* (Chinese), No.1, pp. 33.

MacFarquhar, R. (1993), *The Politics of China*, Cambridge University Press.

Macve, R. and Liu, Z.Y. (1995), "A Proposal to form a Unified Chinese Public Accountancy Profession: An Academic Perspective", *The Intentional Journal of Accounting*, Vol.30, No.11, pp.48-61.

MaLhattan, R.D. (1987), "The JIT philosophy", *Management Accounting*, September, pp. 20-26.

Maschmeyer, R.A. and Yang, J. (1991), "Responsibility Accounting During the Economic Transformation in the People's Republic of China" in R.S.O. Wallace, J.M. Samuels and R.J. Briston (eds), *Research in Third World Accounting*, London: JAI Press, Vol.1, pp.141-156.

Mathews, M. R. and Perera, M. H. B. (1993) *Accounting Theory and Development*, Nelson Press, Melbourne.

Mattessich, R. (1984), *Modern Accounting Research: History, Survey and Guide*, The Canadian Certified General Accountants' Research Foundation.

_____ (1991), *Accounting Research in the 1980s and Its Future Relevance*, The Canadian Certified General Accountants' Research Foundation.

Ministry of Finance (1984), *Cost Management Regulations For State-owned Enterprises*.

_____ (1991), *Accounting Standards for Business Enterprises No.1: Basic Standards (draft)*, Beijing.

_____ (1992a), *Accounting Standards for Enterprises*, Chinese Economy and Finance Publishing.

_____ (1992b), *Uniform Accounting System Industrial Enterprises*, Chinese Economy and Finance Publishing.

_____ (1992c), *General Rules of Financial Management for Enterprises,* Chinese Economy and Finance Publishing.

_____ (1992d), *Financial Management Regulations For Industrial Enterprises*, Chinese Economy and Finance Publishing.

_____ (1993a), *Detailed Rules for the Implementation of the Provisional Regulations of the People's Republic of China on Value-Add Tax*, Chinese Statistics Press.

_____ (1993b), *The Personal Income Tax Act of the People's Republic of China*, The People's Publishing.

Moore, C. A. (1967), *The Chinese Mind: Essentials of Chinese Philosophy and Culture*, East-West Center Press, University of Hawaii Press.

Mueller, G.G. (1967), *International Accounting*, Macmillan.

Myers, R.H. (1980), *The Chinese Economy, Past and Present*, Wadsworth Press, Belmont.

National People's Congress, *The Accounting Law of the People's Republic of China*, (Chinese), Beijing, Chinese and Economic Press, 1985, 1993.

Needham, J. (1954), *Science and Civilisation in China*, Cambridge: Cambridge University Press.

Niu, R. L. (1994), "Unemployee's Living on Creditor's Rights", *Economic Research Journal*, No.10, October, pp. 13-21.

Pacioli, L. (1494), *Summa de Arithmetica, Geometria, Proportionalita, Paganinus de Pagninis*.

Pattillo, J. W. (1977), *The Role of Applied Research in Accounting* in Courtis, J.K. (1980), *Research and Methodology in Accounting and Financial Management*, Financial Management Research Center, Armidale, pp. 9-22.

Peragallo, E. (1983), *Origin and Evolution of Double Entry Bookkeeping*, New York: American Institute Publishing Co.

Perera, M.H.B. (1989), "Towards a Framework to Analyse the Impact of Culture on Accounting", *The International Journal of Accounting Education and Research*, Vol.24, pp.42-56.

Popper, K.R. (1968), *The Logic of Scientific Discovery*, London: Hutchinson.

Previts, G.J., Parker, L.D. and Coffman, E.N. (1990), "Accounting History: Definition and Relevance", *Abacus*, Vol.26, No.1, pp.136-158.

Radebaugh, L.H. and Gray, S. J.(1993), *International Accounting and Multinational Enterprises*, Third Edition, John Wiley and Sons, Inc.

Riahi-Belkaoui, A. (1997), *Research Perspectives in Accounting*, Quorum books.

Roberts, C.B., Adams, C.A., Woo, R.W.K. and Wu, X. (1995), "Chinese Accounting Reform: The Internationalisation of Financial Reporting" in Doupnik, T.S. (eds), *Advances in International Accounting*, Vol.8, London: JAI Press Inc.

Roxas, M., Stoneback, J. and Tulin, P. (1997), "Culture and Accounting Values: Hofstede and Trompenaars", *Eighth World Congress of International Association for Accounting Education and Research*, Paris, 23-25 October.

Salter, S.B. and Niswander, F. (1995), "Cultural Influence on the Development of Accounting Systems Internationally: A Test of Gray's (1988) Theory", *Journal of International Business Studies*, Second Quarter, pp. 379-397.

292

Scapens, R.W. (1990), "Researching Management Accounting Practice: The Role of Case Study Method", *British Accounting Review*, Vol.22, pp.259-281.

Scapens, R.W. and Hou, B.L. (1995), "The Evolution of Responsibility Accounting Systems in China" in Wallace, R.S.O., Samuels, J.M. and Briston, R.J. (eds), *Research in Third World Accounting*, Vol.3, London: JAI Press.

Scapens, R.W. and Meng, Y. (1993), "Management Accounting Research in China", *Management Accounting Research*, No.4, pp. 321-341.

Schermerhorn, J.R. and Nyaw, M.K.(1991), "Managerial Leadership in Chinese Industrial Enterprise", *Organisation and Management in China 1979-1990*, M.E.Sharp, Inc.

Scorgie, M.E. and Ji, X.D. (1996), "Production Planning in Seventeenth Century China", *Accounting History*, Vol.1, No.2, November, pp. 37-54.

Sekaran, U.(1992), *Research Methods for Business: A Skilled-building Approach*, Second Edition, John Wiley and Sons, Inc.

Shanghai University of Finance and Economics and Center for International Accounting development, The University of Texas at Dallas (1987), *Accounting and Auditing in the People's Republic of China: a review of its practices, systems, education and development*, Dallas: Centre for International Accounting Development, University of Texas.

Shao, L. (1994), "Mainland State-Owned Enterprises Almost Completely Lost Their Role as Locomotive of the Economy", *Zhongguo Tongxun She*, 22 April.

Simyar, F. (1988), "Joint Ventures in the People's Republic of China", *Recent Accounting and Economic Development in the Far East*, Centre for International Education and Research in Accounting, Urbana-Champaign, Ill, The University of Illinois, pp.170-196.

Skinner, D.J. (1993), "The Investment Opportunity Set and Accounting Procedure", *Journal of Accounting and Economics*, Vol.16, pp.407-445.

Skousen, C.R. and Yang, J.L. (1988), "Western Management Accounting and the Economic Reforms of China", *Accounting, Organisations and Society*, Vol.13, No.2, pp. 201-206.

Skousen, C.R., Yany, J. and Dai, X. (1991), "Auditing in China: Recent Developments and Current Problems" in Wallace, R.S.O., Samuels, J.M. and Briston, R.J. (eds), *Research in Third World Accounting*, Vol.1, London: JAI Press, pp.157-169.

Skousen, C.R., Brackner, J.W. and Hu, R.K. (1993), "Financial Accounting in State-owned Enterprises in China" in Wallace, R.S.O., Samuels, J.M. and Briston, R.J. (eds), *Research in Third World Accounting*, London: JAI Press, Vol.2, pp.313-332.

Solomons, D. (1952), *Studies in Costing*, The Law Book Co. of Australia Pty. Ltd.

Spair, E. (1960), *Culture, Language, and Personality*, University of California Press.

Standford, M. (1987), *The Nature of Historical Knowledge*, Oxford: Basil Blackwell.

State Council of the People's Republic of China (1993), *Provisional Regulations of the People's Republic of China on Value-Add Tax*, Chinese Statistical Press.

293

State Statistical Bureau, PRC (1995), China Statistical Yearbook, China Statistical Publishing House.

Sterling, R. (1970), *Theory of the Measurement of Enterprise Income*, Kansas: University Press of Kansas.

Tang, Q. L. (1993), "Economic Consequences of the International Harmonization of Accounting Standards: Theory and Its Chinese Application", *The Intentional Journal of Accounting*, Vol.29, No.2, pp.146-160.

Tang, Q. L. and Fang, Z.L. (1987), "Accounting and Auditing Organisations and Research" in *Accounting and Auditing in the People's Republic of China: a review of its practices, systems, education and development*, Joint Research Study by Shanghai University of Finance and Economics and Center for International Accounting development, The University of Texas at Dallas, pp. 139-153.

Tang, Y.W., Cooper, B.J. and Chow, L. (1994, 1996), *Accounting and Finance in China: A Review of Current Practice*, Longman.

Taussig, R.A., Yang, D.C. and Mao, X.H. (1994), "Financial Standards in Contemporary China", in Doupnik, T.S. (eds) *Advances in International Accounting*, Vol.7, London: JAI Press.

Taylor, D.W. and Liu, K.C. (1992), "Management Autonomy and Financial Performance Criteria: the Case of State Commercial Enterprise in China", Asian Review of Accounting, Vol.1, No.1, pp. 87-98.

The People's Daily (1994) (Chinese) 20 May.

The Research Group of The Ministry of Finance (1994), "The Basic Thinking On How to Establish to Social Security System", *Economic Research Journal* (Chinses), No.10, pp.20-23.

The World Bank (1985), *China: Long Term Development Issues and Options*, The John Hopkins University Press.

_____ (1996), *China: Internal Market Development and Regulation*, Washington.

Thomas, A.L. (1966), *Revenue Recognition*, Ann Arbor: University of Michigan Press.

Tomasic, R. (1992), "Auditors and Reporting to Illegality and Financial Fraud", *Australian Business Law Review*, June, pp. 203.

Trompenaars, F. (1994), *Riding the Waves of Culture: Understanding Diversity in Global Business*, Irwin.

Tsang, S. and Cheng, Y. (1994), "China's Tax Reforms of 1994", Breakthrough or Compromise?", *Asian Survey*, September, pp.769-188.

Tung, R. (1993), "Transforming the Management of Mainland China's State-owned Enterprises", *Issues and Studies: A Journal of Chinese Studies and International Affairs*, Institute of International Relations, Taipei, Vol.29, No.12, pp. 20-28.

Wagdy, M.A. (1992), *"Management Accounting Problems in China"*, Management Accounting, April, pp.58-66.

Wallace, R.S.O., Samuels, J.M. and Briston, R.J., *Research in Third World Accounting*, Vol.1 (1990), Vol.2 (1993), Vol.3 (1994) London: JAI Press.

Wallace, W.A. (1991), *Accounting Research Methods: Do the Facts Speak for Themselves?*, Richard D. Irwin, Inc.

Wang, L.L. (1994), "The Ownership of Housing, From Unclear to Clear", *Economic Research Journal* (Chinese), No.10, pp.31-36.

Wang, S.N. and Qian, J.F. (1987), "Financial Accounting and Reporting", in *Accounting and Auditing in the People's Republic of China: a review of its practices, systems, education and development*, Joint Research Study by Shanghai University of Finance and Economics and Center for International Accounting development, The University of Texas at Dallas, pp. 9-30.

_____ (1987), "Education and Training of Accounting and Auditing Personnel", in *Accounting and Auditing in the People's Republic of China: a review of its practices, systems, education and development*, Joint Research Study by Shanghai University of Finance and Economics and Center for International Accounting Development, The University of Texas at Dallas. pp.127-138.

Watne, D.A. and Baldwin, B.A. (1988), "University-Level Education of Accountants in the People's Republic of China", *Issues in Accounting Education*, Vol.3. pp. 139-155.

Watts, R. (1995), *Nature and Origins of Positive Research in Accounting*, in Jones, S., Romano, C. and Ratnatunga, J. (eds), *Accounting Theory: A Contemporary Review*, Harcourt Brace and Company, Australia.

Watts, R.L. and Zimmerman, J.L. (1978), "Towards a Positive Theory of the Determination of Accounting Standards", *Accounting Review*, Vol.53, pp.112-134.

Watts, R. L. and Zimmerman, J. L. (1979), "The demand and Supply of Accounting Theories: The Market for Excuses", *Accounting Review*, Vol.54, pp.273-305.

Wei, Z.X. (1984), *Chinese Bookkeeping Methods* (Chinese), Beijing: Chinese Finance and Economics Press.

Williamson, O.E. (1975), *Markets and Hierarchies: Analysis and Anti-trust Implications*, New York, NY, The Free Press.

Winkle, G.M., Huss, H.F. and Tang, Z. (1992), "Accounting Education in the People's Republic of China: An Update", *Issues in Accounting Education*, Fall, Vol.7, pp.179-192.

Winkle, G.M., Huss, H.F. and Chen, X.X. (1994), "Accounting Standards in the People's Republic of China: Responding to Economic Reforms", *Accounting Horizons*, Vol.8, No.3, September, pp. 48-57.

Wolk, H., Francis, J.R. and Tearney, M.G. (1992), *Accounting Theory: A Conceptual and Institutional Approach*, Cincinnati, Ohio: South-Western Publishing.

Wong, J. (1988), "Political Costs and an Interperiod Accounting Choice for Export Tax Credit", *Journal of Accounting and Economics*, Vol.10, pp.37-51.

Wu, C.E. (1983), *Travelling Towards the West*, The People's Publishing.

Xiao, J.Z.Z. and Pan, A. (1995), "The Chinese Approach to Accounting Standards and a Conceptual Framework", *Perspectives on Accounting and Finance in China*, Routledge, pp. 178-199.

Xiao, Z., Young, D.O., Dyson, J.R. and Pan, A. (1995), "Chinese Accounting Reform: The Internationalisation of Financial Reporting" in Doupnik, T.S. (eds) *Advances in International Accounting*, Vol.8, London: JAI Press Inc.

Xing, Z. J. and Huan, S.G. (1951), "How to Establish New Chinese Accounting", *New Accounting*, January, pp. 15-20.

Xing-De (1995), "Issues on Chinese Enterprise Reorganisation and Listing Overseas", Journal of Certified Public Accountants, No.1, pp. 20-26.

Xinhua (1994), "Government Reports State-owned Assets Increase Rapidly", *Xinhua News*, 13, May.

Xu, Z. (1995), "The Development of the Certified Public Accountant System in the People's Republic of China", in A. Tsuji and P. Garner (eds) *Studies in Accounting History*, Greenwood Press, pp. 58-70.

Yang, C. (1981), "'Mass Line' Accounting in China", *Management Accounting*, May, 1981, pp. 13-17.

Yang, J. L. (1982), "Making Western Management Accounting Serve China", *Shanghai Accounting (Chinese)*, No. 8. August, pp.2-8.

Yang, J. W. (1983), "The Current Situation of Accounting in China and Some Problems of Accounting Concerning Chinese-Foreign Joint Venture Enterprises", Speech Delivered to Hong Kong Society of Accountants, March, 1983.

_____ (1988), *Modern Chinese Accounting Handbook*, Beijing, Chinese Finance and Economics Press.

_____ (1992), "Address on the International Symposium on Chinese Accounting Standards", *Accounting Research* (Chinese) No.2, pp.3-4.

_____ (1994), "Moving Towards Accounting Internationalisation", *The Hong Kong Accountant*, Vol.5, No.5, pp.33-39.

Yin, R.K. (1994), *Case Study Research: Design and methods*, Second Edition, Sage Publications.

Yu, S.L. (1994), *Chinese Taxation Law* (Chinese) Economic Management Publishing.

Yu, X.Y. (1988), "The General Character of Chinese and U.S Management Accounting and an Analysis of the New Chinese Management Accounting Style", *Recent Accounting and Economic Development in the Far East*, Centre for International Education and Research in Accounting, Urban-Champaign, Ill, The University of Illinois, pp. 51-64.

Zarsekei, M.T. (1996), "Spontaneous Harmonisation Effects of Culture and Market Forces on Accounting Disclosure Practices", *Accounting Horizons*, Vol. 10, No.1, pp. 18-37.

Zhang, L. Z. (1997), "Research on Chinese Security System", *Sociology Research* (Chinese), No.2, pp.1-23.

Zhang, Y.C. (1993), "Speech in the International Symposium of Accounting Standards" *Accounting Research* (Chinese), Vol.2, p.1.

Zhao, L.B. (1988), "Accounting in the People's republic of China - Contemporary Situations and Issues", *Recent Accounting and Economic Developments in the Far*

East, Centre for International Education and Research in Accounting, The University of Illinois, pp.27-50.

Zhao, Y.L. (1987), "A Brief History of Accounting and Auditing in China", *Accounting and Auditing in the People's Republic of China: a review of its practices, systems, education and development*, Joint Research Study by Shanghai University of Finance and Economics and Center for International Accounting development, The University of Texas at Dallas, pp. 165-191.

_____ (1992), *The History of Accounting and Auditing in Ancient China* (Chinese), Lixing Accounting Publishing.

Zhou, H.Z. (1988), "Chinese Accounting Systems and Practices", *Accounting, Organisations and Society*, Vol.13, No.2, pp.207-221.